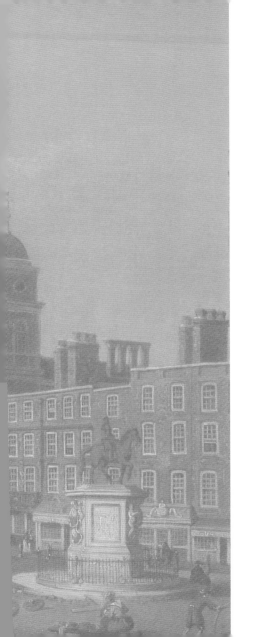

London

A History in Paintings & Illustrations

STEPHEN PORTER

AMBERLEY

ACKNOWLEDGEMENTS

In preparing this book I have drawn on the work of so many previous authors and observers of the London scene, that, alas, space precludes me from including a comprehensive bibliography, but I am nonetheless grateful for their efforts. Jonathan Reeve at Amberley encouraged me to appreciate that a brief history of London, its districts and buildings, combined with a range of illustrations, was a viable project. Peter Day kindly read the text, offered wise advice and prevented me from making several errors, and Stanley Underhill at Sutton's Hospital and Adrian James at the Society of Antiquaries of London efficiently supplied the images which I requested. I am especially grateful to the Governors of Sutton's Hospital, the Society of Antiquaries of London, the Yale Center for British Art and the National Gallery of Art for making their images available. Exhibitions by the Charterhouse, on philanthropy in London, and by the Kunstmuseum at Bern, of the works of Samuel Hieronymus Grimm, were informative and timely. And, of course, such a book would be impossible without the much-appreciated service provided by libraries and booksellers, large and small.

My wife Carolyn has, once again, given unstinting and invaluable help and encouragement, especially in dealing with the images, as well as succour and support in so many other ways.

First published 2014

Amberley Publishing
The Hill, Stroud
Gloucestershire, GL5 4EP

www.amberley-books.com

Copyright © Stephen Porter, 2014

The right of Stephen Porter to be identified as the Author of this work has been asserted in accordance with the Copyrights, Designs and Patents Act 1988.

ISBN 978 1 4456 3274 2 (hardback)
ISBN 978 1 4456 3285 8 (ebook)

British Library Cataloguing in Publication Data.
A catalogue record for this book is available from the British Library.

Typeset in 11pt on 12pt Sabon LT Std.
Typesetting by Amberley Publishing.
Printed in the UK.

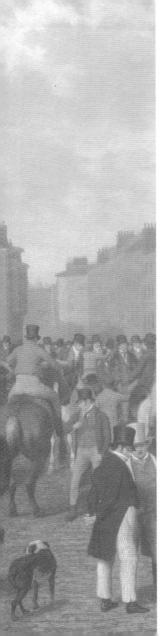

CONTENTS

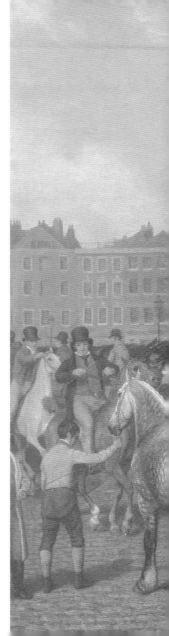

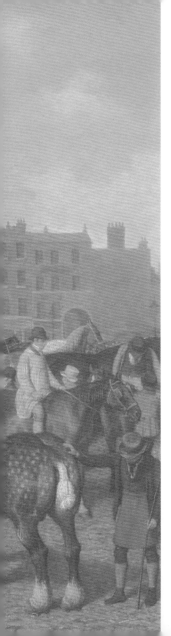

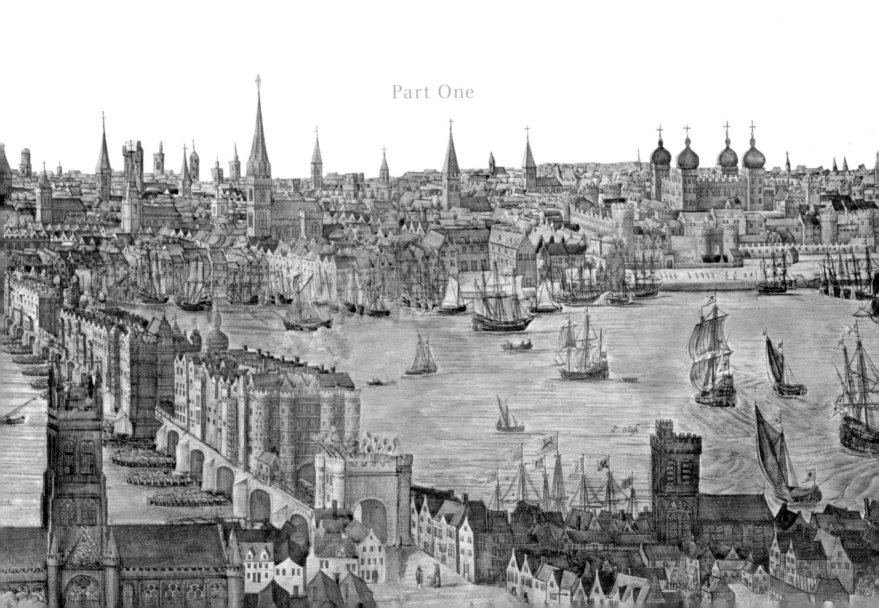

Part One

LONDINIUM

London was a creation of the Romans. Until their invasion of Britain in AD 43, there was no settlement on the site where the city was to develop. The tribal societies of pre-conquest Britain did not generate urban communities and overseas trade was carried out through landing places in Dorset and around the south-east coast, not from the Thames. The first military intervention by the Romans came in 55 BC, when Julius Caesar, the governor of Gaul, launched an invasion with a force of perhaps 10,000 men, which landed on the coast of Kent. He remained only for a short time, but in the following year repeated the exercise, with a larger force, penetrating much further inland. Crossing the Thames at a ford, despite resistance, he pushed on and captured a fortified camp at Wheathampstead, in Hertfordshire. Cassivellaunus, his most determined adversary, then came to terms with Caesar, who did not attempt to consolidate his position, and the Roman army was withdrawn. The ford over the Thames may have been at Westminster, or perhaps on the site where Londinium was to develop.

The Romans did not launch another military campaign in Britain until the reign of Claudius, who was created Emperor by the imperial bodyguard in AD 41, after the assassination of Caligula. The reason for his invasion in AD 43 is not entirely clear. When describing Britain, the Roman historian Tacitus noted that 'the earth yields gold, silver and other metals; the rewards of victory', but conquest was not required to secure the supply of metals, slaves, corn, cattle and hides from there. It is more likely that Claudius needed a military victory to strengthen his authority, and an invasion of Britain could be justified by the fact that it provided a base from which raids were launched against Gaul. To guard that province's long coastline would have taken as many men as did the conquest, and once Britain was incorporated into the empire it could yield taxes to offset the cost of its garrison.

The Roman army which landed at Richborough, Kent, was under the command of Aulus Plautius, and may have consisted of as many as 40,000 men. Despite determined opposition from the Britons and at least two major clashes, the legionaries reached the Thames. But they were unable to find the ford which Caesar had mentioned in his account of the campaign in 54 BC. The Thames was then much wider than it is today and its banks, especially on the south side, consisted of low islands and mudflats, many of which were inundated at high tide. It is likely that shifting of the banks, mudflats and water channels over the intervening years had removed the ford, or the approaches to it. Nevertheless, the army crossed the Thames and, after Claudius himself had joined his troops to emphasise his role as conqueror, it gradually occupied much of southern Britain, which was steadily assimilated into the empire.

By the time of the Claudian invasion the tribal societies of pre-conquest Britain had developed centralised settlements, known as *oppida*, at Colchester, Verulamium (close to the future St Albans) and Silchester, in Hampshire. Within a few years of the conquest an embryonic town had also been formed on the north bank of the Thames, at the river's lowest bridging point, which was known as Londinium. The name was not a Latin one and may have been derived from pre-Celtic elements which referred to a place at the navigable river. It was retained, in various forms, throughout the Anglo-Saxon period, and subsequently became standardised as London, applied to the city on the north bank, but for centuries not generally used to describe the whole of the built-up area, as the metropolis grew.

The importance of the location, where the tidal river could be bridged, was recognised by the Roman engineers. On the north side of the river the two low, gravelly hills of Ludgate Hill and Cornhill were separated by the Walbrook. Cornhill would have been a suitable site for a camp for the army after it had crossed the river during the Claudian invasion. Across the Thames from Cornhill was a peninsula, or possibly an island, which projected northwards into the river among the mudflats, and those two dry sites were connected by a bridge by around AD 50. The settlement which then grew up on its south side was to develop as the suburb of Southwark.

Streets were laid out on Cornhill by around AD 47, but the new town was not the Roman headquarters in Britain, which was established at Colchester. Nevertheless, Londinium grew rapidly as a trading town; the historian Tacitus explained that it 'did not rank as a Roman settlement, but was an important centre for businessmen and merchandise'. The main street ran from east to west across the two hills and the Walbrook valley, continuing to the west along Newgate Street and becoming Watling Street, which connected Londinium with Verulamium and had a branch that led to Silchester, and to the east along the line of Fenchurch Street to Colchester. The street from the bridge continued northwards on the line of Bishopsgate and became Ermine Street, connecting Londinium with York and Lincoln; across the bridge it continued through Southwark and on to Canterbury and Richborough. A grid of streets was set out around a marketplace on Cornhill. The steep descent to the river was terraced and its banks were consolidated with piles, to provide landing places, and warehouses were built, while on the south side of the river timber piling was used where necessary to raise the roadways above the marshy surface. By around AD 60 Londinium's population may have reached 10,000 and new building was continuing.

The development of the town then received a severe setback with the revolt of Boudica, the queen of the Iceni, in East Anglia. This erupted in AD 60 and continued into the following year. Having defeated the Roman force which attempted to quell the uprising, her army captured and burnt Colchester and then advanced towards Londinium. The Romans prudently withdrew from the unfortified town, and 'the inhabitants were allowed to accompany them. But those who stayed because they were women, or old, or attached to the place, were slaughtered by the enemy.'

Boudica's followers burned both Londinium and Southwark and then moved north, torching Verulamium, before being defeated at a battle in the Midlands. Londinium then began the process of recovery, which initially was sluggish; the revolt must have sharply jolted the confidence of the inhabitants and traders. But after ten years or so the town again began to grow. During the last few decades of the first century it recovered and prospered, serving as an important port for the province and as the focus of its developing road network. It also had an important administrative role, with the procurator, who was the principal tax collector, based there, and that was increased when the headquarters of the governor of the province was moved to the town from Colchester. By the early second century its population may have been as high as 30,000.

The period of growth and prosperity was marked by considerable investment in public buildings, perhaps reflecting the recognition that Londinium was the province's most significant town. A forum and basilica were constructed on the site of the market on Cornhill and were soon replaced by a much grander complex which was unusually large even within the context of the empire, taking thirty years to build. In around AD 70 a wooden amphitheatre was erected, on the site of Guildhall Yard, and public baths were built close to the river. A temple erected during the period was also situated west of the Walbrook. It seems that building density on Cornhill prevented the construction of those three complexes in that area. The amphitheatre was rebuilt in stone and to a larger plan in the early second century; it then had space for perhaps as many as 8,000 spectators.

Londinium was gradually drawn into the Roman world, trading not only with northern Europe but also with ports in the Mediterranean, from where imports included olive oil, wine and fish sauce; bronze lamps were brought from Italy and emeralds in a necklace found at Cannon Street came from Egypt. An amphora used for transporting fish sauce, made from mackerel, carried the inscription 'Lucius Tettius Africanus supplies the finest fish sauce from Antibes'. Lucius Pompeius Licetus, a soldier buried at Londinium, was born in Arezzo in Tuscany, and Aulus Alfidius Olussa, who may have been a merchant, was born in Athens and was seventy years old when he died, commemorated in a tombstone found at Tower Hill.

The majority of houses, shops and workshops were built of timber and roofed with thatch; their water supply came from wells. Craftsmen using the workshops included goldsmiths, coppersmiths, leather workers (especially shoemakers), potters, enamellers and iron forgers. Fires occurred from time to time in the crowded urban environment and the town's prosperity was checked by a major blaze which occurred at some time in the years AD 125–30, destroying buildings between Newgate Street in the west almost to the edge of the built-up area in the east. A fort constructed in the Cripplegate area may have been built earlier and was untouched by the conflagration, or its erection could have been prompted by the disaster, to provide a secure base separate from the town's flammable buildings. It covered twelve acres and was built to house the garrison and possibly, too, the governor's staff. In the aftermath of the fire, and in the context of changes in trade, Londinium experienced a decline that lasted for much of the second century. Its public buildings were not only left unrepaired but, in some cases, were demolished, while the riverside embankments were neglected. The population may have fallen by as much as two-thirds after around 150 and some districts were all but abandoned.

Political instability within the empire and struggles for power by rival claimants backed by sections of the army may have contributed to Londinium's malaise. The governor of Britain, Decimus Clodius Albinus, became embroiled in the civil wars which followed the assassination of Emperor Commodus, on the last day of 192, and those of his two successors within the next six months. In 196 Albinus took much of the army of Britain to Gaul to advance his claims, but he was defeated by his principal rival, Lucius Septimius Severus, in a bloody battle near Lyon. Severus, an able reformer and administrator, crossed to Britain in 208 and spent the last four years of his life campaigning beyond the northern frontier. The events of that period and the Emperor's presence in the province may have prompted the erection of a defensive wall encircling Londinium. It was two miles long, nine feet thick and twenty-one feet high and enclosed 330 acres, incorporating the Cripplegate fort. The principal gates were at Ludgate, Newgate, Bishopsgate and Aldgate; Cripplegate was the northern gate of the fort and Aldersgate was made later. The cemeteries lay outside the gates, following the customary Roman practice. Skeletal remains show that the citizens typically were of good physique and had an adequate diet; but only roughly one in ten were more than forty-five years old when they died.

Londinium revived after around 200 and the third century was a relatively prosperous period during which large houses were built, floored with fine mosaics and decorated with wall paintings. The early third century saw the arrival in Britain of the cult of Mithras, which had originated in Persia before being adopted throughout much of the empire. It was an exclusively male cult which appealed particularly to soldiers and merchants; a Temple of Mithras was built close to the Walbrook in the 240s, in a district that revived during the third century, after the period of stagnation. Londinium contained a number of temples serving the various beliefs and cults from around the empire, which during the third century included Christianity, and in 313 the Edict of Milan permitted the practice of the faith without persecution.

Despite that prosperity, further political upheavals and an increasing inability to prevent raids across the North Sea produced, from roughly the middle of the third century, a growing insecurity. That was shown by the construction of a defensive wall along the riverside as far west as Blackfriars, to provide protection against the raiders. Londinium's administrative role was diminished as the province was divided, first into two provinces in the early third century and then into four around 300. A fall in the water level of the Thames made the loading and unloading of cargoes more difficult; the waterfront had been built further out, but it may be that in time transhipment became easier downstream, at Shadwell. Patterns of overseas trade were changing as well, with Gaul and Germany becoming relatively more important as trade with the Mediterranean declined. Nevertheless, commerce continued throughout the fourth century and there was new building, including a large basilica in the east of the town, close to the wall, which was strengthened in that area by the addition of bastions around 371–75.

As well as the military threat from outside the empire, the changing political situation within it affected Britain. On four occasions after 340 the army in Britain was deployed on the Continent to support rival forces and candidates for the imperial throne. The last of such interventions came in the summer of 407 when Constantine III, proclaimed Emperor in Britain, took the army to Gaul to repel an invasion by tribes from Germany and stabilise the Rhine frontier, and then to put down revolts in Spain. Thereafter, the situation in Britain was such that, according to the Byzantine historian Zosimus, it 'forced the inhabitants of Britain and some of the tribes in Gaul to secede from Roman rule and to be independent, obeying Roman laws no longer … expelling the Roman officials and establishing whatever government they wished'. Paying taxes for an army which was no longer present and was unlikely to be replaced was futile, and without troops the Roman officials could not maintain their authority. In Italy Emperor Honorius was increasingly beleaguered and in 410 Rome was sacked by the Visigoths under Alaric. Neither Honorius nor Constantine could deal with the problems of provinces on the north-west edge of the empire, and in 410 Honorius advised the Britons that they should 'guard themselves'. The ending of Roman rule was followed by a decline in conditions within Londinium, which was gradually deserted during the fifth century.

2

ANGLO-SAXON AND NORMAN LONDON

The raids of the late third and early fourth centuries developed into invasions by the Angles and Saxons. These did not go unopposed, but in 456 the Britons were defeated by the army of the Saxon leader Hengist and his son Aesc at a major battle in Kent: 'The Britons then abandoned the land of Kent and in great terror fled to the stronghold of London.' It could not remain a refuge, however, for the line of the walls was too long to be defended by the small and steadily falling population of the town, and at some point the bridge was either partially demolished or simply fell into decay. London was abandoned as the Roman provinces became a number of Anglo-Saxon kingdoms. Hengist's kingdom of Kent stretched as far as the Thames, with that of the East Saxons established north of the river and including the site of Londinium. But the town's buildings and streets were deserted and trees and scrub grew on the site.

A part of the town was again occupied following the reconversion of England to Christianity, which began when the Pope sent a mission under the Benedictine monk Augustine, in 597, with the goodwill of Ethelbert, king of Kent, and Saebhert, king of the East Saxons. A second group of monks followed in 601 and a member of that group, Mellitus, was consecrated by Augustine in 604 as bishop of the East Saxons, with his seat at London. It is likely that the cathedral which he founded, dedicated to St Paul, was on, or near to, the site of the later cathedral buildings, prominently placed on the hill on the east side of the valley of the River Fleet. But following the death of both Ethelbert and Saeberht, in 616 Mellitus was expelled by Saeberht's sons, who reverted to paganism. It was not until Theodore of Tarsus, Archbishop of Canterbury from 669, consecrated Erkenwald as bishop around 675 that the see was effectively re-established and secured. Erkenwald was abbot of Chertsey; additions to the abbey's holdings in recent years had included a length of frontage on the Thames 'at the port of London'.

By the late seventh century control of London had passed to the kingdom of Mercia; a later tradition held that Offa, king of Mercia from 757 to 796, had a palace in the vicinity of the modern Wood Street, within the Cripplegate fort. The area just to the east of Wood Street did evolve as the administrative centre of the city: a guildhall was referred to in 1128 and a hall for public meetings was in existence to the east of Aldermanbury before the end of the twelfth century.

The historian Bede later described the East Saxon capital at the time of Mellitus as being 'the city of London, which is on the

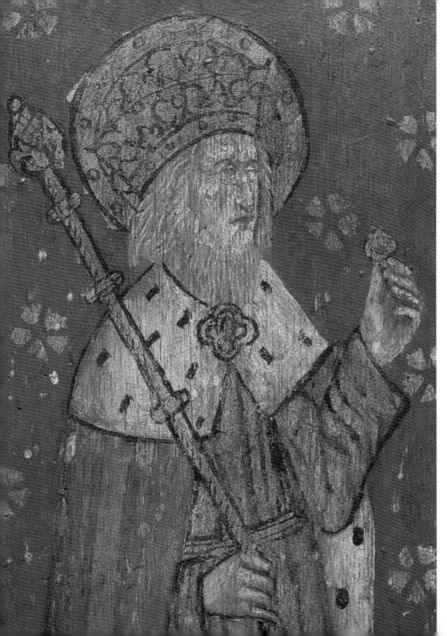

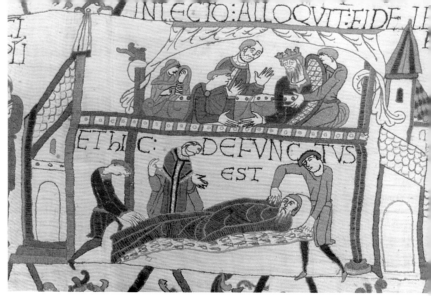

Above: 1. These scenes from the Bayeux Tapestry illustrate Edward the Confessor's final illness and death in 1066, in the palace which he had built at Westminster. The way in which the building's towers are shown conveys a sense of its scale. (City of Bayeux)

Left: 2. Edward the Confessor, who refounded St Peter's abbey at Westminster and began the building of Westminster Palace. This later portrait of the king is on the screen in St Catherine's church, Ludham, Norfolk. (Jonathan Reeve, JR 1117slide 10001100D)

banks of that river and is an emporium for many nations who come to it by land and sea'. A grant of land near to the river made in 672–74 referred to 'the port of London, where ships come to land'. From the same period, coins began to come into use once more after what seems to have been a long period without coinage, during which transactions were made by barter. The settlement described was not on the site of Londinium, but to its west. Known as Lundenwic, this covered roughly 150 acres in an area centred on the modern Aldwych, the name of which means 'old trading settlement', between Kingsway and Trafalgar Square and the Thames and Oxford Street. By 800 it had a population of roughly 4,000 and was a settlement of artisans as well as traders, who had connections to the lower Rhine, the Meuse valley and northern France. The gravelly foreshore provided a landing place for ships, for the river level had risen after the recession during the Roman period, and the tidal head was at least as far upstream as Lundenwic. It seems that the bridge did not prevent seagoing vessels from reaching the town, and so it was partially ruined, if not completely collapsed.

The city's security was threatened by the Danish coastal raids, which became increasingly common during the early ninth century. In 842 'there was a great slaughter in London' and in 851 'for the first time the heathen men stayed over the winter'; that year they landed from 350 ships and 'stormed Canterbury and London, and put to flight Beorhtwulf king of Mercia with his army'. The kingdom of Wessex had been putting growing pressure on Mercia and had gained control of the south side of the Thames. The Mercians were also under attack from the Vikings and were powerless to prevent the 'great army' that

landed in 865 from occupying London in 872; it may have remained in Danish hands in the following years. In 871 Alfred became king of Wessex and his principal task was to stem the encroachment of the Norsemen, which had seen the occupation of Northumbria and East Anglia, the loss of much of Mercia and incursions deep into Wessex itself. In May 878 Alfred defeated the Danish king Guthrum at Edington in Wiltshire and in 886 his forces occupied London, which he then entrusted to his son-in-law Aethelred, ealdorman, or ruler, of the Mercians. Aethelred retained control of the city after Alfred died in 899 and until his own death in 911.

During Aethelred's period in charge of London the inhabitants moved within the Roman walls of what was now known as Lundenburg, 'the fortified town', and Lundenwic was gradually abandoned, in the face of the threat from Viking raids. New streets were set out on Ludgate Hill and Cornhill, but not following the Roman street plan, except for the streets leading from the gates. Cheapside became the main east–west thoroughfare, and streets were set out south of it, east of Bread Street and down to the river, where the quay at Queenhithe was referred to in 898 as 'Aetheredes hyd'. A market space was set out in the late ninth century south of Cheapside and Poultry, its eastwards extension. East of the Walbrook, streets were built south of Eastcheap around Fish Street Hill and down to the river at Billingsgate. The bridge was also repaired or, as seems more likely, was rebuilt during this period, probably during Alfred's reign. A river bridge acted as a defensive feature, providing a barrier to ships, a platform from which approaching vessels could be attacked and a means of moving troops swiftly from one side of the river to the other.

Its commercial benefits were at least as important as its defensive value and Southwark, which seems not to have been occupied since the fifth century, revived; it is first mentioned by name in a list of burhs established by Alfred.

During the tenth century commerce expanded; a royal ordinance to regulate trade and fix tolls was issued in the late tenth or early eleventh century. It mentions Billingsgate, where a jetty was built in around 1000. The quay at Queenhithe also saw considerable changes in the early eleventh century. Ships from London once again traded with the Mediterranean, as well as with the ports of northern France and Germany; the Emperor's subjects were given special privileges.

The city within the walls continued to develop, with new streets set out north of Cheapside in the tenth century. The early and middle years of the tenth century were a relatively peaceful period, but the citizens still faced various perils, as in 962, when there was not only 'a very great pestilence among men', but also 'the great fatal fire in London, and Paul's minster burned down; and it was founded again the same year'. Just twenty years later, in 982, a chronicler recorded that 'London town burned'. Viking raids had resumed in 980 and in 981 'great harm [was] done everywhere along the sea-coast'. In the period of warfare which followed, London was attacked in 994 by Oláf, later King of Norway, and Swein 'Forkbeard', King of Denmark. But although they arrived with a considerable force in ninety-four ships, the Londoners beat them off and 'they suffered more harm and injury than they ever imagined any town-dwellers would do to them'. King Aethelred then came to terms with the Vikings, paying them £16,000 in tribute.

The Vikings seem to have withdrawn from England during the great famine in 1005, but their raids were renewed in 1006, under Swein's leadership. London fought off attacks in 1009 and in 1013, when 'the inhabitants of the town … held out against them with full battle', but later in 1013 they did submit. Swein died in 1014 and Aethelred in 1016; Aethelred's son Edmund was elected king in London, although the Danes chose Swein's son Cnut as king. Cnut attempted to capture London in 1016, but the citizens successfully resisted his forces, even after they had 'dug a great ditch on the south side and dragged their ships to the west side of the bridge'. A second attempt to capture the city was also unsuccessful. But after Edmund's defeat later that year the Londoners did submit to Cnut, agreeing to make a payment and providing winter quarters for his troops. With Edmund's death at the end of November 1016 Cnut became king of the whole country, bringing the period of warfare to an end.

The wars of the early eleventh century confirmed London's importance, militarily, politically and economically. Its defences had proved to be strong, with a large enough population to provide or reinforce an effective garrison. And it was a prize to be held, for its resources and status, and not sacked. From the tenth century London was England's largest and wealthiest town; in the levy imposed in 1018 it was to pay £10,500 and the rest of the country £72,000.

That heavy taxation may have had a detrimental economic effect and Cnut also did London a disservice by removing, in 1023, the body of St Aelfeah, or Alphage, from St Paul's to Canterbury Cathedral. He had been Archbishop of Canterbury,

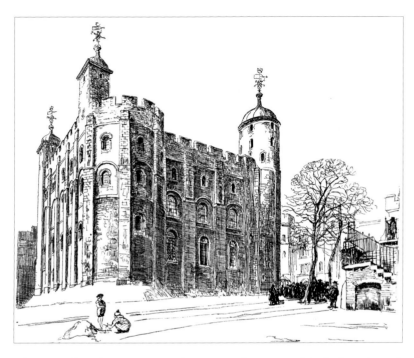

Above: 3. The White Tower was the Norman keep erected in the late eleventh century. (Stephen Porter)

Right: 4. St John's chapel in the White Tower, painted by John Fulleylove around 1907, was used for a time for storing records, but when they were removed the appearance of this part of the Norman building could again be appreciated. (Stephen Porter)

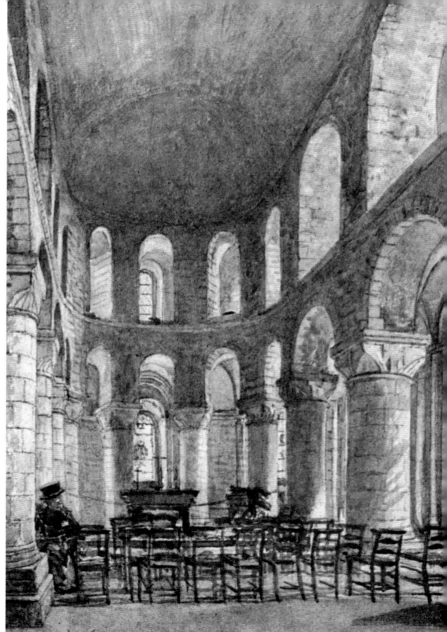

murdered during a drunken Viking feast in 1012 and buried in St Paul's, where reverence of his memory quickly developed into a cult so strong that Cnut arranged for troops to be at the ready in case of popular disturbances when his body was removed.

Cnut died in 1035 and his reign was followed by those of Harold Harefoot and Harthacnut. After Harthacnut's death in 1042 Edward the Confessor, Aethelred's seventh son, became king. He had spent twenty-five years in exile in the Norse Duchy of Normandy, and Norman influences were a feature of his reign. They were checked to a certain extent by a crisis in 1051–52, which culminated in Earl Godwine of Wessex and his son Swein being outlawed. Godwine went to Flanders, but returned with a fleet which reached London in September 1052. The citizens were broadly sympathetic and allowed his army to set up camp in his manor of Southwark. Edward's support disintegrated and the Frenchmen at court fled from the city; the crisis left Earl Godwine and his sons in a strong position and the pro-Norman elements weakened. The reign was, in most other respects, peaceful and favourable for both internal and external trade, which benefited London, which had a population of perhaps 15,000 by the middle of the century.

Edward instigated a major development by refounding the Benedictine abbey of St Peter's at Westminster and rebuilding it on a grand scale and in the Norman style. This stood on an island between two branches of the River Tyburn, which bifurcated before reaching the Thames. The site had the advantage of being near to London but separate from it, and Edward also built a royal palace close to the abbey. The new abbey church was dedicated on 28 December 1065, but the king was too ill to attend and he died a week later. He was buried in the church on 6 January; Earl Godwine's son Harold was crowned king there on the same day. With the abandonment of Lundenwic, the reoccupation of Lundenburg and the development of Southwark, London had consisted of two components; the development of a royal enclave at Westminster added a third.

Harold's right to the crown was challenged by Duke William of Normandy, and he also had to deal with an invasion by his disaffected brother Tostig and Harald Hardrada, King of Norway; both were killed when Harold defeated their army at the Battle of Stamford Bridge near York on 25 September 1066. He returned with his army to London and then advanced into Sussex to confront Duke William's army, which had landed at Pevensey. In the ensuing battle near Hastings, on 14 October, Harold was killed and his army was defeated. The Norman army then advanced through Kent to Dover and Canterbury before moving westwards towards London.

Opposition to the invaders was organised in London by Asgar, an exceptionally wealthy nobleman who held the position of staller, the principal officer in the royal household. Edgar the Aetheling was chosen king; he was the grandson of Edmund Ironside and great-nephew of Edward the Confessor. The Londoners' own 'numerous and formidable force' was reinforced by many others who were willing to defend 'this large town', which, because of its walls and the Thames, 'neither fears enemies nor dreads being taken by storm'. The Normans could not hope to force a crossing at the bridge, although a detachment set Southwark on fire, and so carried out a wide encircling movement through Berkshire into Bedfordshire and Hertfordshire before occupying Westminster, where they prepared to attack the city. That was not necessary, for negotiations between William and Asgar resulted in the opening of Ludgate to the duke's troops. But the advance guard was attacked in an open space, or perhaps a wide street such as Cheapside, where the Normans 'at once engaged them in battle, causing no little mourning to the City because of the very many deaths of her own sons and citizens'.

Despite that resistance, the Normans prevailed and William was crowned in Westminster Abbey on Christmas Day. But the great shout within the abbey when he was acclaimed was misunderstood by his soldiers, who feared that it could be the beginning of a riot, or even a rebellion. The Normans evidently felt that the Londoners' antagonism towards them still lingered. The soldiers' response was to set nearby houses on fire and in the confusion which followed most of the congregation fled, leaving only the senior clergy and some monks in the sanctuary to complete the coronation ceremony.

William was understandably distrustful of the citizens and withdrew to Barking until fortifications had been built. These were Baynard's Castle and Montfichet's Tower, close together west of Ludgate, and an irregularly shaped enclosure in the south-east corner of the city, just within the city walls. They provided accommodation for a garrison and strongpoints from which the city could be policed and the citizens overawed. The enclosure in the south-east corner was the site of a great stone keep, the White Tower, begun by William the Conqueror in 1078 and completed during the reign of his son, William II (William Rufus, 1087–1100). The White Tower became the principal building of the Tower of London, a castle which served as a defensive feature protecting the city, a restraint upon the citizens and a royal palace. It also came to function as the state prison, a military arsenal and a safe deposit for bullion and the records of government and the courts.

The other major building works carried out under the Norman kings were the erection of Westminster Hall by William Rufus and, also during his reign, the rebuilding of St Paul's Cathedral, destroyed by fire in 1087, 'with many other churches and the largest and noblest part of all the city'. A blaze ten years earlier was then said to have been the worst that the city had experienced. William Fitzstephen's description of his native city in the twelfth century included 'the frequent fires' as one of only two 'inconveniences' of London; the other was 'the immoderate drinking of foolish persons'. The new cathedral took many years to complete, but when it was eventually finished, in the early fourteenth century, it was the largest building in England. The city also contained more than a hundred churches and the dedications of some of them, to St Botolph and St Oláf, for example, show a pre-Conquest origin, probably as private churches from which the parish structure evolved in the eleventh and twelfth centuries. In addition, according to Fitzstephen, 'almost all the bishops, abbots, and great men of England … have magnificent houses there, to which they resort, spending large sums of money'.

London's size and affluence, and the royal palaces at Westminster and the Tower, gave it a major role as a focus of political power, but Fitzstephen's description of it as 'the capital of the kingdom of England' was misleading. Winchester, the chief city of Wessex, retained an important function as a royal centre, with its strategic position enhanced by the unification of England and Normandy in 1066. Only after the loss of Normandy in 1204 could London justly be described as the unrivalled capital of England.

3

MEDIEVAL LONDON

The Norman kings and their Plantagenet successors needed both to control London and draw on its considerable wealth; Fitzstephen described it as having 'abundant wealth, extensive commerce, great grandeur and magnificence'. Stable and strong government protected the city from ambitious noblemen and created the peaceful conditions in which commerce could flourish. The city's privileges were set out in royal charters, and the citizens negotiated with the Crown on such matters as the right to trade within England free from tolls and the annual levy imposed upon the city, attempting to fix it at no more than £300. This they obtained as a concession from kings in a weak political position, such as Stephen and John, while those firmly in control, such as Henry II, set it at more than £500. The post of staller, introduced by the Danes, was discontinued under the Normans, with two sheriffs, appointed by the Crown, deputed to collect the levy.

An innovation during the Danish monarchy had been the Court of Hustings, first mentioned during Cnut's reign, and that did become established, dealing with disputes such as those over property, debt and trade. By the twelfth century it met weekly and had superseded the much older assembly of citizens known as the folkmoot, now limited to three meetings a year, in the open air north-east of St Paul's. In addition, by Fitzstephen's time the city was subdivided into twenty-four wards, where local courts were held under the direction of an alderman, many of whom had a connection with the royal household. The size of the wards reflected the density of occupation. Several of them lay both within and outside the walls; Farringdon was the largest ward, containing Ludgate and Newgate, which reflected the sparser development in the western part of the city. In 1394 it was divided into two and in 1550 Southwark became Bridge Ward Without, bringing the number of wards up to twenty-six.

The Londoners' attempts to gain greater control over their affairs bore fruit during the years of monarchical weakness in the late twelfth and early thirteenth centuries. Soon after Richard I's accession in 1189 he went off to join the Third Crusade, appointing the unpopular William Longchamp as chancellor and joint justiciar. A power struggle developed between Longchamp and Richard's brother and heir Prince John, and in the summer of 1191 Longchamp was forced to retreat to the Tower, while John confidently swept into London and held a meeting in St Paul's. He had the Londoners' support, but to retain it he needed to make concessions, granting the city commune status. A commune was an association of citizens who swore to uphold or extend their rights, which were taken to include choice of a civic leader, known as a mayor. London briefly had such a status in 1141, granted by Stephen, and the Londoners had responded by not only preventing the coronation of his rival the Empress Matilda, in Westminster Abbey, but driving her and her supporters away from the city. No mayor was recorded as being chosen then and the first mayor was Henry Fitz Ailwin, an alderman since 1168, who was described as mayor in 1194 and held the post until his death in 1212. John succeeded to the throne in 1199 and in a charter granted in 1215 he conceded the principle of an elected mayor. He was then in the throes of his dispute with the barons, who received London's support, despite that new charter. The struggle culminated in the granting of Magna Carta, a clause of which stated that taxes could be levied only by the 'common counsel' of the realm, and specifically included London within that provision, and another declared that 'the city of London is to have all its ancient liberties and free customs both by land and water'.

The mayor was chosen from among the aldermen at an annual gathering of the freemen (the term lord mayor came into use during the sixteenth century). A smaller group of 'respectable men' emerged as an element in the city's government before the end of the thirteenth century and in time was to become the Common Council. The mayor was senior to the sheriffs; John also accepted that the sheriffs should be chosen by the city, not the Crown. From the early thirteenth century a mayor's court developed, handling business not dealt with by the Court of Hustings. And so by the end of John's reign in 1216 London had become a self-governing city, albeit subject to occasional taxation by the Crown in addition to the regular levy, but with its principal officers chosen from among its own citizens. From those arrangements, the Court of Aldermen had emerged as the city's ruling body, providing the agenda for the much larger Common Council, the legislative body, and having the right of veto over its proceedings. Common Council was called and dissolved by the mayor and its members were elected by the Court of Common Hall, with the right to vote restricted to the freemen of the city. The Guildhall was the meeting place of the Court of Aldermen and the Court of Common Council, and the place where elections were held.

Another element in the administration of the city was the craft and trade guilds, the earliest of which, the weavers and the bakers, were established in the mid-twelfth century. They became more numerous from the thirteenth century, until there were roughly sixty-five of them around 1300. They limited access to their trade, and so controlled the numbers entitled to work, by regulating apprenticeships and the journeymen; they also maintained the quality of their products and provided help for needy widows and children of deceased members. The guilds, which came to be known as livery companies in the fifteenth century, developed an important role in the government of the city, for increasingly their leaders became the powerful men in its administration. They also played a growing part in London's social and ceremonial life.

Disputes with the Crown continued intermittently, with a serious breakdown when a faction among the city's rulers opted to side with the barons, under the leadership of Simon de Montfort, in their dispute with John's son, Henry III (1216–72), in 1263. Civil war ensued, until the barons' defeat and de Montfort's death at the Battle of Evesham in 1265. Henry's son and successor Edward I (1272–1307) restored the Crown's authority and asserted his control over London when he took the city's government into his own hands in 1285. It was administered by royal wardens for the next thirteen years, until the Crown returned it to its mayor and officers in 1298.

As well as intervening in London's affairs, the Crown retained a strong presence in the city at the Tower. Henry III extended its area by enlarging the outer ward and created a new royal palace within the inner ward, and Edward I pushed the walled area even further out, into the city, and during his reign the Tower attained the size and form which it still retains. At Westminster Henry III developed the cult of Edward the Confessor, who had been canonised by Pope Alexander III in 1161, by rebuilding the abbey church, which included a new tomb for the saint's remains, which were placed there in 1269.

Edward's cult and shrine were primarily royal concerns; the Londoners' own especial saint was Thomas à Becket, Archbishop of Canterbury, following his murder by Henry II's knights in 1170 and canonisation in 1173. His shrine was in Canterbury, but he was born in Cheapside and the Londoners regarded him as one of their own. Pilgrims making the journey from Southwark to Canterbury were to provide the setting for Geoffrey Chaucer's *The Canterbury Tales*, which he wrote towards the end of the fourteenth century.

The monarchs and members of the court had a role in establishing monastic foundations in and around London. William I's request to the abbot of Cluny to send twelve monks to England led to the founding of the priory of St Saviour's in Bermondsey, in 1082, and Holy Trinity, Aldgate, was founded by Matilda, Henry I's queen, for the Augustinian canons. Another Augustinian house was St

Bartholomew's priory, founded in 1123 by Rahere, who had been a member of Henry I's court, and the priory of St Mary Overy was established in Southwark around 1106. Both contained hospitals, but in the early thirteenth century St Mary Overy's hospital was moved away from the priory and developed separately as St Thomas's. The hospital of St Mary without Bishopsgate was established in 1197 and was run by the Augustinians to provide care for the sick poor and women in childbirth, and for the children of mothers who had died giving birth. Initially there were twelve or thirteen inmates, but in 1253 the hospital was refounded on a much larger scale, with infirmaries for men and for women, each containing thirty beds. The city authorities contributed to the foundation of the Dominicans, or Black Friars, on the site of Baynard's Castle and Montfichet's Tower, demolishing those buildings in 1275 and giving the site to the monks, who moved there from Shoe Lane. The citizens were also associated with the monasteries by donations and bequests, and by choosing to be buried within them. The monastic houses and hospitals became an integral part of the community.

Another significant project was the building of a new bridge, in stone. The pre-Conquest bridge was destroyed by a surge of water in 1091, its replacement was damaged in a general conflagration in 1135 and a new timber bridge was built in 1163, overseen by Peter de Colechurch, a parish priest. That succession of problems demonstrated the need for a more durable structure and so a stone bridge was built, between 1176 and 1212, under de Colechurch's direction. At just over 300 yards long, it was by far the largest stone bridge in England and unusually large by European standards. A gatehouse with a drawbridge was built at

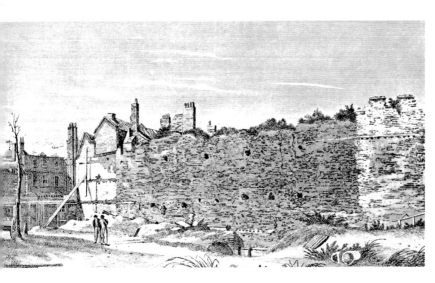

Above: 5. The medieval city wall at Tower Hill, exposed when the buildings adjoining it were destroyed by a fire in 1818. (Stephen Porter)

Right: 6. The circular church of the Knights Templar was built around 1160–85 and a rectangular chancel or choir was added around 1240. A community of lawyers grew up nearby, which evolved into the Inner Temple and Middle Temple; the lawyers were permitted to continue to use the chapel after the Knights Hospitaller were suppressed in 1539. (Stephen Porter)

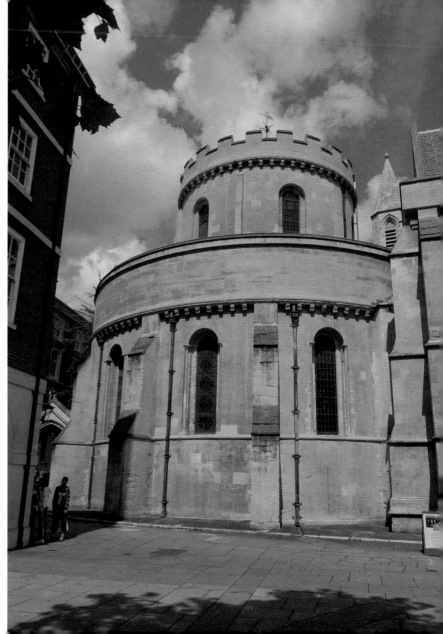

its south end and in 1426 a second, larger gatehouse was added. A chapel dedicated to St Thomas à Becket was erected on the bridge, probably in the early thirteenth century, and rebuilt in 1384–97. What made the bridge unusual were the shops which lined the roadway on both sides. It drew admiring comments from most visitors to London, for its structure and the richness of the goods for sale in those shops.

The bridge prevented seagoing vessels from sailing further upstream. In 1275 Edward I introduced a levy on wool, effectively initiating a national system of customs, and the quays on the north bank between the bridge and the Tower became the Legal Quays, where goods liable for customs duties were loaded and unloaded, and where a custom house was built around 1382. The quays were steadily enlarged and improved and that stretch of the river was designated as the Pool of London. Edward I also intervened in English trade when, in 1270, Flemish merchants were arrested during a dispute between England and Flanders. They had considerable control of the wool trade, preferring to ship it to the clothmaking towns of Flanders from Lynn and Boston, rather than London. By the time that the dispute was settled and they were readmitted to the trade, seven years later, Italian merchants and those from the Hanseatic ports had taken their place, and they operated through London. The Hanseatic League was formed in 1241 as a loose grouping of northern European cities trading abroad, directed by a diet that met in Lübeck. German merchants were operating in London by the 1150s and were granted concessions in 1194, 1260 and 1303, which included the freedom to trade throughout England and partial exemption from taxation. They were based at the Steelyard, on the Thames, and among the reciprocal obligations was the maintenance of the gate at Bishopsgate by the merchants, who paid for its rebuilding in 1479.

The Italian and north European merchants also took over some functions, such as the granting of loans, from the Jewish community, who suffered from both official and more general persecution during the mid-thirteenth century. In 1275 the Statute of the Jewry prohibited them from taking interest and granting mortgages. Many members of the community were imprisoned in the Tower over the following two years, and they were subject to a further bout of persecution in 1279–80, when a contemporary chronicler recorded that more than 280 were hanged. In 1290 Edward I expelled the entire community from England; the Constable of the Tower took a toll from the 1,461 Jews who embarked within his jurisdiction.

Despite disruptions such as the dispute with Flanders, London's trade prospered during the thirteenth century. Imports included Baltic grain, cloth from Flanders, furs from Russia, wine from Germany and increasingly from Bordeaux, following the addition of Gascony to English possessions with the marriage of Henry II and Eleanor of Aquitaine in 1152. Luxury items such as silks, gold, precious jewels and enamels were also imported. With the prosperity of overseas trade and the output of London's skilled artisans, the city's economy grew, as did its population, which may have risen in the twelfth century to around 40,000 and then continued to grow, so that by 1300 it had reached roughly 80,000, perhaps even 100,000. Provisions were drawn from south-east England and beyond, and the water supply from wells was augmented by that from conduits; the great conduit in

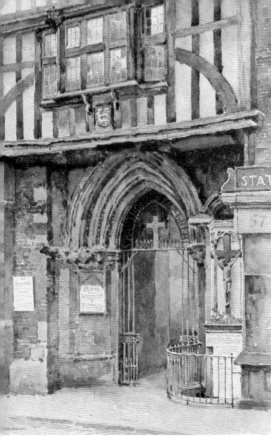

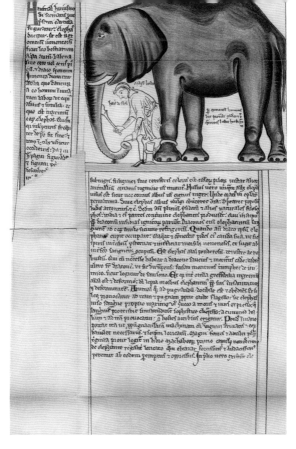

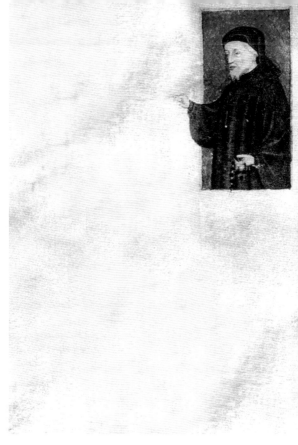

7. The gatehouse of the church of St Bartholomew the Great in Smithfield; the stone doorway was the west entrance to the priory church and was retained when the nave was demolished around 1543. The painting is by E. W. Haslehust, around 1924. (Stephen Porter)

8. The elephant given to Henry III by Louis IX of France in 1255, drawn by Matthew Paris, who described it as 'the only elephant ever seen in England'. (Jonathan Reeve JR2225b99plateXVI 12001300)

9. Portrait of Geoffrey Chaucer, who was a customs officer when, from 1374 to 1385, he lived in the rooms over Aldgate as a tenant of the corporation; he wrote *Troylus and Cryseyde* during those years. The portrait is from Thomas Hoccleve's *The Regiment of Princes* of 1412. (Jonathan Reeve, JR991b1p2 13001400)

Cheapside was built in 1236–45 and rebuilt in 1286, and that at Cornhill in 1282, by Henry le Waleys, who served three terms as mayor. Other environmental matters were dealt with, such as the removal of garbage, and thatched roofs, which were prohibited in building regulations promulgated in 1189. Despite such attention to conditions in the city, the burials of more than 2,000 bodies in pits at St Mary Spital from the late thirteenth century show how vulnerable the metropolis was to epidemic disease.

That weakness was exposed during the fourteenth century, which saw a quite different demographic pattern. Poor harvests for several years before 1315 had led to high prices for corn and other foodstuffs, but it was the almost incessant rain during the summer and autumn of that year which caused a catastrophically bad harvest across much of northern Europe. According to an English account, there was 'a gret derthe of corn and other vitailes … and the poure peple eten for hunger cattes and hors and houndes … stal [stole] children and eten them, and thanne anon after there fille a gret pestilence among the peple'. The famine and epidemic lasted through the next two years and checked population growth. Subsequently, Edward III's decision in 1334 to assert his claim to the French throne by force began the series of campaigns which became known as the Hundred Years War. They were expensive to sustain and disruptive of London's trade, such as the wine imports from Bordeaux, because of the devastation of the vineyards in Gascony and the depredations of pirates.

After the mid-fourteenth century London had a much smaller population from which taxes could be levied, for the Black Death reached the city in the autumn of 1348 and in less than a year killed at least one-third, and possibly half, of its inhabitants. A chronicler recorded that the 'violent pestilence' had broken out over the whole country 'and especially in the city of London where people superabounded, so great a multitude eventually died there that all the cemeteries of the aforesaid city were insufficient for the burial of the dead'. Victims had to be buried wherever space could be found, some in unconsecrated ground, and, it was said, corpses were even thrown into the Thames. During this 'grete pestylence at London' thousands were interred in three new burial grounds opened outside the walls. Monasteries were subsequently founded adjoining two of them, a Cistercian one at East Smithfield and a Carthusian priory at West Smithfield. Further epidemics followed. That in 1361 killed roughly one-third of the depleted population, another in 1368 was less deadly, but in 1375 'a large number of Londoners, from among the wealthier and more eminent citizens, died in the pestilence'. London's population may have fallen to below 40,000 and was not to recover its former level before the sixteenth century.

In the wake of the Black Death, the reign of Edward's grandson Richard II was a turbulent one, both nationally and within London. During the late 1370s the authority of the aldermen was undermined by changes to the electoral procedure for membership of the Common Council and a rule that aldermen should be elected for only one year, not for life. Then in 1381 the Peasants' Revolt erupted, a popular uprising provoked partly by the imposition of a poll tax. The rebels from Kent ran amok in London: they looted the shops, set fire to John of Gaunt's palace of the Savoy, destroyed 'several fine houses', attacked the Archbishop of Canterbury's palace at Lambeth, captured the Fleet and Marshalsea prisons, burned the lawyers' books at the Temple, and threatened to 'burn and destroy everything'. They even broke into the Tower, releasing prisoners and murdering Simon Sudbury, Archbishop of Canterbury and chancellor, along with the treasurer, a serjeant at law who was held responsible for the poll tax and John of Gaunt's physician. Perhaps as many as 150 people were beheaded across London on the same day. The revolt petered out after its leader, Wat Tyler, had been wounded by the mayor, Sir William Walworth, during a meeting with the king at Smithfield, and subsequently dragged out of St Bartholomew's priory and executed.

The electoral changes were reversed after the revolt, but factionalism within the elite continued, with one group supporting the five dissident leading nobles known as the lords appellant, who defeated the king's army in 1387 and were able to occupy London, where they confronted Richard, who had withdrawn to the Tower. The mayor, Sir Nicholas Brembre, a supporter of the king, was one of five men accused by them of treason. Tried by Parliament and convicted, he was executed in 1388. Richard survived the crisis and wrested power back from the lords in 1389, punishing the city by suspending its government and levying the huge fine of £10,000. But in 1399 he was deposed by one of the lords, Henry Bolingbroke, who took the throne as Henry IV. The changes of the 1370s had been reversed, the city's elite again held unchallenged control and after Henry's accession relations with the Crown improved.

A relatively stable period followed. London's smaller population was advantageous for wage earners and there were no serious food shortages. A municipal granary was erected at Leadenhall after the market rights were acquired by Sir Richard Whittington and transferred by him to the corporation; the building was completed in 1455. The city also supervised the market at Blackwell Hall, where cloth brought to London was sold. It acquired the building in 1396 and an arrangement by which the market was controlled by the mayor was formalised during Whittington's first term in that office, in 1397–98. That was intended to avoid dubious and dishonest bargains and to control the quality of the cloth, which became England's most valuable export commodity. From the mid-fourteenth century England's clothmaking industry developed rapidly, while wool exports steadily declined. Cloth exports rose eightfold during the second half of the century, and then quadrupled by the 1490s, an overall rise from 5,000 to 160,000 cloths per year. The trade increasingly was in the hands of London merchants, and by the mid-sixteenth century 89 per cent of cloth was exported through the city, an arrangement which applied to other sectors of overseas trade.

Whittington served as mayor on four occasions, but after his last term of office, in 1419–20, the pattern changed from the earlier period, when men had held the post for successive years, or were re-elected a number of times. In the fifteenth century they held the office once, or at most twice. Nor did dynasties emerge among the civic elite, for the second or third generations of a successful family typically chose to invest in land and become country landowners, rather than continue a civic dynasty. And so London did not have overmighty families that vied with each other for power and influence within the city. By the fifteenth century its leaders came from the livery companies. They had confidence and wealth, building halls for their companies and a new guildhall for their city, which was the largest guildhall in medieval England. Begun in 1411, it took almost twenty years to complete.

Londoners donated some of their wealth for charitable purposes, directly or through a livery company, with gifts and bequests to the forty or so monastic houses, as well as to the religious fraternities which were attached to them and to the parishes. Through such donations roughly a quarter of the property in the city came to be held by the monasteries, providing them with rental income. Almshouses for the elderly and writing schools, grammar schools and music schools for the young were established. Although music played a significant part in the life of the city, drama apparently did not. Yet literacy extended beyond the wealthy mercantile classes and the livery companies came to require a basic level of education for would-be apprentices; for example, in 1478 the goldsmiths' company forbade its members to enrol an apprentice 'wtout he canne writte and Rede'. Probably more than 50 per cent of the adult male population and a lower, but significant, proportion of women were literate. Women were active economically and were permitted to take up the freedom of the city, so they enrolled as apprentices and traded alone, and a widow could continue her husband's business.

The literate Londoners provided a market for printed books, which were being imported into the city before William Caxton set up his printing press at the sign of the Red Pale in Westminster in 1476. In 1479–80 two merchants imported at least 1,200 books, and Caxton was an importer as well as a printer, bringing in 1,161 books and 'one container with books' through the port of London in the space of two months in 1488. Wynkyn de Worde took over Caxton's business after his death in 1492 and in 1500–01 he moved to premises at the sign of the Sun in Fleet Street. Other printers followed, beginning that district's long connection with the printing trade.

The stability of the fifteenth century was disturbed occasionally. During Jack Cade's rebellion, in 1450, rebels from Kent occupied the city, but their behaviour provoked the citizens, who 'did arise and came out upon them' one evening and 'until the morrow eight of the bell they were ever fighting upon London Bridge'. That response by the Londoners effectively suppressed the rebellion. During the Wars of the Roses, which began in 1455, Londoners probably were more sympathetic to the Yorkists than to the Lancastrians. They helped to besiege a Lancastrian force in the Tower in 1460, enduring a bombardment in the process, and in the following year closed Cripplegate against a delegation of Lancastrian knights. They also impounded a convoy of supplies that was to be sent to their army, while allowing the Yorkist leader and his supporters to enter the city, where he was proclaimed king as Edward IV.

During the dynastic quarrels the Tower was the scene of the violent deaths of Henry VI, Edward IV's brother the Duke of Clarence, and, most probably, his sons, Edward V and the Duke of York. The Plantagenet dynasty came to an end with the defeat and death of Richard III by Henry Tudor at the Battle of Bosworth in August 1485. Henry had to take control of London to be secure, but there was no other force to oppose him and, according to Sir Francis Bacon's account, 'the mayor and companies of the city received him at Shoreditch, whence, with great and honourable attendance and troops of noblemen and persons of quality, he entered the city'. His coronation, as Henry VII, took place in Westminster Abbey on 30 October.

Below right: 10. The west front of St Paul's Cathedral is shown on this redrawing from an early fourteenth-century manuscript describing the foundation of the city. (Jonathan Reeve, JR329b11p385 13001350)

Below left: 11. In Convers Lane, later Chancery Lane, Henry III established a Converts House with a chapel around 1231, for Jews who had converted to Christianity. After the expulsion of the Jews in 1290 the house was closed and in 1377 it was assigned to the Keeper of the Rolls of Chancery. The Chancery records were stored in the chapel. The illustration is from the *Chronica Majora* of Matthew Paris, who died in 1259. (Jonathan Reeve, JR1021b11p392 13501450)

Right: 12. The illustration of Charles, Duke of Orléans, nephew of Charles V, imprisoned in the Tower was drawn in the late fifteenth century and shows not only the Tower itself but also London Bridge and a part of the city beyond it. (Jonathan Reeve JR992b4p640 14501550)

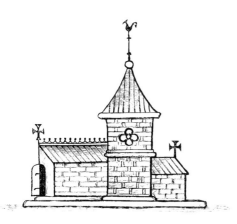
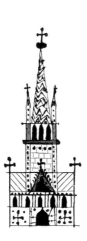
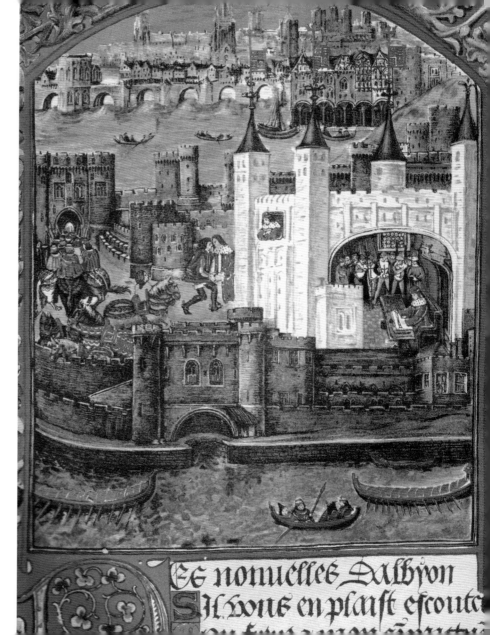

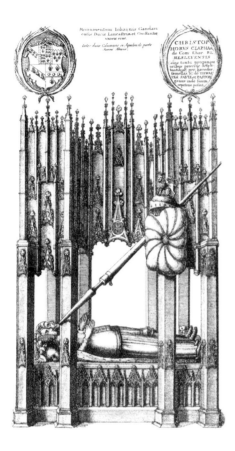

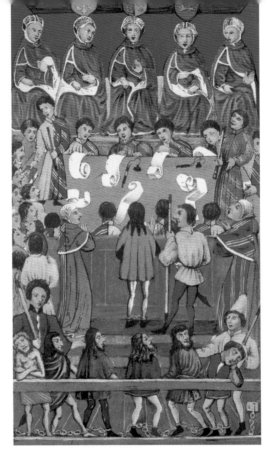

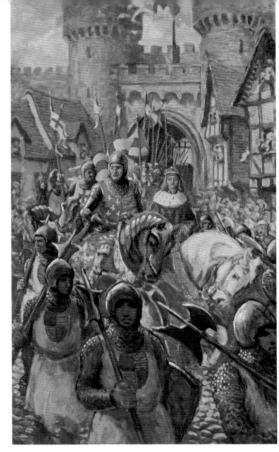

13. John of Gaunt, Duke of Lancaster, the third son of Edward III, was involved in London politics and became an unpopular figure; his great palace at the Savoy was burned during the Peasants' Revolt of 1381. Yet he was buried in St Paul's Cathedral, alongside his first wife, Blanche. Their tomb was destroyed during the Great Fire. (Stephen Porter)

14. The Court of King's Bench sitting in Westminster Hall around 1460. (Jonathan Reeve, JR1579b4fp564 14501500)

15. Control of London was essential for any government and after Edward IV's death his brother Richard, Duke of Gloucester, took charge of the new king, his nephew Edward V, and brought him into the city in May 1483. (Jonathan Reeve, JR1581b61fp592 14501500)

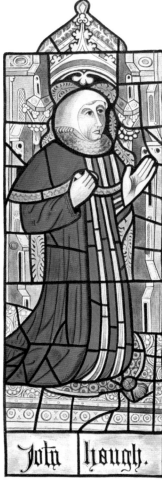
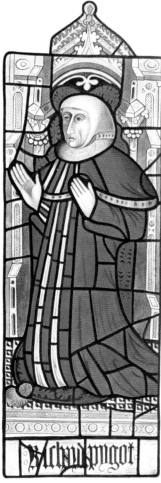
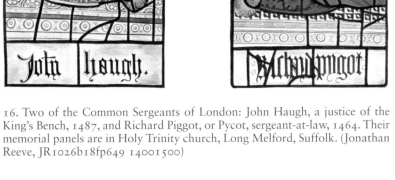

John hough. Richard pigot

16. Two of the Common Sergeants of London: John Haugh, a justice of the King's Bench, 1487, and Richard Piggot, or Pycot, sergeant-at-law, 1464. Their memorial panels are in Holy Trinity church, Long Melford, Suffolk. (Jonathan Reeve, JR1026b18fp649 14001500)

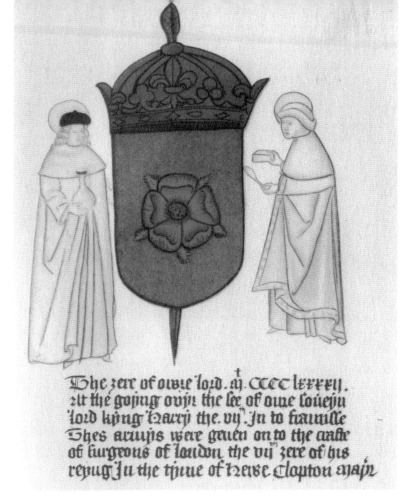

The zere of owre lord. M. CCCC lxxxij. at the goyng oujr the see of owre soueju lord kyng Harry the vij in to fraunce Thes armys were geuen on to the crafte of surgeons of london the vij zere of his reyug Jn the tyme of Herre clopton mair

17. The arms of the Barber-Surgeons' Company, granted by Henry VII and illustrated in 1492, depicting the company's patron saints, St Cosmo and St Damian. (Stephen Porter)

4

TUDOR AND JACOBEAN LONDON

Any rejoicing at Henry VII's victory was marred by the appearance of a fatal disease in London before the end of 1485, which was blamed on his troops. Probably a viral infection, it was described as 'a gret dethe and hasty, called swettyng syknes'. The sweat, as it became known, was feared not only because of the high mortality rate, with 'scarcely one in a hundred' of those who contracted the disease surviving, but also because its victims died so quickly, generally within twenty-four hours. The disease struck both the prosperous and the poor, whereas the plague was thought of as mostly afflicting the poor, because the well-to-do took evasive action, by leaving.

Severe epidemics of both the sweat and plague occurred intermittently through the late fifteenth and early sixteenth centuries. An epidemic in 1498, probably of the plague, carried off perhaps 10,000 people in London, the sweat returned in 1508–09 and during a 'great plague' in 1513 the daily death toll reached as high as 300 to 400. In the summer of 1517 another outbreak of the sweat was swiftly followed by a plague epidemic, with Sir Thomas More commenting that it was safer to be on the battlefield than in London. Such eruptions prompted the introduction of measures designed to prevent the spread of diseases during an epidemic and to provide for the sick during their illness. Although the first

such steps were taken in 1518 and the government pressed the authorities in the city to enforce them, a codification of the orders for London was not issued until 1583. That was twenty years after the worst plague outbreak in the capital during the Tudor era, in 1563, when 23,660 people died, 85 per cent of them from plague, or roughly one-fifth of the population.

Despite the death toll during such outbreaks, and the high mortality levels during non-epidemic years, London's population grew remorselessly during the sixteenth and early seventeenth centuries, at first steadily and then increasingly rapidly. The number of inhabitants rose from roughly 80,000 in 1550 to 200,000 in 1600 and perhaps 260,000 by 1625. That growth came to be a major concern to the government. It feared the threat to public health, for polluted air and a foul environment were thought to be among the causes of disease, exacerbated by the overcrowding in such a large city and by the problem of rubbish disposal. Another concern was the rising numbers of poor, which placed a strain on the system of poor relief and raised the spectre of social instability and unrest. The problems of ever-expanding suburbs, containing 'filthy cottages' and rubbish dumps, overcrowding and the consequent subdivision of houses could not be ignored. To curb the city's growth, a proclamation was issued in 1580 which prohibited new building and ordered that a house should be occupied by only one family. Despite attempts to enforce this and subsequent orders, London's growth was inexorable, and in the early seventeenth century the fines levied for breach of the edicts against new building came to be seen by the authorities as a means of raising revenue rather than curbing expansion.

In contrast to the scruffy and disreputable suburbs, the centre of the city contained timber-built houses of three and four storeys, roofed with tiles. The finest group was Goldsmiths' Row in Cheapside, erected in 1491, which had ten houses, with fourteen narrow shops, and was four storeys high, 'uniformly built'. But that was an exception and the lack of uniformity in the street frontages was criticised by visitors. A proclamation issued in 1605 attempted to improve the city's appearance by ordering that the fronts of houses should be of brick or stone and that 'the forefront thereof in every respect shall be made of that uniforme order and forme, as shall be prescribed unto them for that Streete'. But that could only be applied to new or rebuilt houses and so the change which was envisaged would take time to achieve. Enforcement of that and other policies was hindered by the refusal of the city's government to expand its boundaries, and so while the area governed by the mayor and aldermen, which for convenience could be described as the City, was closely regulated, the built-up area beyond was administered by the Middlesex and Surrey justices of the peace, with less authority and fewer resources in larger parishes. In the mid-sixteenth century 75 per cent of Londoners lived in the City, but the proportion fell as the population increased, and by 1700 it was only 25 per cent.

The authorities did not have to face a famine crisis and only occasionally were troubled by protests against high prices, for population growth did not produce food shortages. Supplies were drawn from a wide area of England, and increasingly from Wales and Scotland, too, and kept pace with the city's expansion. Market gardens were developed around the city from the late sixteenth century, providing its fruit and vegetables, and by 1617 they were said to employ 'thowsands of poore people'. The markets were regulated and the aldermen intervened when necessary to limit price increases. Water supplies were augmented, most notably with the opening of the New River in 1613, which brought water from Hertfordshire to Clerkenwell.

London had become busy and congested. Jacob Rathgeb, from Würtemberg, was just one of several visitors from abroad who commented on how crowded it was, writing that 'it is a very populous city, so that one can scarcely pass along the streets, on account of the throng'. The growth was fuelled largely by those drawn to London from the provinces for economic reasons. A far smaller number came from the Continent, with about 3,000 'strangers' living in the city in 1500. But although their communities were small and some were of long standing, they attracted attention and resentment. The Evil May Day riot of 1517 was directed against the strangers, with the apprentices' anger being taken out chiefly on the Flemish community. That outburst had precedents in the fifteenth century, with anti-Italian flare-ups in 1456 and 1457 and attacks on the Steelyard in 1462 and 1494. Yet no similar anti-immigrant riot occurred after 1517, although one was threatened in a pamphlet distributed in 1593, which demanded that all the French and Flemish should leave, or else 'all the apprentices and journeymen will down with the Flemish and strangers'.

During the second half of the sixteenth century anxiety about the numbers of strangers prompted the city authorities and the government to organise enumerations. But one covering the year to Easter 1567 showed that out of 2,750 incomers, only 232 settled in London. At a count taken in 1573 the city contained 7,143 strangers and an enumeration twenty years later produced a similar figure, but did not include Westminster, and the true number may have been around 10,000. The 1593 return revealed that twice as many strangers had arrived from the Low Countries as from France, and fewer still from Germany. The Dutch and Flemish community was settled chiefly east of the Tower and in Southwark. Religious refugees came to form a significant proportion of the incomers; a commission of the mayor and aldermen in 1551 noted that the strangers were 'for the most part heretics out of other countries'. They arrived from France, where the Wars of Religion dragged on from 1562 to 1598, and the Low Countries, as Spain attempted to reassert its authority over its rebellious provinces there. Yet the economic motive remained a strong one, with roughly a third of those recorded in 1573 stating 'that their coming hither was onlie to seeke woorke for their livinge', drawn by London's prosperous and expanding economy.

Among the forces driving that economy was the presence of the royal court, which for much of the year was fixed at Westminster Palace, until its living apartments were destroyed by fire in 1512. Briefly thereafter it was at the new Bridewell Palace and from 1529 at Whitehall Palace, which became the principal royal residence. Parts of Westminster Palace escaped

the flames, including Westminster Hall, St Stephen's chapel (which became the meeting place of the House of Commons after 1547), the Painted Chamber, the White Chamber (where the House of Lords sat) and the Court of Requests. And so the sittings of Parliament, which became more frequent from the reign of Henry VIII, continued to be held in Westminster, as did the courts of law.

The aristocracy and the country gentry began to bring their families with them on their visits to London for the meetings of Parliament or for social and business reasons, and to stay longer, producing a growing market for suitable accommodation and luxury goods, and business for the steadily developing professions. Those goods were supplied by London's burgeoning overseas trade and skilled craftsmen; its economy was summarised by Lupold von Wedel, from Pomerania, in 1585 as consisting of 'great trade and many handicrafts'. The city contained a range of manufacturing and service trades, skilled and semi-skilled workers, and wholesalers and retailers, who were described by the historian of London John Stow as 'mercers, vintners, haberdashers, ironmonger, milliners, and all such as sell wares growing or made beyond the seas'.

Long-standing trade routes connected the city with northern Europe and Iberia, but world trade expanded as European traders financed voyages to the Americas, the Indian Ocean and the East Indies, and increasingly London's merchants 'have sought out the East and West Indies and made now and then suspicious [exploratory] journeys not only unto the Canaries, and New Spain, but likewise unto Cathaia, Muscovia, Tartaria and the regions thereabouts'. A visitor in 1597 wrote that they 'trade also in Poland, Muscovy, and as far as Persia'. The merchants met in the open in Lombard Street until the completion of the Royal Exchange, in 1568. It provided a focus for the merchants, who transacted their business in the courtyard, and also served as a convenient meeting place, where information and opinions could be exchanged.

Trading companies were formed for the commerce with the new regions: the Muscovy Company was established in 1555, the Eastland Company for trade with Scandinavia and the Baltic in 1579, the Turkey Company in 1581, the Venice Company in 1583 (the Turkey and Venice companies became the Levant Company in 1592), the East India Company in 1600 and the Virginia Company in 1609. Trade with Morocco began in 1551, but the Barbary Company, established in 1585, was dissolved twelve years later, perhaps because it had made little impact on the trade and the merchants felt that they would be as well off without it. The range of goods imported steadily widened, with pepper, currants, spices, silk, cotton, indigo, calico, dyes and sugar being brought in. Wine imports rose fivefold between 1563 and 1620 and as tobacco increased in popularity it became one of the more valuable imports. By the end of the sixteenth century London handled roughly 80 per cent of England's imports and exports.

Embedded in cargoes imported in the 1520s and 1530s were caches of prohibited Protestant books clandestinely brought from Antwerp, including the New Testament translated into English by William Tyndale and printed in 1525–26. Rose Hickman later remembered those days, when her mother would read to her and her sisters from the 'good books very privately for fear of troble'. They had been sent to Rose's mother by her husband's agents

'from beyond the sea'. John Wycliffe had translated the Bible into English in the 1380s and the supporters of his reforming ideas, dubbed Lollards, were persecuted as heretics. Yet their beliefs survived and the numbers of religious dissidents were augmented in the early sixteenth century by a small but growing number of Protestants, especially after Martin Luther went public with his criticism of the Church in 1517. In the 1520s Henry VIII's concerns over his lack of a male heir and fears for the survival of the Tudor dynasty led to his seeking an annulment of his marriage to Katherine of Aragon. The Pope was unable to oblige, for Katherine's nephew was the Emperor Charles V, whose troops sacked Rome in 1527. Henry's solution was to break from the papacy and make himself head of the English Church. Persecution of Protestants gradually eased during the 1530s and the policy regarding English Bibles changed from having them burnt to the authorisation in 1539 of the 'Great Bible', which was in English.

Having supplanted the Pope as head of the Church, Henry proceeded to expel the monastic orders, dissolve the religious houses and their hospitals and appropriate their lands and buildings. Most monks acquiesced, but members of the Carthusian order opposed the king. The prior of the London Charterhouse, John Houghton, was convicted of treason and executed in May 1535, together with the priors of Beauvale and Axholme. During that summer three other senior members of the London house were executed. In 1536, fourteen of its monks and lay brothers were removed to other Carthusian houses and in the following year ten more were imprisoned in Newgate, where nine of them died; the tenth was executed in 1540. In all, ten monks and six lay brothers of the

London Charterhouse lost their lives. No other order followed their example and any popular sympathy for their suffering did not translate into official support: the Court of Aldermen decided that 'no labour shalbe made by thys Cytye yn that bihalf'.

The Court of Augmentations was established to oversee the disposal of the monastic property. Its sale released those houses on to the market, while the sites of the monasteries themselves were generally converted to grand houses by the wealthy. Not all monastic property was disposed of in that way. The Austin Friars was obtained by William Paulet, but the nave of the church was granted by the Crown in 1550 to the Dutch community. The Greyfriars in Newgate Street was given to the corporation and the grant was confirmed by Edward VI when he established Christ's Hospital there, for 'poor fatherless children'. Bridewell, Bethlehem hospital and St Thomas's hospital were also presented to the city. A conspicuous example of the changes to the townscape in the wake of the Reformation was the demolition of the chapel of Thomas à Becket on the bridge, in 1553. Coincidentally, during the 1530s the ecclesiastical palaces which lined the Strand were acquired by members of the aristocracy and leading courtiers.

The redistribution of property could not be reversed during the reign of Mary Tudor (1553–58), when England was returned to the Catholic faith. Popular dissatisfaction and hopes that Mary would be replaced by her sister Elizabeth fuelled a rebellion in Kent in 1554, led by Sir Thomas Wyatt. A detachment of Londoners sent to suppress it defected to the rebels, encouraging Wyatt to think that he might capture the city. His force occupied Southwark, but was prevented from crossing the bridge. After a long detour through Kingston, the rebels eventually were able to make their way along the Strand, only to find Ludgate closed and defended against them. The rebellion fizzled out and Wyatt was executed.

Mary's reign was punctuated by other executions. During the reigns of the first three Tudor monarchs, between 1485 and 1553, 102 heretics were burnt, but the burnings of Protestants in the mid-1550s made a far deeper impression. The first took place in February 1555 and by the time of Mary's death, in November 1558, 283 people had been burnt, seventy-eight of them in London, of whom fifty-six were executed in Smithfield. Although only roughly a fifth of the Protestant martyrs were burnt there, 'the fires of Smithfield' came to symbolise those burnt to death for their faith during Mary's reign.

Elizabeth did indeed come to the throne, in 1558; Protestantism was then restored and became firmly established during her long reign, until she died in 1603. But Catholic writers continued to criticise the religious settlement, not least by claiming that charitable giving had been adversely affected by the Reformation. In fact, the monasteries had given only very small amounts in alms, in some cases less than 1 per cent of their revenues, and even Westminster Abbey gave only 3.3 per cent of its income to the poor. The pace of charitable giving increased after the Reformation, with donations and bequests to support the poor and elderly. They included casual almsgiving, funeral doles, collections taken in response to charitable appeals read after church services and formal giving through the establishment of charities, such as those for the distribution of bread, or, at the top of the scale, the founding of schools and almshouses. Endowments were received from Londoners and also those who had left the capital and become country gentry, who continued to establish and support charities in the city where they had made their fortunes. John Stow proudly noted, at the end of the sixteenth century, that London 'relieveth plentifully, and with good policy, not only her own poor people ... but also the poor that from each quarter of the realm do flock unto it'. The most spectacular charity, for its scale and setting, was the almshouse for eighty men and school for forty boys established by Thomas Sutton in 1611 in the mansion built on the site of the Carthusian priory. Sutton had made his fortune from various strands, including lending money at 10 per cent, as permitted by the Usury Act of 1571, and set himself up as a Cambridgeshire gentleman towards the end of his life. Poor relief was also administered through the parishes, with a rate levied from householders for the purpose, a practice which was adopted by the government as a policy in 1572. The Poor Law arrangements were confirmed by legislation in 1598 and 1601.

Yet not everyone was happy with the level of giving and Stow himself complained, in this context, that the citizens were now spending money for show and pleasure, on such buildings as summer houses. His comment referred to a growing enjoyment of prosperity and leisure. The citizens turned out in large numbers to watch the annual procession celebrating the inauguration of a new mayor. In the fifteenth century the mayors had taken a barge to Westminster to swear their oath of office, and during the sixteenth century that developed into a numerous and colourful armada of boats, with the mayor returning to the Guildhall in a procession that contained exotic animals, floats and a variety of entertainers. The event was staged by the mayor's livery company, which provided a theme appropriate for his trade, and the companies also observed their own round of celebratory occasions during the year. Another popular annual event was Bartholomew Fair in Smithfield, which lasted for three days, centred on St Bartholomew's Day, 24 August. It combined a range of entertainments, such as puppeteers, conjurers, actors, balladeers, wrestlers, tightrope walkers and fire-eaters, with trading, especially in cloth, leather, pewter, livestock, butter and cheese. It was followed in early September by Southwark Fair, also a three-day event, which had been held from at least as early as the 1440s.

More regular entertainments included archery, dancing, music, bell-ringing and football, and watching cockfighting, animal baiting and the theatres. Londoners most often went to Bankside, on the south side of the river, for their recreation. The district was only sparsely developed until the mid-sixteenth century and attracted attention chiefly because of its brothels, but it then became increasingly popular, for its bull- and bear-baiting and then its theatres. Stow mentioned the two arenas for animal baiting, 'wherein be kept bears, bulls, and other beasts, to be baited; as also mastiffs in several kennels, nourished to bait them'. The earliest purpose-built playhouse was erected in Whitechapel in 1567 and others followed, in Shoreditch, Newington Butts, Clerkenwell and Bankside, and later indoor theatres at Blackfriars and in Drury Lane. The number open at any one time varied, with theatres closing and new ones being built; the Globe was erected in Shoreditch in 1595 and was dismantled and reassembled on Bankside, where it reopened in 1599. Plays ran for only a few performances and so writers needed to produce a steady flow of new material, for audiences which probably numbered 21,000 per week by the early seventeenth century, when three playhouses and two hall theatres were open. The playgoers came from a wide social range, and the players were also conscripted to play before the court.

The social range of the playgoers did not reflect universal approval of the theatres, however, for the puritans, who were increasingly prominent in the city, found them repugnant on moral grounds, and both national and civic governments disapproved because of the risk they posed to public health. That objection extended to any large gathering of people, so that in 1610 Robert Cecil, Earl of Salisbury, could condemn Bartholomew Fair as 'this filthy Fair ... continual origin of the plague'. Theatres were closed during plague epidemics, which occurred in 1592–93, the worst since 1563; in 1603, in the early months of James I's reign; and in 1625, soon after his son Charles had come to the throne. The outbreaks in 1603 and 1625 each killed roughly one-fifth of London's population, but in both cases it returned to its pre-plague level within two years, because of the numbers drawn in to replace those who had died. Neither such devastating epidemics nor government policy on building checked the city's growth, which emphasised its economic power and unassailable position as the country's dominant city.

18. Henry VIII developed an enthusiasm for jousting. In 1511 he participated in the great tournament at Westminster depicted here, to celebrate the birth of his son, Henry. But the infant died before he was eight weeks old. (Jonathan Reeve JR1098b2fp204 15001550)

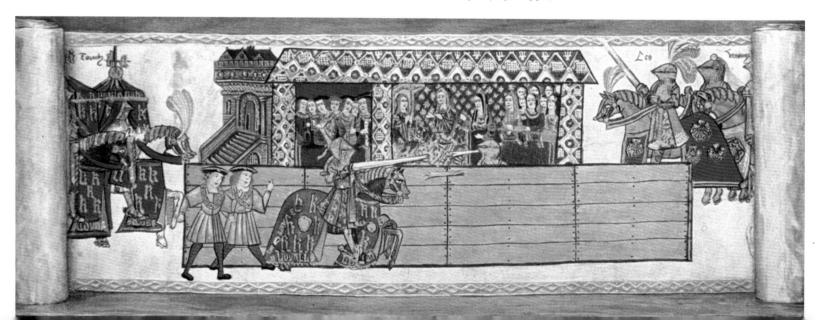

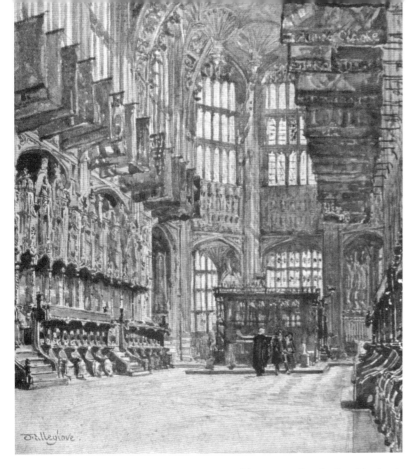

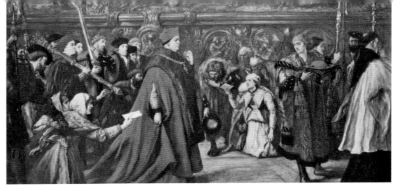

20. Cardinal Wolsey gained a dominant role at Henry VIII's court and greatly enlarged the Archbishop of York's palace at Westminster. In this painting, exhibited in 1887, Sir John Gilbert depicted him in his robes 'on his way to Westminster Hall'. (Stephen Porter)

19. The Henry VII chapel in Westminster Abbey, completed after his death in 1509, contains his tomb, with his queen, Elizabeth of York; the stalls and misericords are contemporary. In the aisles are the tombs of Henry VII's mother, Lady Margaret Beaufort, Mary, Queen of Scots, Elizabeth I and a monument containing bones discovered in the Tower of London in 1678 and believed to be those of Edward V and his brother Richard, Duke of York; depicted by John Fulleylove. (Stephen Porter)

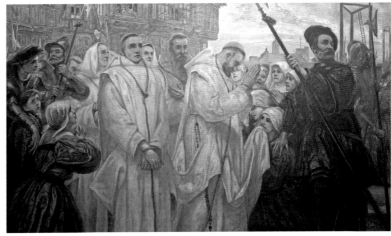

21. The Carthusian Martyrs at Tyburn, by Andrew Benjamin Donaldson (1840–1919). Convicted of treason, the priors of the London Charterhouse, Beauvale and Axholme were hanged, drawn and quartered, together with a monk from Syon Abbey, on 4 May 1535. (The Governors of Sutton's Hospital)

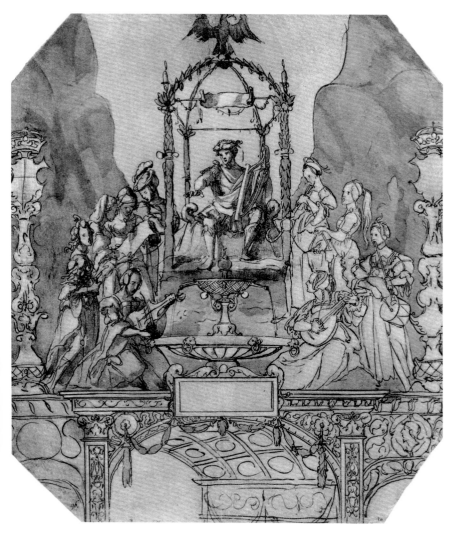

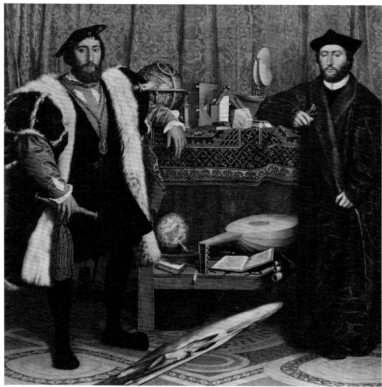

Above: 22. The French ambassador, Jean de Dinteville, lived in Bridewell Palace intermittently from 1531 to 1539. Hans Holbein's double portrait of de Dinteville and Georges de Selve, Bishop of Lavaur, was probably painted there in 1533. (Stephen Porter)

Left: 23. Design by Hans Holbein for a pageant tableau, probably for the merchants of the Steelyard for Anne Boleyn's coronation procession from the Tower to Westminster, 1533. (Elizabeth Norton and the Amberley Archive)

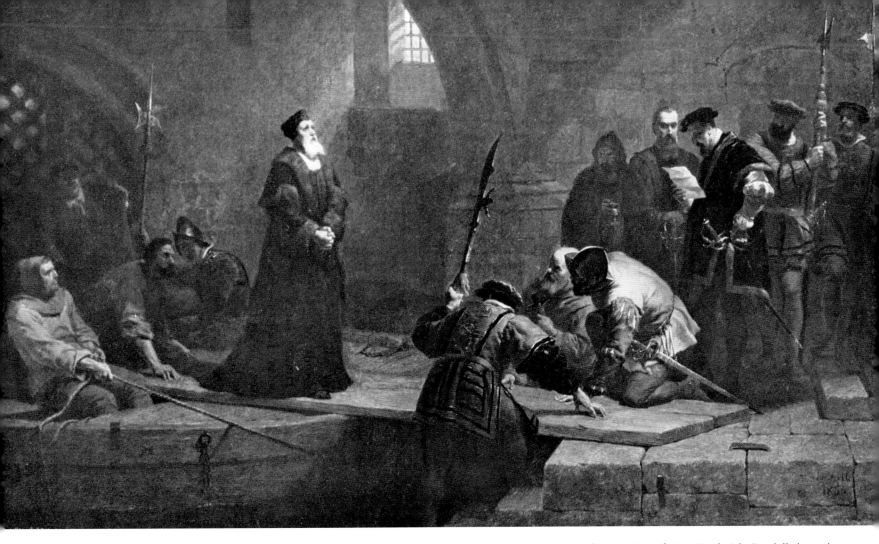

24. Scenes from national and London history became increasingly popular during the nineteenth century. In this painting of 1856 Frederick Goodall showed Archbishop Thomas Cranmer arriving at Traitor's Gate in the Tower of London, following his arrest in 1553. (Stephen Porter)

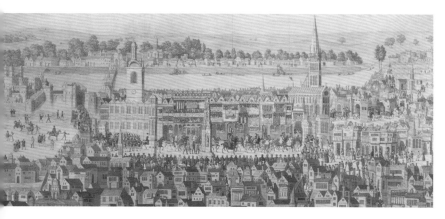

Above: 25. A panorama of Tudor London, looking south, illustrating the coronation procession of Edward VI from the Tower to Westminster, in 1547. The procession leaves the Tower, passes along Cheapside, through St Paul's churchyard, through Ludgate and Temple Bar to Westminster. Copy by Samuel Hieronymus Grimm (1733–94) of the (now lost) original. (Society of Antiquaries of London)

Right: 26. Sir Francis Vere was one of England's leading soldiers of his generation and served for many years in the Low Countries under Dutch command. After his death in 1609 he was buried in Westminster Abbey; the design of his tomb was based on that of Engelbert of Nassau at Breda. (Stephen Porter)

Opposite: 27. A wedding feast at Bermondsey, across the Thames from the Tower of London, by Joris Hoefnagel around 1570. It shows the feast being prepared, the dining area adjoining, musicians playing beneath a tree and much detail on the clothing of the participants on a holiday. This copy is by Samuel Hieronymus Grimm. (Society of Antiquaries of London)

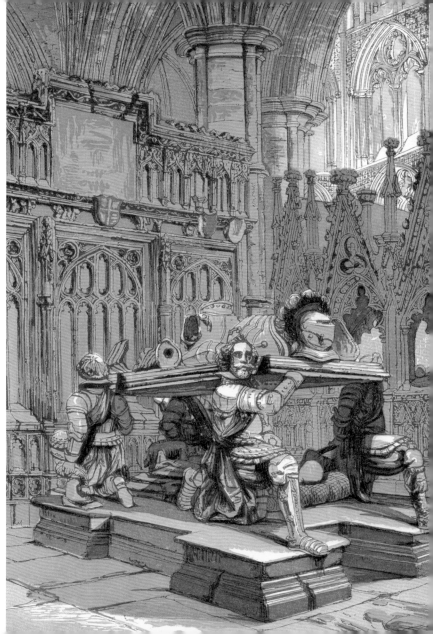

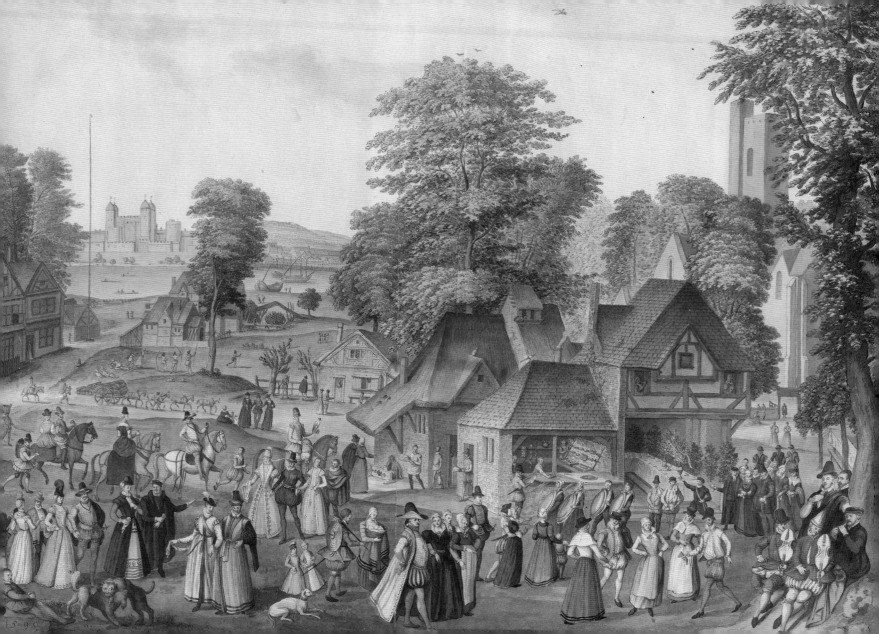

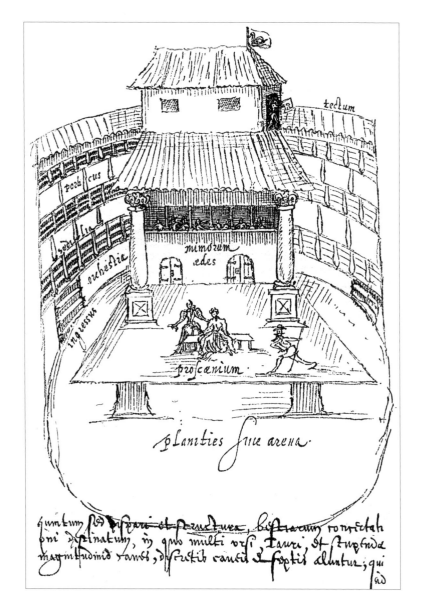

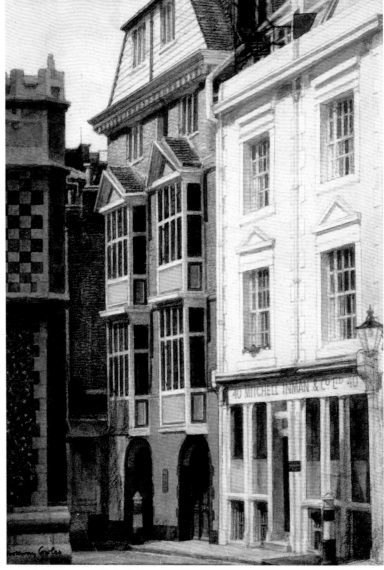

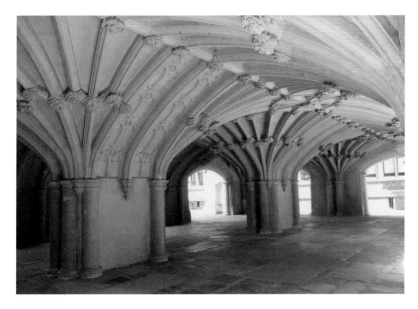

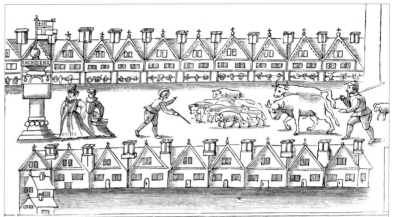

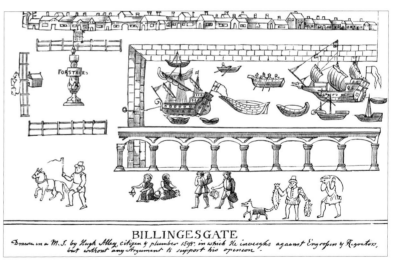

Above: 30. The undercroft of Lincoln's Inn chapel, built in 1619–23, was designed to be a place where lawyers, clients and students would meet. (Stephen Porter)

Above right: 31. Eastcheap Market, drawn in 1598, was one of the butchers' markets; livestock are being driven along the street and there are carcasses in the butchers' shops. (Stephen Porter)

Opposite left: 28. The Swan Theatre on Bankside was built in 1595 and Johannes de Witt attended a performance there in the following year. He drew a sketch of the interior, which a friend of his copied into his commonplace book. That copy is the only contemporary illustration of the interior of a playhouse of the Elizabethan and Jacobean period. (Stephen Porter)

Opposite right: 29. Numbers 41–42 Cloth Fair were built in 1614, when that part of Smithfield was first developed. They were restored by the architects Seely & Paget around 1930 and used as their offices. Drawn by Harold Hookway Cowles (1896–1987), from 1970 a Brother of Charterhouse. (The Governors of Sutton's Hospital)

32. Billingsgate market in 1598, with three-masted vessels as well as smaller craft in the dock, and a figure carrying away two large fish. Billingsgate developed as both a specialist fish market and a market for other foodstuffs brought to London along the Thames. (Stephen Porter)

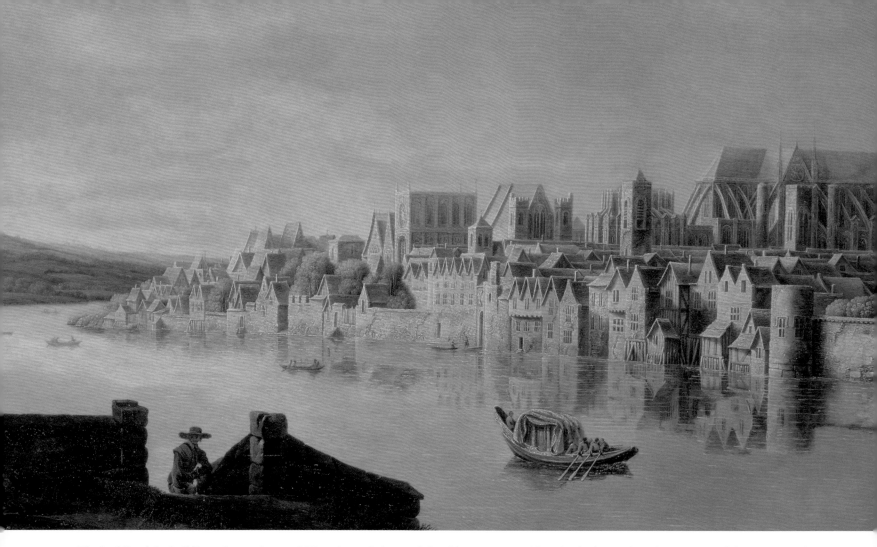

33. The huddle of the buildings clustered around Westminster Palace and the abbey is conveyed by Claude de Jongh in this painting of the 1630s. (Yale Center for British Art, Paul Mellon Collection)

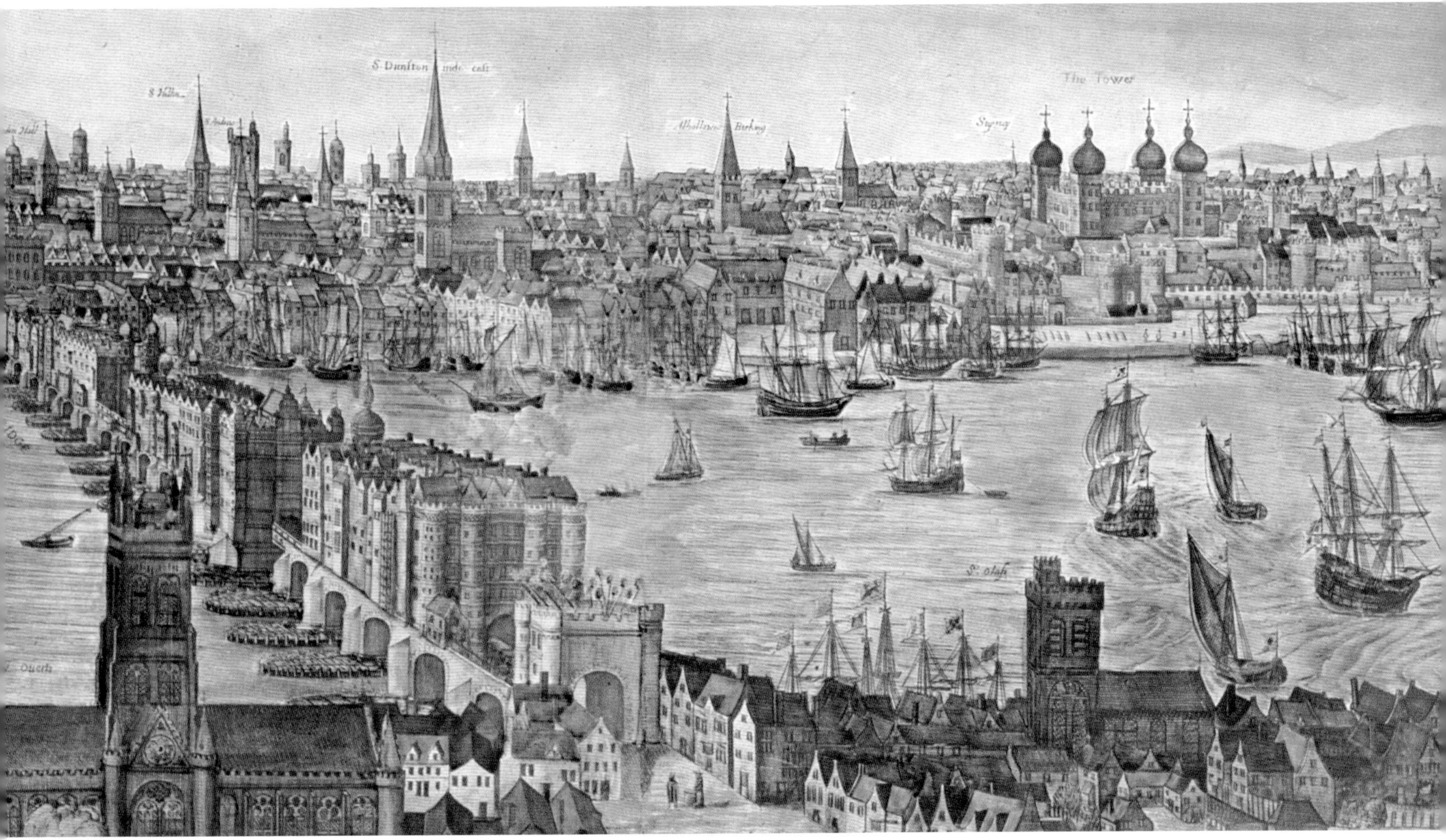

34. A section of Claes Visscher's panorama of London of 1616, showing Southwark in the foreground, London Bridge, the Tower and the varied steeples of the City's churches. (Stephen Porter)

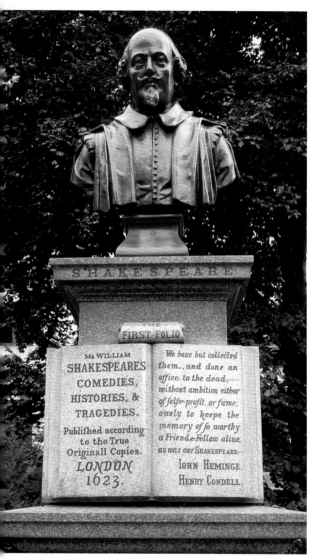

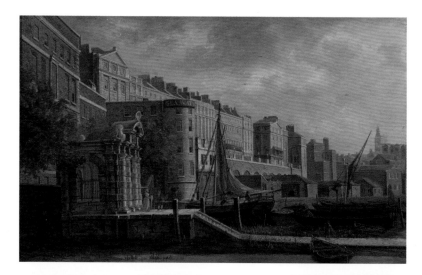

Left: 35. The first edition of William Shakespeare's works was published in 1623; known as the First Folio, it was one of the most important books ever published. Its editors were his friends and fellow actors John Hemming and Henry Condell, who lived in the City parish of St Mary Aldermanbury, where a monument to them was erected in 1896. (Stephen Porter)

Top right: 36. The watergate built in 1626–27 served the Strand palace built for the Duke of Buckingham and survived when the palace was pulled down in 1676; beyond is the Adelphi. Painted by Daniel Turner, around 1800. (Yale Center for British Art, Paul Mellon Collection)

Bottom right: 37. The York Watergate of the Duke of Buckingham's palace now stands in a public park, bereft of any context. (Stephen Porter)

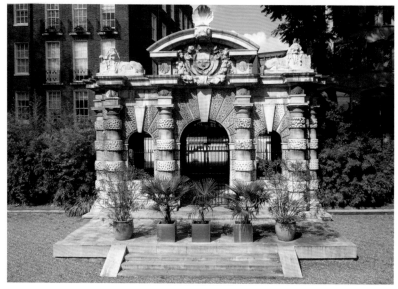

5

THE CIVIL WAR AND BEYOND

Like other capital cities, London could pose a threat to a government, which required its taxes and the loans from the wealthy merchants as well as the political acquiescence of the city's leaders and potentially tumultuous citizens. Throughout the Tudor period London had not acted against the monarch, failing to support Sir Thomas Wyatt in 1554 and the Earl of Essex in his futile attempt to displace the ageing Elizabeth's leading councillors in 1601. But during the 1630s it became increasingly detached from Charles I's court, and when his attempt to impose the Book of Common Prayer on the Scots led to the two Bishops' Wars, in 1639 and 1640, and consequent financial crisis, many Londoners aligned with Parliament, which the king called after an interval of eleven years.

The City's senior figures were unhappy with several aspects of the Crown's policies, such as rule through the Privy Council without calling Parliament, support for privileged concessionaires of patents and licences, and trades being organised separately from the oversight of the livery companies. The plantation of Ulster after 1608 had included considerable investment from London, through the City of London joint stock company and by the livery companies. An acrimonious dispute with the Crown over its management of the plantation culminated in a Star Chamber case in 1635, which resulted in the City's forfeiture of its Irish lands and a fine. In the following year the Crown established the New Corporation of the Suburbs, which the City regarded as a potential rival administration to the Court of Aldermen. The citizens were concerned about the effects of the economic recession and Archbishop Laud's High Church policies, initially as Bishop of London and then as Archbishop of Canterbury.

As the confrontation between Crown and Parliament became increasingly tense, Londoners attacked the archbishop's palace at Lambeth and turned out in their thousands at Westminster to demonstrate against the king's ministers. An enormous crowd assembled on Tower Hill in 1641 to watch the execution of the Earl of Strafford, Charles's leading advisor. One cause of anxiety for the citizens was removed when Royalist attempts to gain control of the Tower were prevented. In January 1642 the king went to Parliament with soldiers intending to arrest his leading opponents, who had been forewarned and left for the City. He then went to Guildhall to demand that they be handed over, only to be refused and suffer the further humiliation of being heckled in the streets. Thwarted, Charles left London and by the summer the country had descended into Civil War.

The political manoeuvres in Parliament were matched by changes within the City's ruling élite, with the pro-Royalist aldermen, including the lord mayor, supplanted and replaced by those who supported the parliamentary leadership. The citizens did not oppose those changes and by the time that the war began, Guildhall was aligned with Parliament. Some of the London militia regiments were in the army that stopped the Royalist advance on the city at Turnham Green, in November 1642, and in the following summer thousands laboured to create earthwork defences which entirely encircled the city. Yet the war had a deleterious impact through high taxation, labour shortages as men joined the forces, losses of merchant ships to Royalist privateers and an influx of displaced people who took refuge in the city. Coal had steadily replaced wood as London's chief fuel, brought in colliers down the east coast from the Tyne and the Wear, but when the coalfields were in Royalist hands, Parliament's ships blockaded the ports to prevent it being shipped out. Only when the Scots joined the war on Parliament's side in 1644 and captured Newcastle were supplies resumed. But the war generated business, too, and London benefited from the presence of Parliament, its role as the headquarters of Parliamentarian administration and by supplying the armies.

London's Royalists lacked organisation, cohesion and leadership and the city remained Parliamentarian throughout the war and its aftermath, which saw a potential counter-revolution in London in 1647 suppressed by the New Model Army. London did not support the Royalist cause in the Second Civil War in 1648, nor intervene in the political crisis that culminated in the execution of the king and the abolition of the monarchy and the House of Lords in 1649. The organisation of the Church, too, was abolished and an attempt to impose a Presbyterian structure was only partially successful in London. The protestant dissenters who had attracted growing support before the war now achieved freedom of worship, a policy that was maintained by the republican governments after 1649, with the Jews formally readmitted to the country in 1656. But that toleration did not extend to Roman Catholics.

The collapse of the Church's authority saw the breakdown of censorship of publications, which had been in the hands of the Archbishop of Canterbury, the Bishop of London and the Stationers' Company. This saw a veritable explosion of publishing: the London bookseller George Thomason acquired twenty-four titles in 1640, 721 in 1641 and 2,134 in 1642. When the Bohemian intellectual Jan Comenius arrived in London in 1641 he was impressed by the number of bookshops. Comenius had been invited to London to share in the new intellectual freedom and plans for reform. John Milton described scholars 'sitting by their studious lamps, musing, searching, revolving new notions and ideas wherewith to present … the approaching Reformation; others as fast reading, trying all things, assenting to the force of reason and convincement'. Proposals were put forward for the establishment of a university in London, but they were not taken further, although adult education in non-classical subjects was provided at Gresham College, in Old Broad Street, where lectures had begun in 1597. Its rooms were the meeting place for the Royal Society, which developed from the intellectual ferment of the 1640s and 1650s, receiving its first royal charter in 1662.

The post-war years saw an economic revival, partly stimulated by the Navigation Acts of 1651 and 1660, which required that imports to England must be carried in English vessels or those of the country of origin. London remained dominant in overseas trade and so its merchants were the chief beneficiaries of the policy. Trade continued to increase despite three wars with the Dutch, the chief carrying nation, between 1652 and 1674. Both exports and imports increased during the second half of the century, but the re-export trade expanded at a far greater rate and became an important element in London's economy. Another change in the structure of the economy was a growth in employment in domestic service, so that a higher proportion of the incomers during the second half of the century were young women, while the numbers of young men taking apprenticeships in crafts regulated by the livery companies began to wane. The city continued to grow and had 575,000 inhabitants by 1700. As the national population was no longer increasing, the proportion of the total living in the metropolis rose to over 11 per cent by the end of the seventeenth century. In the 1690s the French visitor Henri Misson wrote that 'one may safely venture to affirm, that London, including Westminster, is the biggest City in Europe'.

An indication of London's economic strength was the speed with which it recovered from two major disasters in the 1660s. An outbreak of bubonic plague in 1636 was a serious, but not major, eruption, and appearances of the disease in the 1640s did not develop into epidemics. Concern about plague on the Continent, especially in Amsterdam, prompted the government to implement the established policy of naval quarantine to prevent the disease reaching England. But the early signs of an outbreak in London in the closing months of 1664 heralded the city's most deadly plague epidemic. Those who could leave the stricken city did so, but many did not have that option. For the period 27 December 1664 to 19 December 1665, 97,306 deaths were recorded, 68,956 attributed to plague, although the number of plague deaths almost certainly was understated. It represented roughly 20 per cent of the population and the number of burials was almost six times the annual average. Yet the losses were replaced within two years, as they had been after the earlier epidemics in the seventeenth century. Once again, incomers were not deterred by the possibility that the disease would strike again, and they were correct, for the Great Plague of 1665 was the last plague epidemic in London.

The second disaster was a conflagration, which began early on the morning of 2 September 1666, a Sunday, and so a day when not many people were up and about early. That was a factor in the progress of the fire, for failure to tackle the blaze in its early stages by demolishing nearby buildings and a serious misjudgement of the extent of the danger (not least by the lord mayor, Sir Thomas Bludworth) contributed to the scale of the catastrophe. But most of all it was a strong gale blowing from the estuary and driving the flames onward which defeated the firefighters' efforts and made it the most destructive fire in the city's history. Only when the wind dropped on the following Wednesday could the fires be extinguished.

The Great Fire consumed four-fifths of the City, from the Tower to the Temple along the riverside and as far inland as the city wall. The losses included 13,200 houses, eighty-seven churches and six chapels, fifty-two livery company halls, the custom house and the Royal Exchange, Blackwell Hall, three prisons, Bridewell and the Sessions House. The Guildhall was gutted. St Paul's Cathedral had suffered a blaze in 1561, when the steeple was destroyed and the roof damaged. Repairs had been carried out, but the steeple was not replaced then or in the 1630s, when Inigo Jones's additions to the exterior included new façades for the west front and the transepts. The fire swept through the building and also the chapel of St Faith in the crypt, where the booksellers and printers had moved their stocks, hoping that they would be safe there. Like others who moved their goods insufficiently far, their efforts were in vain. Between 65,000 and 80,000 Londoners were burned out and the value of the buildings, trade and household goods destroyed may have been almost £8 million. Even so, 80 per cent of the metropolis escaped untouched, and the homeless quickly found accommodation.

An Act of Parliament of 1657 had attempted to revive the policy initiated in 1605 by stipulating that new buildings should be 'built with Brick or Stone, or both, and straight up, without butting or jetting out into the Street, Lane or place'. The conflagration now provided an unprecedented opportunity to implement those requirements on a large scale. To regulate the rebuilding, an Act of Parliament was passed in 1667 which classified the new houses into four types, based on size. All of them were to have external walls of brick or stone, with roofs covered with tiles, and the party walls were to remain intact, ensuring the integrity of each house, for the earlier interconnections between houses was recognised as one of reasons why the fire could not be halted. Some streets were widened, a new one was created leading from Guildhall, and the marketplaces were re-sited, but imaginative plans to set out a new street plan were impractical. A duty imposed on coal landed in the port of London financed the public buildings and a fire court was set up to quickly settle ownership, liability and boundary issues so that they would not delay the rebuilding.

Reconstruction was initially sluggish because of shortages of materials and perhaps, too, a lack of confidence caused by Dutch naval successes in the summer of 1667. But the war was brought to a conclusion in July and thereafter the pace quickened. Most of the new houses were built by 1672 and the majority of the livery companies' halls by the late 1670s, together with the Royal Exchange, custom house, Guildhall and other public buildings. To commemorate the fire a slender Doric column, dubbed the Monument, was built close to the site of the bakehouse where it had begun. The opportunity was taken to reduce the number of churches, with fifty-one rebuilt, all of which were in use by 1696, although some steeples and towers were added later, and St Paul's, begun in 1675, was not completed until 1710. Sir Christopher Wren was the architect for the cathedral and all of the churches.

Fewer houses were built than had been lost; in a sample of eight parishes, there was a fall of 22 per cent between 1638 and 1695. The rebuilding regulations prevented the erection of the small dwellings that had previously stood in the back alleys and courts, although the fall in number also indicated a decline in demand, reflecting a move away from the City, stimulated, but not initiated, by the Great Fire. That trend produced a division, for the retailers of high-value goods moved west, to be nearer to their wealthy customers, while the merchants remained in the City.

The aristocracy and gentry had gradually been moving to fashionable new developments west of the City. Covent Garden was set out on the Earl of Bedford's estate in the 1630s, with a licence authorising the building of houses for 'Gentlemen and men of abillity'. Similar developments followed, including 'a spacious street, called Long Acre, and then Pickadilly, full of fair

Houses round about'. South of Piccadilly, in 1661 Pall Mall was laid out and St James's Square and the adjacent streets were built between those two streets from 1665. Squares and rectangular grid layouts became the favoured form of development in the growing West End, but with a contrast at Seven Dials near St Giles-in-the-Fields church, in which 'seaven streetes make a starr from a Doric Pillar plac'd in the middle of a Circular Area'. Many of the mansions along the Strand which had been transferred from clerical to aristocratic occupation in the 1530s were now demolished and replaced by streets of substantial houses.

The most prominent developer of the period was Nicholas Barbon, whose manipulation of credit and the collaboration of 'a gang of clercks, attorneys, scriveners, and lawyers, that were his humble servants and slaves to comand' allowed him to operate on a large scale. As he remarked, 'it was not worth his while, to deal litle, that a bricklayer could doe. The gaine he expected was out of great undertakings.' Barbon's example was copied by other developers and the face of London was gradually transformed through their projects, the building regulations and a change in taste which decried timber and plaster fronts and favoured brick and stone, with a symmetrical appearance. That was seen in the rebuilding after other fires, the most serious being a blaze in Shadwell in 1673, which gutted almost 100 houses, and a far worse one in Southwark three years later which destroyed 624 houses. The great Tudor palace at Whitehall, the focus of the monarchy and court since the 1530s, was destroyed by fire in 1698, but it was not rebuilt.

As well as the fabric, the political atmosphere was changing, for although the restoration of the monarchy was welcomed by enthusiastic crowds in 1660, Charles II's reign was marked by intermittent partisan strife, played out in Guildhall and on the streets. It saw the emergence of two groupings, not yet formal parties, dubbed the Whigs and the Tories, which, in general terms, were supported by the merchants and the landed gentry respectively. The restoration of the Crown was, of course, accompanied by the re-establishment of the Church, which imposed penal measures on Nonconformists, but a substantial minority of Londoners nevertheless remained outside the Church of England. One sect, the Fifth Monarchy Men, staged an uprising in the City in 1661, which provoked harsh retaliation. There were tumultuous riots and demonstrations during the Popish Plot scare of 1678–79 and the subsequent Exclusion Crisis, when leading Whig politicians attempted to remove Charles's Roman Catholic brother James, Duke of York, as heir to the throne. The king was able to ride out the storm and in the early 1680s his supporters came to power at Guildhall and he struck a blow at the City by withdrawing its charter.

James succeeded Charles unopposed in 1685 and pursued a policy favouring his co-religionists and Nonconformists, hoping that they would combine to neutralise the power of the Church of England. That failed and he provoked such opposition that in 1688 his son-in-law William of Orange was invited by a group of peers and the Bishop of London to intervene. When his Dutch troops marched into London they were welcomed by the crowds, bells were rung and bonfires were lit, accompanied by 'all the public demonstrations of joy imaginable'. James was deposed by this Glorious Revolution and William and his wife, James's daughter Mary, took the throne as joint monarchs. The political settlement which followed included the restoration of the City's charter and promised greater political stability.

A dominant theme of William's foreign policy as Stadholder of the United Provinces, from 1672 until his death in 1702, was hostility to France. England was inevitably drawn into this after the Glorious Revolution and within a few months of William's accession war was declared on France. James II's policy had been to oppose the Dutch, because of their commercial strength, but Louis XIV's aggrandising policies were now seen as the greater threat and the war had the support of the City. That was as well, for it was very expensive and the cost could be met only by drawing, as never before, on the resources of the City's wealthy goldsmith-bankers and merchants.

The solution was the creation of a joint-stock bank, the Bank of England, authorised by an Act of Parliament of 1694, by which the government received an initial loan of £1.2 million; the interest was to be paid from duties levied on shipping and alcohol. Other loans followed, on the security of parliamentary taxation, not the credit of the Crown, and the government was able to tap the wealth of the City, as the early Stuarts had been unable to do. The bank could also deal in bullion and bills of exchange, and issue paper money. During the 1690s there was a great increase in the establishment of joint-stock companies. London attracted capital not only from within the country, but also from abroad. Trade with Portugal, which was drawing in gold from mines in Brazil, expanded after the signing of the Methuen Treaty in 1703 and that produced a trade surplus which significantly contributed to the capital available in London. The Nine Years War, or King William's War, which ended in 1697, was a struggle financially, but the city's wealth, with the innovations in public finance put in place during the 1690s, enabled the country to meet the unprecedentedly high costs of the War of the Spanish Succession, which began in 1701 and continued until 1713. A rival to the East India Company was created in 1698 and traded in competition with the company until the two were merged in 1708 as a 'new' East India Company, with trading privileges from the government in exchange for loans. Similarly, in 1711 the South Sea Company was launched, which, it was believed, would tap the riches of the Pacific and South America; as part of the arrangement £9 million of government debt was converted into company stock.

Trading in the joint-stock companies' and Bank of England's stocks, and investments in the government debt, especially through Exchequer Bills and lottery tickets, saw the emergence of 'brokers and stock-jobbers', who specialised in trading in stocks. They were mistrusted and in 1698 were expelled from the Royal Exchange; they then shifted their base to coffee houses in Exchange Alley nearby. Not until 1773 did they acquire a building which became known as the Stock Exchange.

The brokers' choice of coffee houses was not an eccentric one, for they were places where men met, to transact business, socialise and exchange news and gossip. The first coffee house in London was opened in 1652, by 1663 there were eighty-two of them in the City and by 1739 the number had risen to 551 in the whole of London. By 1658 Thomas Garraway's coffee house in the parish of St Bartholomew by the Exchange was selling tea as well as coffee; he may have been the first retailer of tea in England. Marine and fire insurance was another branch of business which developed during the later seventeenth century; shipping news and insurance was based at Edward Lloyd's coffee house, which he moved to Lombard Street in 1691.

As well as becoming the financial quarter, the area around Cornhill also developed as a centre for publishing, printing and bookselling. The freedom of publication in the 1640s did not last and subsequent governments attempted to impose some control of publications. A Licensing Act of 1662 banned all books deemed to be heretical or seditious and the Restoration regime introduced the licensing of coffee houses in 1663, fearful that they were places where 'false news' was spread. But the licensing of publications lapsed in 1695, bringing press censorship to an end. The only newspaper at the time was the official *London Gazette*, but within the next fifteen years around twenty appeared in London, including the first regular daily, the *Daily Courant*, in 1702.

London's intellectuals and literati had their own favourite coffee houses; the poet John Dryden and his circle met in the early 1660s at 'the great Coffee house' in Covent Garden. In 1675 John Banister, a violinist, moved his public concerts to Covent Garden from the Whitefriars district, where he had inaugurated them in 1672. They were the first public concerts; hitherto such performances had been held in private houses. Banister and others, including Henry Purcell, the foremost English composer of the seventeenth century, also composed for the theatres: more than fifty suites of theatre music were published in the first decade of the eighteenth century, as music publishing expanded. The theatres had been closed in 1642 and reopened in 1660, with women acting on stage for the first time. A new repertoire was developed, including comedies which contrasted the bright and cunning rakehells of the West End with the worthy but naïve and plodding City men. A marked division was opening between the genteel West End, inhabited by the well-to-do and

fashionable, and the mercantile world of the City. In the early eighteenth century Sir Richard Steele drew attention to the contrasting characters of London's various districts, describing the city as 'an Aggregate of various Nations distinguished from each other by their respective Customs, Manners and Interests … the Inhabitants of St. James's, notwithstanding they live under the same Laws, and speak the same Language, are a distinct People from those of Cheapside, who are likewise removed from those of the Temple on the one side, and those of Smithfield on the other, by several Climates and Degrees in their way of Thinking and Conversing together'.

Another division, between the Church of England and the Nonconformists, had not been closed and it continued to reflect political loyalties during Queen Anne's reign (1702–14). Pro-Tory demonstrations in 1710 were accompanied by the wrecking of Nonconformist chapels and anti-Catholic demonstrations occurred after a failed Jacobite uprising in 1715. Those early eighteenth-century riots were later described by the French philosopher Voltaire as 'only a few murmurs of a sea still choppy long after the storm has passed', compared to what had gone before. The numbers of Nonconformists was swelled by the influx of French Protestants, the Huguenots, after Louis XIV's 1685 revocation of the Edict of Nantes, which had guaranteed them freedom of worship. By the end of the century 23,000 Huguenot refugees lived in London and the number of congregations had increased from two to twenty-three. They mostly settled in Soho and Leicester Fields, and in Spitalfields, where they established a silk industry. The Jewish community continued to expand; a synagogue was built in Creechurch Lane and enlarged in 1674, before being replaced by a new building

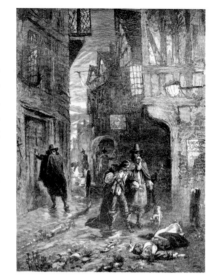
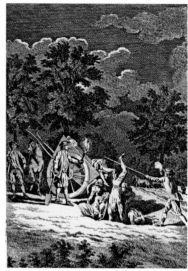

in Bevis Marks, in 1700. Another, in Duke's Place, was erected in 1690, replaced in 1722 and again in 1788–90. London benefited significantly from the immigrants' skills and industriousness, and they were absorbed into the wider community. Voltaire admired that toleration when he visited England in 1726–29, commenting that in the London Stock Exchange 'you will see representatives from all nations gathered together for the utility of men. Here Jew, Mohammedan and Christian deal with each other as though they were all of the same faith, and only apply the word infidel to people who go bankrupt. Here the Presbyterian trusts the Anabaptist and the Anglican accepts a promise from the Quaker. On leaving these peaceful and free assemblies some go to the Synagogue and others for a drink.' He was implicitly criticising the French government's policies, but his point was a strong one, for England benefited from its neighbour's intolerance.

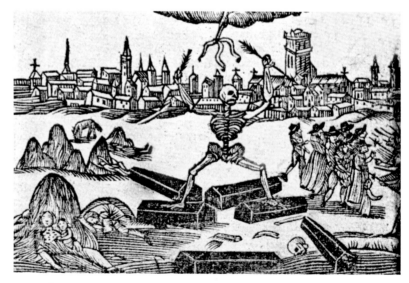

Top left: 38. A later depiction of a London street during the Great Plague of 1665 shows the citizens trying to cover their faces to avoid inhaling the foul miasmic air which was believed to transmit the disease, but a woman in the foreground has already succumbed. (Stephen Porter)

Top right: 39. An eighteenth-century impression of burials in a pit at the burial ground at Holywell Mount in Shoreditch during the Great Plague of 1665. (Stephen Porter)

Right: 40. This woodcut depicting the impact of plague on London was published in both Thomas Dekker's *A Rod for Run-awayes* (1625) and John Taylor's *The Fearefull Summer* (1636). Death is astride the coffins of the victims and citizens trying to leave are confronted by armed countrymen, anxious to keep the disease out of their communities. (Jonathan Reeve, JR1106b21p213 16001650)

Right: 41. The Great Fire began in Pudding Lane and was stopped at Pie Corner in Smithfield, where the figure of the Fat Boy was placed, with the inscription, 'This Boy is in Memmory Put up for the late FIRE of LONDON Occasioned by the Sin of Gluttony 1666.' (Stephen Porter)

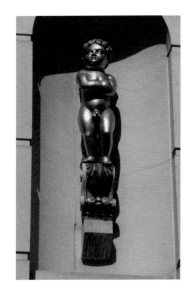

Below: 42. Philippe-Jacques de Loutherbourg painted this dramatic depiction of the Great Fire around 1797. From the viewpoint of an arch in London Bridge, looking towards St Paul's, he shows families in boats with the belongings which they could carry, as described by Samuel Pepys in his contemporary account. (Yale Center for British Art, Paul Mellon Collection)

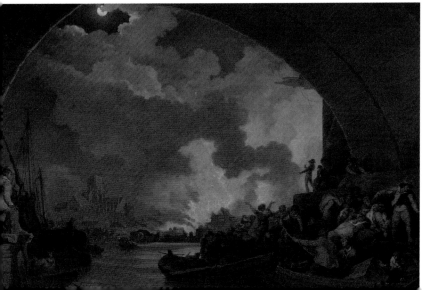

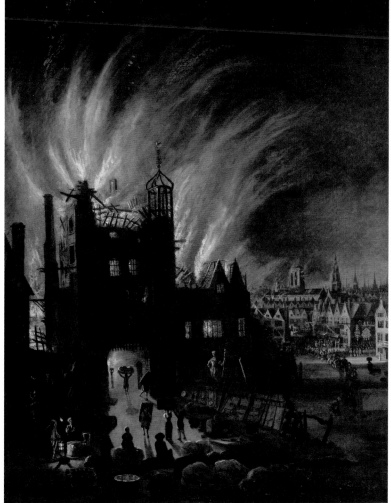

43. A depiction of the Great Fire of 1666, showing citizens carrying their belongings through Ludgate to where piles of goods have been deposited, and a line of people, apparently passing items along the line. Painted by an unknown artist around 1670. (Yale Center for British Art, Paul Mellon Collection)

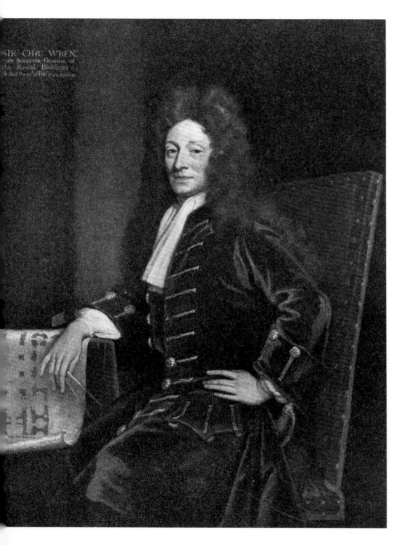

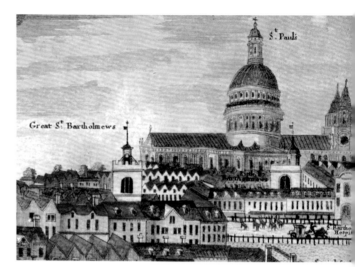

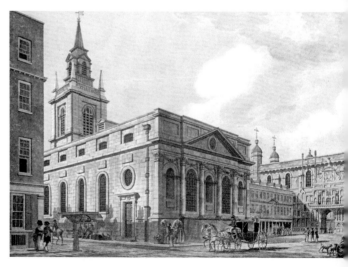

Left: 44. Portrait of Sir Christopher Wren attributed to Michael Wright. (Stephen Porter)

Top right: 45. The Great Fire did not reach St Bartholomew's Hospital and its church, St Bartholomew the Less, or the former priory church of St Bartholomew the Great, but behind them is the area that was destroyed and St Paul's Cathedral. (The Governors of Sutton's Hospital)

Bottom right: 46. The church of St Lawrence Jewry was constructed in 1671–80; it was the most expensive of Wren's parish churches, reflecting its standing as the corporation's church. The east end faces the processional route to Guildhall created after the Great Fire and so is an elaborate design. Drawn by Thomas Malton, 1783. (Stephen Porter)

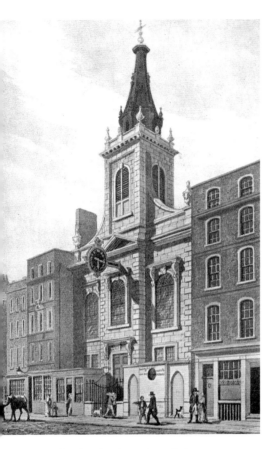

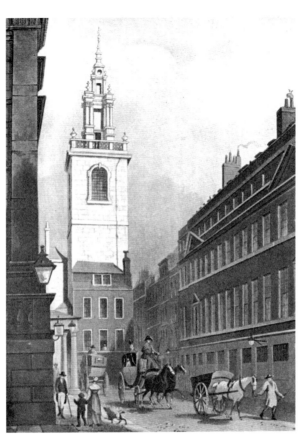

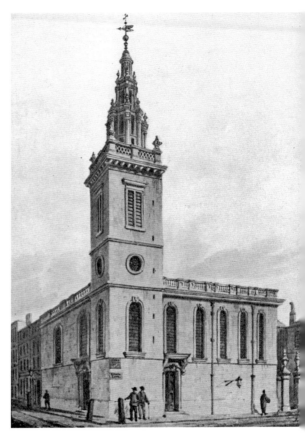

47. The church of St Edmund the King, Lombard Street, was built in 1670–74 to Sir Christopher Wren's designs. The spire was added in 1709. The church, drawn by George Shepherd in 1811, is orientated north–south. (Stephen Porter)

48. Walbrook looking north to St Stephen's church, which was completed in 1680; the tower was added in 1713–15. Drawn by Thomas Hosmer Shepherd, 1811. (Stephen Porter)

49. St Michael Paternoster Royal stands on the east side of College Hill; Paternoster is from the makers of rosaries in the district and Royal probably is a corruption of La Réole in Gascony, from where wine was shipped to London. The church was built to Sir Christopher Wren's designs in 1685–94; the three-stage steeple was added in 1713–17. Drawn by John Coney, 1812. (Stephen Porter)

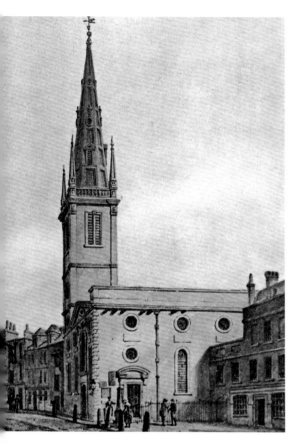

50. The church of St Margaret Patten, which faces Rood Lane, was named for a crucifix which stood in the churchyard until it was broken up in 1538. The church erected after the Great Fire was designed by Sir Christopher Wren and was erected in 1684–87; the spire on the north-west tower was added in 1698–1702. Drawn by John Coney, 1812. (Stephen Porter)

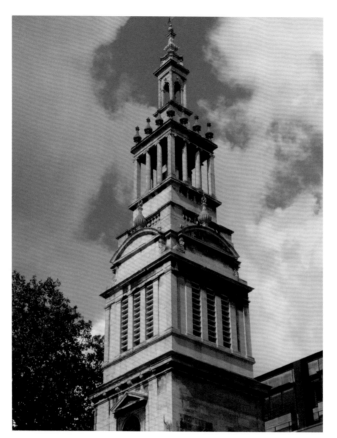

51. The tower and steeple of Christ Church, Newgate Street, added in 1703–04 to the post-Great Fire church erected in 1677–87. The church was not rebuilt after it was destroyed in the Second World War, but the tower and steeple were restored. (Stephen Porter)

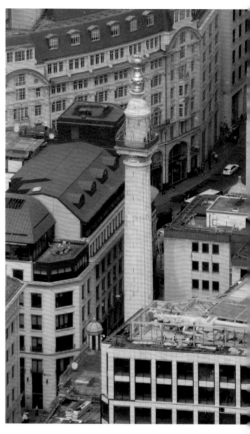

52. The Monument erected to commemorate the Great Fire of 1666 is still visible above the encroaching modern buildings. (Stephen Porter)

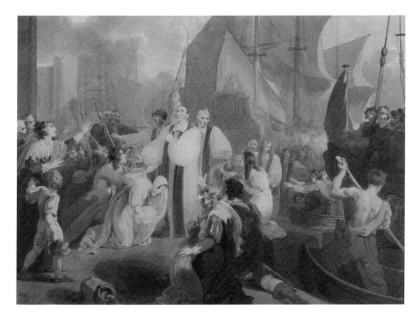

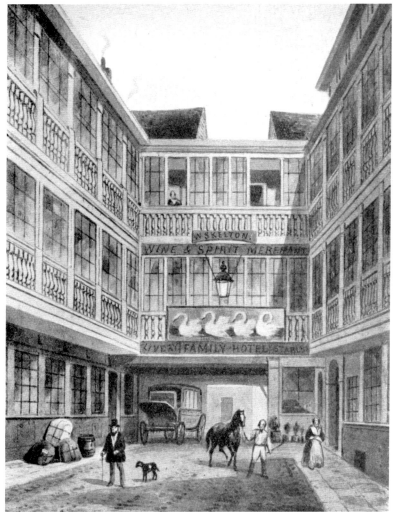

Above: 53. *The Seven Bishops Going To Trial*, painted in 1790 by Richard Westall, depicts the episode in the reign of James II when, in 1688, William Sancroft, the Archbishop of Canterbury, and six bishops of the Church of England were imprisoned in the Tower and tried for refusing to read the Declaration of Indulgence. Their acquittal was greeted with rejoicing, and their treatment contributed to the growing uneasiness with the king's policies. (Yale Center for British Art, Bequest of Joseph F. McCrindle)

Right: 54. The Four Swans was one of three inns in Bishopsgate described in 1720 as 'large, and of a considerable Trade, and resort for Waggons and Stage Coaches that go Northwards'. It was demolished in the 1870s. (Stephen Porter)

6

THE GEORGIAN ERA

The period following George I's accession in 1714 was troubled by the Jacobite rebellion in 1715 and a financial crisis in 1720, when the price of South Sea Company stock rose to giddy heights before suddenly falling back. The company was an integral part of the public finances and so the bursting of the 'bubble' was a serious crisis, but it was skilfully managed by the Whig politician Sir Robert Walpole, who emerged as the first prime minister. He kept Britain at peace until the outbreak of war with Spain in 1739, dubbed the War of Jenkins's Ear, which soon merged into the more general War of the Austrian Succession. That was the first of five major wars with France and her various allies which continued with relatively short intervals of peace until 1815. They were fought in Europe and around the world, and from 1776 to 1782 in Britain's own colonies in North America, as it engaged in a futile attempt to prevent them attaining independence. Their loss was offset by an increasing share of world trade, territorial gains and growing influence; as Britain's political and economic power developed, so London became the capital of an expanding worldwide empire.

In his *Tour thro the whole island of Great Britain* (1724) Daniel Defoe wrote an account of the country and its flourishing economy, pointing out London's predominance within it. The city drew its provisions from every part of the kingdom and its commercial influence was such that, according to Defoe, it 'sucks the vitals of trade in this island to itself'. From the mid-eighteenth century the Industrial Revolution changed the economic structure which he had described, as manufacturing industries developed on the coalfields of the Midlands and the north of England. The cities in those areas grew rapidly, and the rise of the Atlantic economies benefited the west coast ports of Bristol, Liverpool and Glasgow. But London continued to handle by far the largest share of overseas trade and remained the focus of the service sector, cultural and political life. As national population again began to grow, after a period of stagnation, the city continued to expand and had 960,000 inhabitants in 1801, the year of the first national census, and 1,655,000 by 1831. It had outstripped its rivals and become the world's largest city.

London's expansion was not constrained by fortifications, as in some Continental cities, and the pattern of development established in the second half of the seventeenth century continued, with the release of aristocratic and gentry estates in the West End on building leases, whereby the landlords retained ownership and the leaseholders undertook the building, on the security of a long lease and in accordance with its stipulations. Most such developments were around squares and on a rectangular grid of streets. That contrasted with the largely unplanned, piecemeal growth of east London, although some squares were also laid out there, while the riverfront was built up from the Tower to Limehouse. South of the Thames, development was stimulated by the building of Westminster Bridge (1750) and Blackfriars Bridge (1769), followed in the second decade of the nineteenth century by Vauxhall, Waterloo and Southwark bridges, while a new London Bridge was erected between 1823 and 1831 to replace the medieval one. By 1800 only around 17 per cent of London's population lived in the City and the trend continued, as those who worked in the financial sector and the professions began to live elsewhere and commute in.

Some of the new developments included a church, but many did not, and the disparity between the numbers of parishioners and the seating available within the churches had become a problem. When the Tories came to power in 1710 they provided funds for fifty new churches, to help redress the imbalance. In the event just twelve were built, but they included such distinguished buildings as Christchurch Spitalfields, St Anne's Limehouse, and St Mary Woolnoth. The early eighteenth century saw a growing apathy towards church attendance and indifference to organised religion, until the Methodist revival from the late 1730s, inspired by the preaching of the brothers John and Charles Wesley, and George Whitefield. At first their services were held in the open air, until a site in Moorfields was acquired for a chapel. John Wesley's preaching, in particular, drew thousands and so a new and larger chapel was built there; opened in 1778, it was described as the 'cathedral of Methodism'. The early nineteenth century saw a wider revival of attendance at services among Nonconformists, with new chapels erected, and Anglicans, for whom new churches were built following the establishment in 1818 of the Church Building Commission. That produced a far more sustained programme of building than had its predecessor a century earlier, with over 120 churches erected in London and its immediate environs by the mid-1850s.

The most prominent new secular buildings in the City were the Bank of England and the Mansion House. The bank retained its monopoly of joint-stock banking and by the 1760s some 80 per cent of its business came through its connection with the government; almost all of its other transactions were within the city and it was known during the eighteenth century as 'the Bank of London'. The other bankers had been hard hit by the South Sea Bubble, when almost a third of them went out of business, but they recovered and there were fifty by 1770 and seventy by 1800. The Bank of England operated from the Grocers' Company's hall until a new building was erected, opened in 1734, and, although enlarged, that, too, became inadequate. Britain's expenditure during the recurrent wars involved not only the costs of her own armed forces, but also the hiring of mercenaries and payment of subsidies to Continental allies. The national debt increased from £16.7 million in 1697 to £76.1 million by 1748, and by the close of the wars with France in 1815 it had reached almost £800 million. The bank's business grew correspondingly and a new building was erected on an enlarged site in two phases, in 1793–95 and 1808–18. No other bank could match it. Indeed, although the first purpose-built private bank in the City was erected in 1757, by Asgill's in Lombard Street, until the early nineteenth century most banks were still in buildings used for both business and as houses.

For the Mansion House, the corporation cleared a site almost opposite the Bank of England, where the new building was completed in 1753 as an official residence for the lord mayor. It had been the practice for the mayors to use the hall of their livery company, or perhaps their own house, for City business, to receive visitors and host functions. That was no longer necessary, for the Mansion House contained rooms for receptions, accommodation for the lord mayor, and a courtroom for hearings held by him as a justice of the peace. The building was also a centre for civic conviviality; the average consumption of wine there during the years 1774–85 was 5,772 bottles per year. The lord mayor's inauguration procession continued to be a glittering occasion, on the river and through the streets.

The Mansion House was to be surpassed in size by the building in the Strand erected to replace Somerset House, which had been built in the mid-sixteenth century and had served as a royal palace, chiefly for the queen consorts. In addition to St James's Palace and Kensington Palace, which was built for William and Mary beyond the West End, Carlton House in Pall Mall was bought in 1732 for Frederick, Prince of Wales, and in 1762 George III acquired Buckingham House for Queen Charlotte; it became her favourite London residence. There was little likelihood that Somerset House would be needed again for royal occupation, while the government had a pressing need for office accommodation. And so the Tudor palace was replaced by an office building, begun in 1776, which was both the largest public building project undertaken during the Georgian period and the first large purpose-built office building. It accommodated various government departments, including the Navy Office and the Stamp Office, and also housed the Royal Society, the Society of Antiquaries and the Royal Academy of Arts.

The foundation of the Royal Academy in 1768 marked a significant step in the emergence of art as a recognised profession. Its precursor was the St Martin's Lane Academy, founded in 1735 by the portrait painters John Ellys and William Hogarth, and almost all of its members were based in London. Born near Smithfield in 1697, Hogarth established himself as a portrait and history painter before attracting attention through his scenes of London life, with the engravings of his sets of paintings reaching a wide market. That was especially the case with those which he termed 'modern moral subjects', each set having a pictorial narrative. He satirised the well-to-do and the respectable, and drew attention to the plight of those who were exploited by the greedy and unprincipled, such as the country girl procured as a prostitute shortly after arriving in London in *A Harlot's Progress* (1732). Prostitution also features in *A Rake's Progress* (1735), when the would-be social climber Tom Rakewell is robbed in a brothel in Drury Lane, and in *Industry and Idleness* the idle apprentice is seen 'in a Garret with a common Prostitute' before she betrays him to the watch and he is executed at Tyburn. While exaggerating for effect, Hogarth was expressing a contemporary impression of a wanton London. In 1751 he issued *Beer Street*, *Gin Lane* and *The Four Stages of Cruelty*, which, he wrote, were 'calculated to reform some reigning Vices peculiar to the lower Class of People'. The harmful effect of cheap gin was a contemporary issue, as it had become a very popular drink. Attempts to reduce consumption by raising the duty were made in 1729 and 1736, and Hogarth may have produced his illustrations in support of the Gin Act of 1751, which brought in tight licensing regulations. The measure was effective in reducing the number of dram shops and alehouses, and the amount of gin produced, which fell by more than a third within a year.

The playwright and novelist Henry Fielding was prominent in the campaign to reduce gin consumption and in the control of crime. From 1748 he was the magistrate at Bow Street, where the earliest police office had been established in 1740, and was elected Chair of the Westminster Magistrates in 1749. He was succeeded in 1754 by his half-brother Sir John Fielding, known as the 'Blind Beak of Bow Street'. The Fielding brothers were energetic in enforcing the law, for example by raiding street gangs and gaming houses, and developed a reputation for their fairness in administering justice. In 1749 Henry created a force of six men to serve writs and make arrests; known as the Bow Street Runners, these were London's first police force. The brothers were also aware of the social conditions in which the poor lived and drew attention to the problems. The Middlesex Sessions was held in the Jacobean Hicks' Hall in Clerkenwell, but it became too small and in 1782 was replaced by a new Sessions House on Clerkenwell Green. With the growing population and the increasing number of misdemeanours categorised as criminal, the prisons gradually became overcrowded and foul. The Millbank Penitentiary, built according to modern ideas, was completed in 1821, after a long gestation.

In *Roderick Random* (1748), the novelist Tobias Smollett characterised London as a place where the unwary from the country could easily be fleeced by practised swindlers and cardsharps. One of his characters is relieved of all his money within two days of arriving and, on being told 'a great many stories of people who had been seduced, cheated, pilfered, beat, nay even murdered', ruefully remarks that 'surely the devil had set up his throne in London'. Like Hogarth, Smollett exaggerated to add colour to his tale and that was a caricature, rather than a description, of early Georgian London, in the days when the infamous Jonathan Wild achieved considerable notoriety for his various criminal activities. It would not have been appropriate for the later part of the eighteenth century.

Street patrols by the watch were among the responsibilities of the trustees or commissioners empowered by Acts of Parliament to oversee paving, lighting and cleaning of the streets in a district. Improvement was needed, judging by Karl Ludwig Pollnitz's observation after a visit in 1721, when he wrote that London 'cannot be rank'd among the finest Cities; for many of its Streets being dirty and ill-paved, its Houses of Brick, not very high, nor adorn'd with Architecture, but blacken'd with unmerciful Smoke of Coal-fires, gives it a dark Hue, which renders it far less agreeable than it would be otherwise'. The first such body of commissioners was established in 1735 and by 1850 there were approximately 300 of them. They operated independently of the parishes, which continued to carry out their local government functions. From about the mid-eighteenth century, and especially after the first Westminster Paving Act was passed in 1762, a steady improvement could be seen, and the condition of the city's streets now attracted favourable comments. Friedrich Wilhelm von Schütz visited London from Hamburg in 1791 and his impression was far different from Pollnitz's, seventy years earlier, for he remarked on the excellence of its pavements, and also admired its hospitals.

St Thomas's and St Bartholomew's hospitals were rebuilt in the early eighteenth century. At St Thomas's the work began in 1693 and was completed in 1724, while St Bartholomew's was rebuilt between 1730 and 1760. Its new buildings contained twelve wards and 500 beds, and an operating theatre was built in 1791. Among the prominent benefactors of St Thomas's were Thomas Frederick, Thomas Guy and Sir Robert Clayton, an immensely wealthy banker who served as lord mayor in 1679–80 and was described in 1720 as 'the largest and noblest of all modern Benefactors'. Guy surpassed even Clayton's contribution by not only contributing to the new buildings at St Thomas's but also founding a new hospital close by which took his name. He had made a considerable fortune, initially as a bookseller at the end of Lombard Street, printing Bibles for Oxford University. Some of his wealth was invested in seamen's pay tickets, which in 1710 were put into the South Sea Company. Guy sold his stock at a profit before the share price collapsed. His hospital opened in 1725, for those sick requiring long-term care, who were not provided for at St Thomas's. The cost of the buildings and the endowment represented by far the largest example of private philanthropy in London until that time. Defoe described it as 'perhaps, the greatest of its kind that ever was founded in this nation by one person, whether private or public, not excepting the kings themselves'. The royal establishments at Chelsea (1682) and Greenwich (1694) were restricted to retired and disabled servicemen.

Thomas Coram came from a very different background, for he was a seaman and shipbuilder. He established the Foundling Hospital in 1741 as the first institution in the country for unwanted boys and girls whose mothers were too poor to keep them or deserted them out of shame because they were illegitimate. The charity followed the practices of a joint-stock company by raising money from subscribers and initially no public funding was provided. It came to be much admired: the French artist André Rouquet described it in 1755 as 'a noble institution, which this famous metropolis greatly wanted'. Philanthropists were coming to favour hospitals and foundations to help the underprivileged, including the Magdalen Hospital for Penitent Prostitutes, a refuge which opened in 1758. Less evident to an observer such as Rouquet was the growth in the number of charity schools, especially through the efforts of the Society for Promoting Christian Knowledge, founded in 1698, which taught girls as well as boys. Almshouses attracted less attention than in the preceding centuries, but continued to be founded; two were erected in Southwark in 1752. Improved healthcare included a campaign of inoculation against smallpox, which accounted for upwards of 10 per cent of deaths by the 1770s, but a declining number thereafter. With growing charitable provision and a cleaner environment, the overall death rate fell from the mid-century onwards.

Hogarth and other artists donated paintings to both St Bartholomew's and the Foundling Hospital, and the composer Georg Frideric Handel presented an organ for the Foundling Hospital chapel and organised very successful concerts there. Handel had arrived in London in 1710, one of the many singers, instrumentalists and composers drawn to London as Italian opera became increasingly popular. When that waned, after the 1720s, Handel concentrated on the developing musical form of oratorio, based on biblical stories. Francesco Geminiani first arrived in London in 1714 and he also established himself as a composer and performer, organising concerts and publishing treatises on music. Performances of music by both Continental and English composers were held at subscription concerts and by musical societies in such varied settings as taverns and the livery companies' halls. Music reached a wider audience through being an integral part of theatre productions, intermixed with a play and other items on the same bill, and performances at the pleasure grounds, which drew large numbers of Londoners, for relaxation and entertainment. The most fashionable ones were Vauxhall Gardens, known as Spring Garden until 1785, and Ranelagh, at Chelsea, which opened in 1742.

The longest-running success in the theatre was John Gay's *The Beggar's Opera* (1728), a political satire and a counterblast to the current taste for Italianate music. The music was arranged by Johann Christoph Pepusch, a distinguished musical theorist as well as composer, who had come to England as a political refugee. He died at the Charterhouse, where he was the organist, in 1752. Handel died in 1759 and Geminiani in 1762, the year in which Johann Christian Bach arrived in London, where he soon became influential in the city's musical life. With Carl Friedrich Abel, who came to London in 1754, Bach set up the first subscription concerts, in Soho, featuring their music and promoting that of other composers, including Joseph Haydn. Bach died in 1782 and Abel in 1787, but the music which they had fostered remained popular and Haydn made two triumphantly successful visits to London in the 1790s. Ballet became established in the repertoire after the success of John Weaver's *The Loves of Mars and Venus* at Drury Lane theatre in 1717, which employed mime and movement, without spoken or sung dialogue. In contrast, dancing, singing, scenery and impressive special effects were deployed to great effect in *The Necromancer: or, Harlequin Doctor Faustus* at Lincoln's Inn Fields theatre in 1723, and its success established pantomime as a popular genre. During the middle years of the century David Garrick (1717–79) was the dominant figure in the theatre world. He was the foremost actor of his generation as well as a playwright, theatre manager and producer, and established many of the conventions and practices of the modern theatre. Not the least of his achievements was the appreciation of Shakespeare as the nation's greatest dramatist and poet. From 1785 until its closure twenty years later, John Boydell's Shakespeare Gallery in Pall Mall sold engravings of scenes from the plays, from specially commissioned paintings.

Theatre performances were occasionally disrupted by angry audiences, objecting to price increases or rearrangements within the auditorium which offended the more rumbustious patrons. These occurred intermittently until the last outburst in 1808. Street demonstrations also occurred from time to time, with a spell of protests in the 1760s in support of the radical politician John Wilkes and his right to take his seat in the House of Commons. Wilkes was also involved in City politics and a controversy in 1771, when the government tried to uphold the convention that press reporting of parliamentary debates was not permitted. Eventually the right to publish the debates was conceded, but not before the lord mayor, Brass Crosby, had been imprisoned in the Tower, becoming the first lord mayor incarcerated there since the Civil War.

A far more serious and destructive outbreak, in terms of life and property, was the Gordon Riots in June 1780. The extension of Roman Catholics' civil rights in the Catholic Relief Act of 1778 had provoked strong opposition, expressed through the London Protestant Association and its vociferous president Lord George Gordon. A crowd, variously estimated to be between 40,000 and 100,000 strong, gathered in St George's Fields, Southwark, before making its way to Westminster to protest. Although the demonstrators moved off peaceably, a large-scale riot ensued and the property of Roman Catholics was wrecked, including chapels and schools, and the Sardinian embassy chapel close to Lincoln's Inn Fields. Thomas Langdale's distillery in Holborn was burned; 'the inside of the house was consumed, and several dead bodies were lying near; the greater part of those who had made themselves drunk in his premises'. Less conspicuous buildings were not ignored, such as a public house in Golden Lane, and a woman tried for her part in ransacking it told the court that 'it was a Roman Catholick's house and there was nothing but Roman Catholicks in it and it must be pulled down and down it should come'. Newgate and the Fleet prisons, and the Clink and King's Bench prisons in Southwark, were set alight and the Sessions House in the Old Bailey was sacked. Groups of demonstrators mounted three attacks on the Bank of England but were driven off by a detachment of soldiers, directed by Wilkes, now an alderman. After a week of mayhem the outbreak was crushed by troops, with at least 285 people killed, although two years later Philip Moritz was told that 'more people were found dead beside the looted and emptied brandy casks than were killed by the musketry of the troops'. A further twenty-five were hanged, although Gordon was acquitted when tried for high treason.

The association's objectives had been conservative, but other societies were aimed at promoting the causes of religious emancipation and parliamentary reform. Those objectives were not attainable during the wars with France after 1793, or indeed in the immediate post-war years. The wars brought some hardship, especially when trade with Continental Europe was curtailed during the Napoleonic War, but Britain's worldwide trade continued to expand and its merchant fleet doubled in size between 1786 and 1815. London's share of overseas trade had fallen during the eighteenth century, to below two-thirds by value, but in absolute terms it had continued to increase in both value and volume. The number of vessels using the port that were engaged in overseas trade increased from 1,335 in 1705 to 1,682 in 1751 and to 3,663 in 1794, while the cargo tonnage rose more sharply, from 234,639 tons in 1751 to 620,845 in 1794, reflecting the increasing size of ships; the number of ships based in London that were over 200 tons rose from 205 in 1732 to 751 in 1794. Coastal trade also expanded considerably and was said to have doubled between 1750 and 1796, with shipments of coal increasing as the city's population rose.

The river became so congested that docks were built in the first decade of the nineteenth century: the London docks at Wapping, the West India docks on the Isle of Dogs and the East India docks on the site of the East India Company's shipyard at Blackwall. St Katherine's docks were constructed close to the Tower in 1825–28. On the Surrey side the Commercial Docks were built in 1809 and the East Country Dock in 1811. Even so, in 1818 Richard Rush, the newly arrived American minister in London, saw the Thames 'choked up with vessels and boats of every description, much after the manner that I beheld Cheapside and Fleet Street to be choked with vehicles'. Congestion in the streets and on the river, although a cause of delays, reflected the city's thriving economy.

The imports and domestically produced goods fed London's consumer demand, which grew as the population expanded and the middle class became more prosperous. Its shops impressed visitors, such as François de la Rochefoucauld in 1784: 'The London shops are indeed worthy of remark … Everything the merchant possesses is displayed behind windows which are always beautifully clean and the shops are built with a little projection on to the street so that they can be seen from three sides.' Those shopfronts and the retailers' displays could be transformed by plate-glass windows, available from the 1770s, although adopted only slowly. Cheapside, Fleet Street and the Strand remained the principal shopping streets. In the early eighteenth century the Strand contained 150 shops, including the premises opened in 1706 by Thomas Twining, who decided to specialise in selling tea. The consumption of tea increased enormously in the early eighteenth century and the business prospered. The newer shopping streets were Piccadilly, where Fortnum & Mason was opened in 1707, Bond Street and Oxford Street, which only gradually came to rival the existing thoroughfares, although by the 1830s it had around 150 shops.

After the period of reaction from the 1790s, opposition to change eased during the 1820s. Political emancipation for Nonconformists came with the repeal of the Test Acts in 1828, followed by Catholic emancipation in 1829 and Jewish emancipation in 1835. Parliamentary reform was achieved with the Great Reform Act of 1832. Reform seemed to have been accepted, yet when University College was opened in Bloomsbury in 1828 as a non-denominational establishment, it was referred to as 'the godless institution of Gower Street'.

The Anglican response was King's College, founded in the following year adjoining Somerset House. Denominational differences were soon set aside, however, and both became constituent colleges of the University of London, which was granted a charter in 1836. The university added to the city's prestige and was to become widely influential in higher education, through its own achievements and those of its colleges in Britain and the Commonwealth.

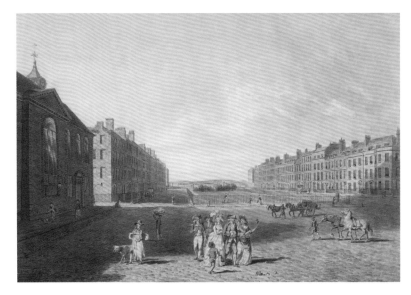

55. Queen Square was planned as early as 1686, but not built up until 1700–30. The north side was left open, allowing views of Highgate and Hampstead, as shown by Edward Dayes in 1786. (Yale Center for British Art, Paul Mellon Collection)

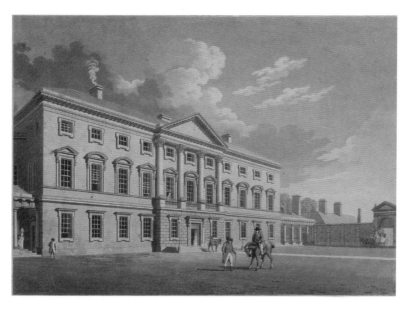

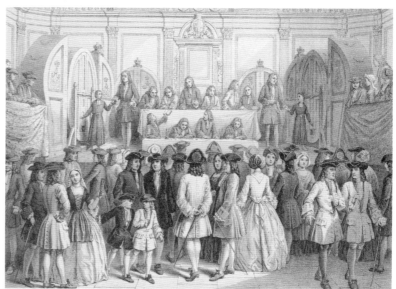

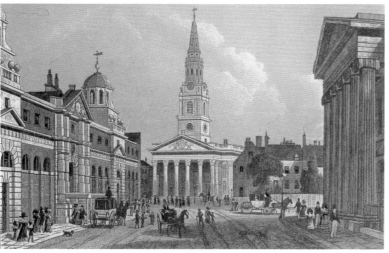

Above left: 56. Buckingham Palace in 1790. The house was built in 1702–05, acquired by the Crown in 1762, and enlarged after 1825. This is the front of the early eighteenth-century house, facing the Mall. (Yale Center for British Art, Paul Mellon Collection)

Above right: 57. The lotteries held in Guildhall were popular in the eighteenth century; the draw was made by the children of Christ's Hospital. (Stephen Porter)

Left: 58. Thomas Shepherd's drawing of St Martin's-in-the-Fields, built in 1721–26 to the designs of James Gibbs, who chose to erect a classical temple, with a Corinthian portico. The design was much imitated for churches across the English-speaking diaspora, despite criticism from the purists that a temple should not have a steeple rising from its roof. (Stephen Porter)

Opposite: 59. In this view of around 1728 Sutton Nicholls gave Charterhouse Square a regularity which is misleading, for the square is not rectangular. But the air of gentility which he conveys is characteristic of London's squares in the eighteenth century. (The Governors of Sutton's Hospital)

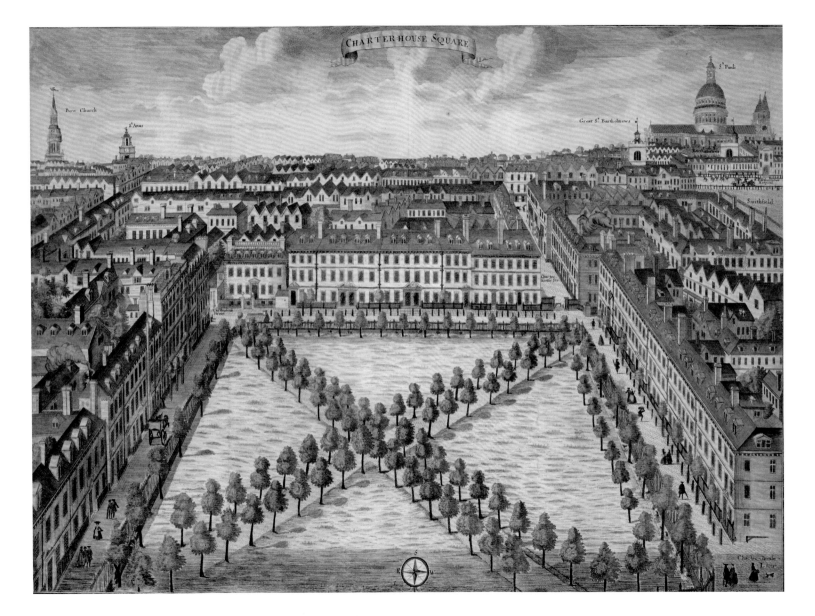

CHARTER-HOUSE SQUARE

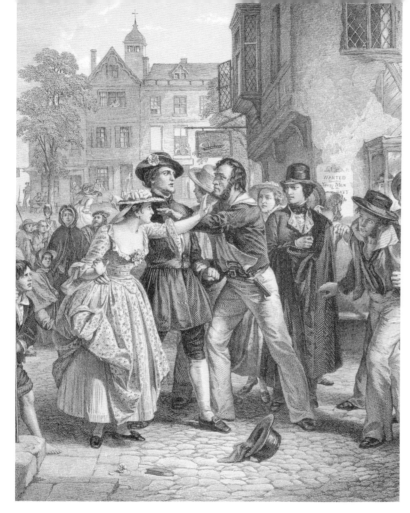

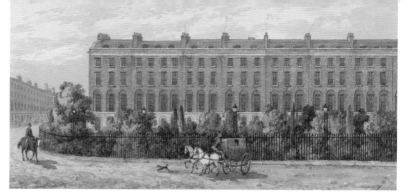

61. Finsbury Square was conceived in 1751 but was not set out before 1777 and building was completed only in the 1790s. With its tall terraces around a rectangular enclosure, it reproduced a typical West End setting close to the City. Painted in 1814 by George Sidney Shepherd. (Yale Center for British Art, Paul Mellon Collection)

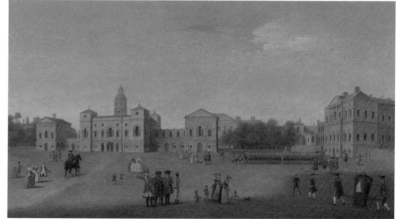

60. Being forcibly taken by the press gang to serve in the Royal Navy was a hazard in the riverside districts during wartime, especially for someone whose clothing suggested that he was a seaman. (Stephen Porter)

62. The expanse of the Horse Guard's Parade, Whitehall, with the Horse Guards building, designed by William Kent and completed in 1760. It had stabling for almost sixty horses and accommodation for the soldiers. View of around 1750, by an unknown artist. (Yale Center for British Art, Paul Mellon Collection)

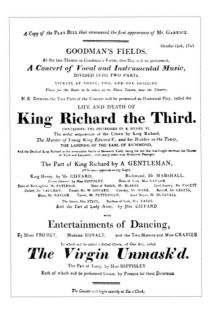

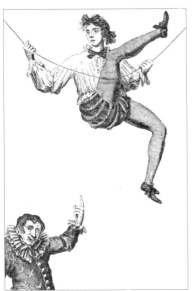

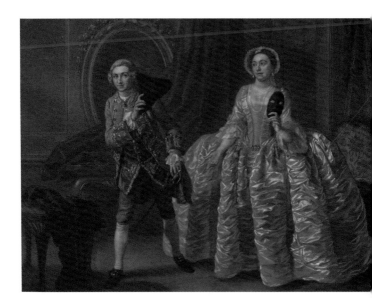

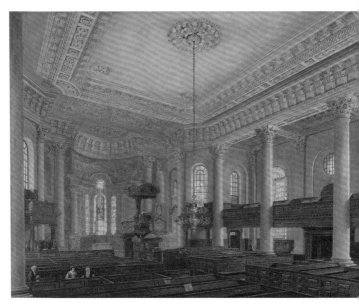

Above left: 63. David Garrick made his debut on the London stage as Richard III at the Goodman Fields theatre, in 1741, with such sensational success that, according to his biographer Arthur Murphy, 'from the polite ends of Westminster the most elegant company flocked to Goodman's Fields'. But at first he was not named in the programme, which ascribed the part to 'A Gentleman'. (Stephen Porter)

Above middle: 64. Sadler's Wells theatre began as a Music House built by Thomas Sadler. It was noted during the eighteenth century for the variety of the entertainments staged there, including tumbling and rope-dancing. (Stephen Porter)

Above right: 65. David Garrick was the leading actor and theatre manager of his generation. He is shown here starring alongside Mrs Pritchard in Benjamin Hoadley's *The Suspicious Husband*, painted by Francis Hayman in 1747. (Yale Center for British Art, Paul Mellon Collection)

Right: 66. St Paul's, Deptford, was designed in 1713 by Thomas Archer for the Commissioners for Building Fifty New Churches and consecrated in 1730. George Johann Scharf's painting conveys the scale of the interior, with its broad nave, Corinthian columns, decorative plasterwork and central chandelier. (Yale Center for British Art, Paul Mellon Collection)

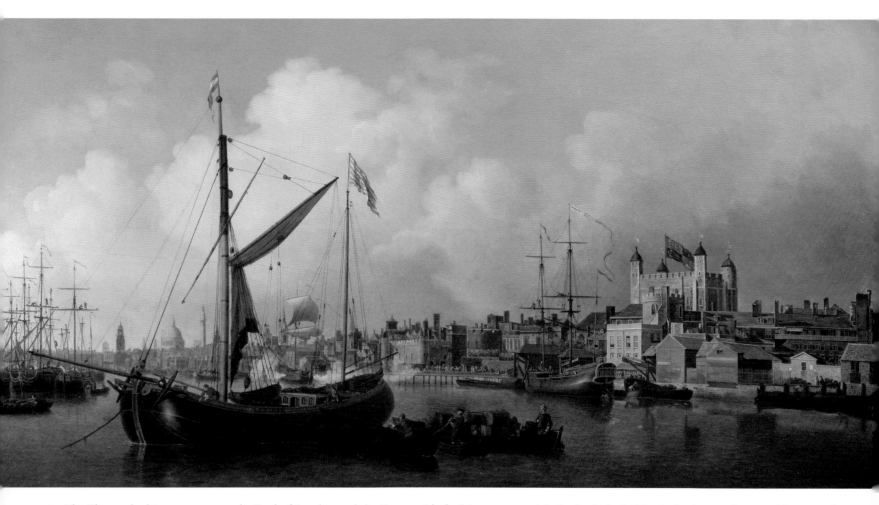

67. The Thames looking upstream to the Pool of London and the Tower, with the Monument and St Paul's Cathedral in the background. Painted by Samuel Scott in 1771. (Yale Center for British Art, Paul Mellon Collection)

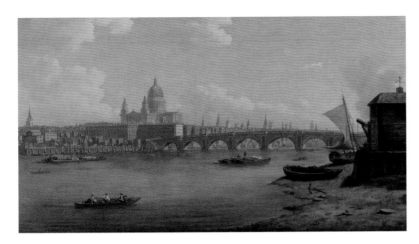

68. Blackfriars Bridge was the third stone bridge across the Thames in London; it is shown by William Marlow looking downstream, with the City behind, just a few years after its opening in 1769. (Yale Center for British Art, Paul Mellon Collection)

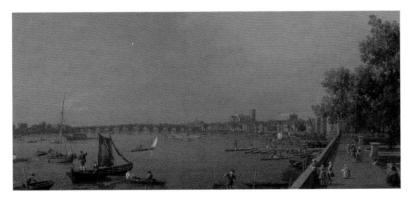

69. The Thames from the terrace of Somerset House, looking towards Westminster, where the prominent buildings are the abbey and the banqueting house at Whitehall; painted by Canaletto, around 1750. (Yale Center for British Art, Paul Mellon Collection)

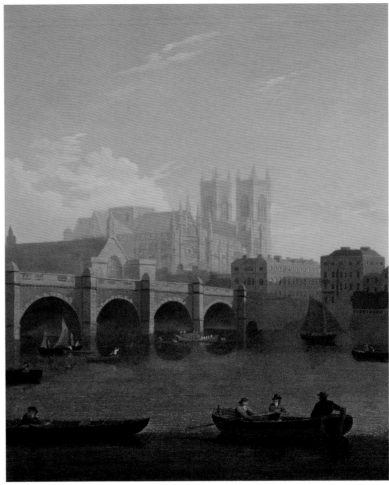

70. Westminster Abbey and Bridge in 1794, painted by Joseph Farington. The abbey's twin towers were completed in 1745. (Yale Center for British Art, Paul Mellon Collection)

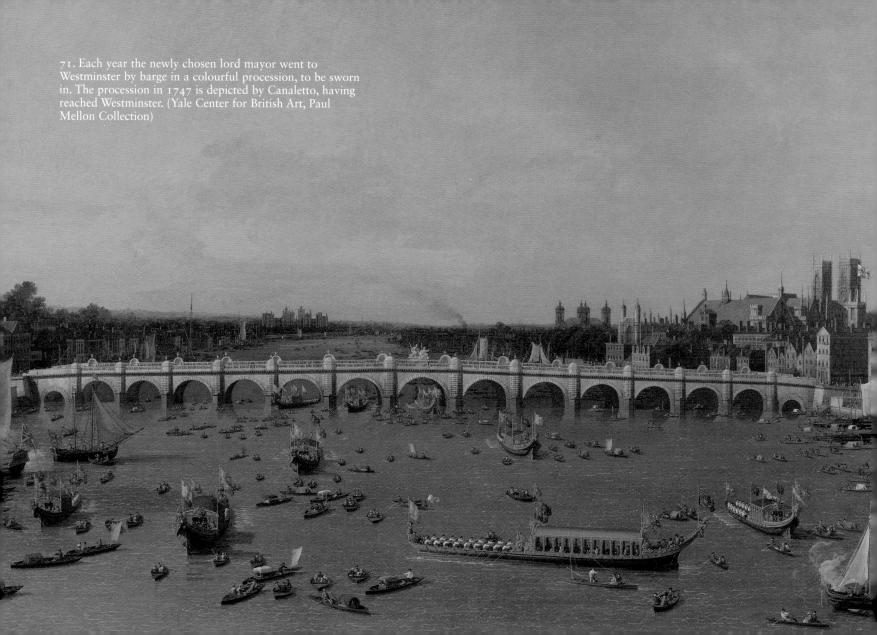

71. Each year the newly chosen lord mayor went to Westminster by barge in a colourful procession, to be sworn in. The procession in 1747 is depicted by Canaletto, having reached Westminster. (Yale Center for British Art, Paul Mellon Collection)

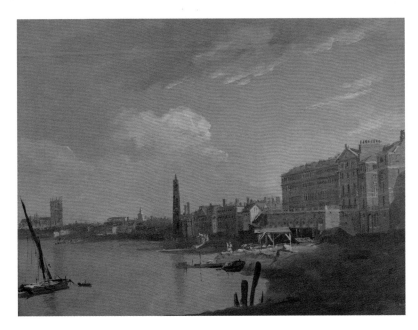

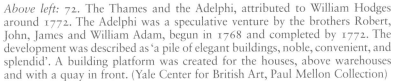

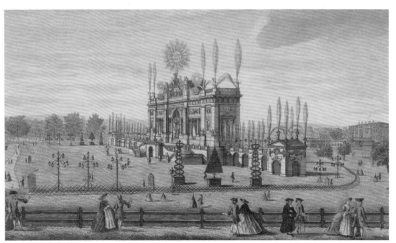

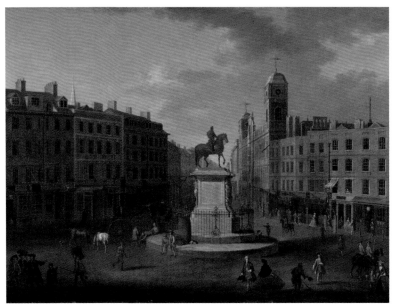

Above left: 72. The Thames and the Adelphi, attributed to William Hodges around 1772. The Adelphi was a speculative venture by the brothers Robert, John, James and William Adam, begun in 1768 and completed by 1772. The development was described as 'a pile of elegant buildings, noble, convenient, and splendid'. A building platform was created for the houses, above warehouses and with a quay in front. (Yale Center for British Art, Paul Mellon Collection)

Above right: 73. *A Perspective View of the Building for the Fireworks in the Green Park*; a print of 1749 by Paul Angier. Plans for a celebration of the peace of Aix-la-Chapelle began in June 1748 and the event took place in the following April. The fireworks were launched from this temporary building of wood and canvas, 410 feet long. (Yale Center for British Art, Yale Art Gallery Collection)

Right: 74. The statue of Charles I on the site of the old Charing Cross at the north end of Whitehall, with the Strand and Northumberland House behind, painted by Joseph Nickolls in 1755. (Yale Center for British Art, Paul Mellon Collection)

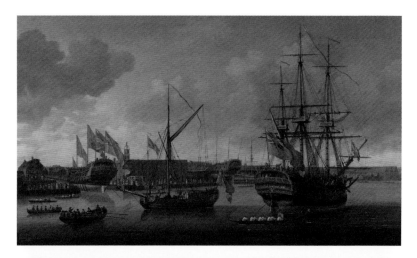

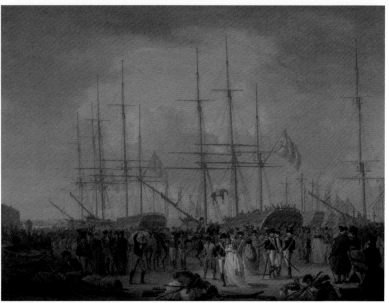

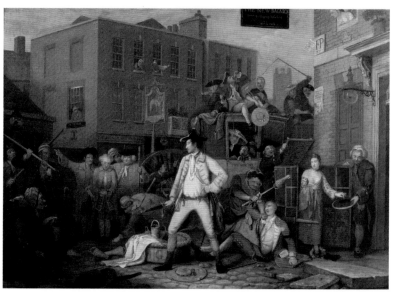

Above right: 75. A turbulent scene in a London street greets travellers arriving in the Bath coach, including a lady emerging from a sedan chair outside a bagnio, or brothel, and the arrest of a thief. The scene was painted by John Collet in 1770. (Yale Center for British Art, Paul Mellon Collection)

Above left: 76. The launch of a man-of-war from a slipway at Deptford shipyard early in the Seven Years War was depicted around 1757 by John Cleveley the elder. (Yale Center for British Art, Paul Mellon Collection)

Left: 77. With the coming of war with France, the dockyard towns downstream from London became even busier than usual. William Anderson shows troops embarking at Deptford in 1793. (Yale Center for British Art, Paul Mellon Collection)

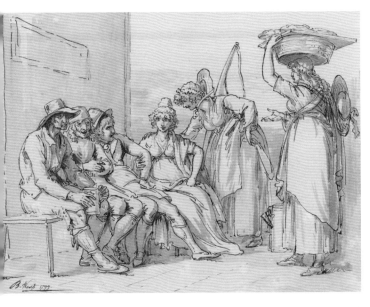

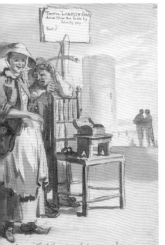

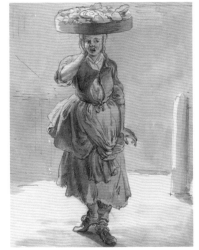

Top left: 78. A drawing by Benjamin West, dated 1799, showing 'Characters in the Streets of London', including a fishseller. (Yale Center for British Art, Paul Mellon Collection)

Bottom left: 79. One of a series of *London Cries* by Paul Sandby, 1759: *Turn your copper into silver now before Your Eyes*. (Yale Center for British Art, Paul Mellon Collection)

Bottom middle: 80. In Paul Sandby's series of *London Cries* of 1759 a girl with a basket on her head is selling food for pets, crying, 'Lights for the Cats, Liver for the Dogs.' Lights are offal, specifically, the lungs of cattle and pigs. (Yale Center for British Art, Paul Mellon Collection)

Right: 81. A street scene from Paul Sandby's *London Cries* of 1759 is entitled *Fun upon Fun*. (Yale Center for British Art, Paul Mellon Collection)

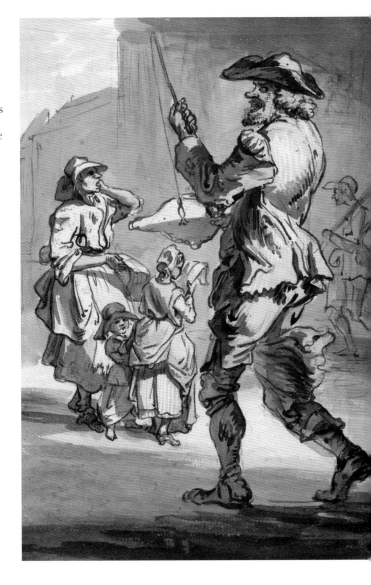

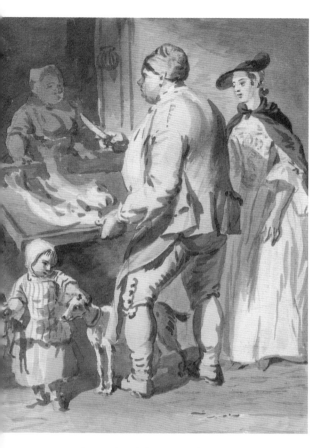

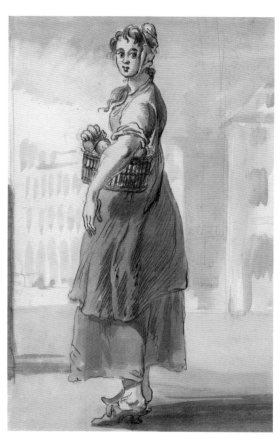

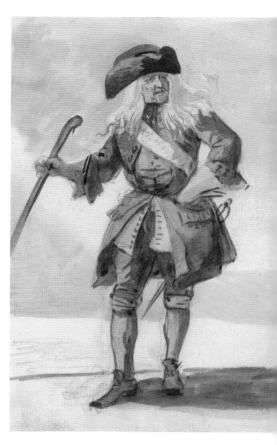

82. A London fishmonger, depicted by Paul Sandby, 1759. (Yale Center for British Art, Paul Mellon Collection)

83. A girl with a basket of oranges, by Paul Sandby, 1759. (Yale Center for British Art, Paul Mellon Collection)

84. *A man swaggering* by Paul Sandby, one of his *London Cries*, 1759. (Yale Center for British Art, Paul Mellon Collection)

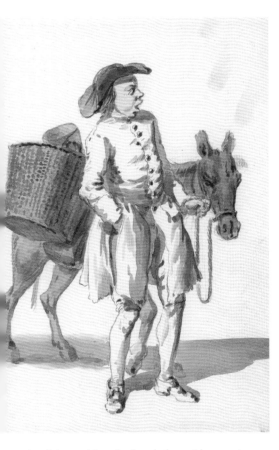

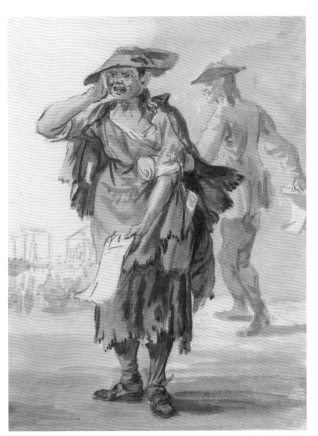

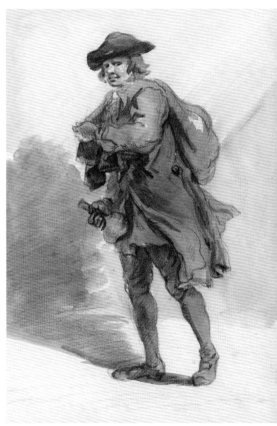

85. A boy with a donkey laden with a panier, by Paul Sandby, from his series *London Cries*, 1759. (Yale Center for British Art, Paul Mellon Collection)

86. The woman street seller is hawking copies of a 'Last Dying Speech and Confession' of a convicted criminal who had been executed, a popular if macabre subject for flysheets in the eighteenth century; by Paul Sandby around 1759. (Yale Center for British Art, Paul Mellon Collection)

87. A man with a bottle and a sack, depicted by Paul Sandby around 1759. (Yale Center for British Art, Paul Mellon Collection)

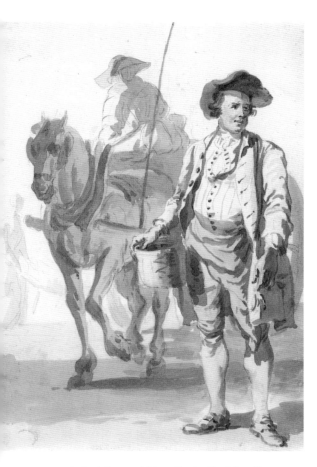

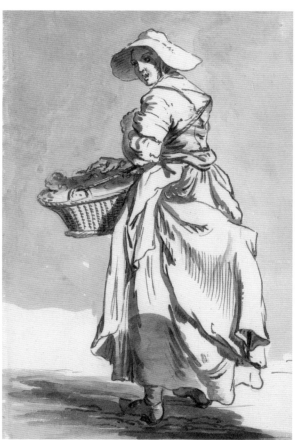

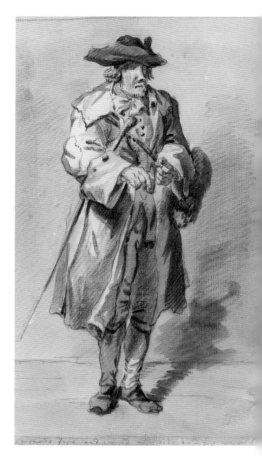

88. A tinker and his wife, by Paul Sandby, around 1759. (Yale Center for British Art, Paul Mellon Collection)

89. In Paul Sandby's *London Cries* series he depicted a girl who was a flower seller, around 1759. (Yale Center for British Art, Paul Mellon Collection)

90. The caption accompanying Paul Sandby's drawing of a rather disconsolate-looking man in his *London Cries* series is 'All Fire and No Smoke', around 1759. (Yale Center for British Art, Paul Mellon Collection)

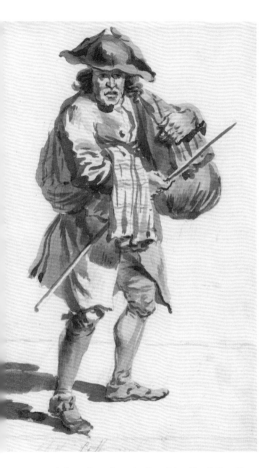

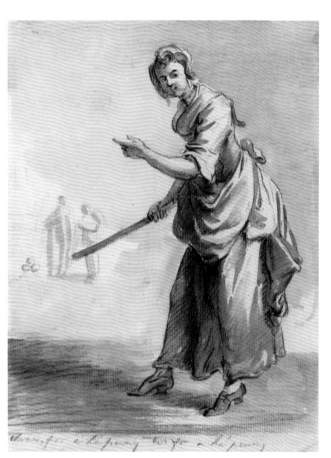

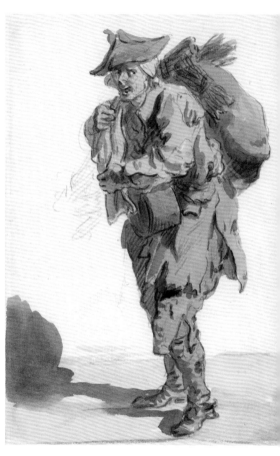

91. A London Cry depicted by Paul Sandby, around 1759: *A Man with a Bundle, Old Clothes*. (Yale Center for British Art, Paul Mellon Collection)

92. In Paul Sandby's *London Cries* series around 1759 the woman invites the onlooker to take 'Throws for a Ha'penny Have You a Ha'penny'. (Yale Center for British Art, Paul Mellon Collection)

93. This London street seller is offering 'Small Coal or Brushes', by Paul Sandby, around 1759. (Yale Center for British Art, Paul Mellon Collection)

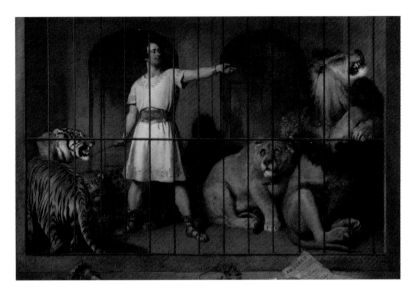

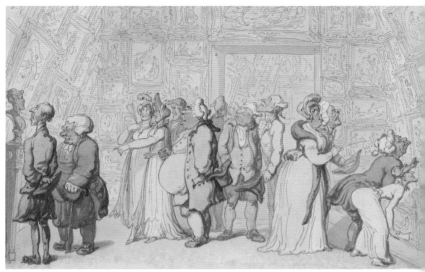

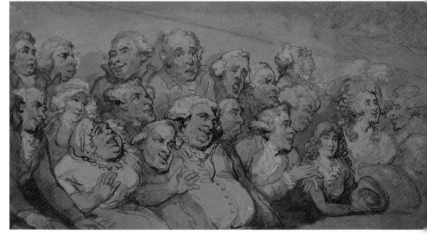

Above left: 94. The American lion tamer Isaac Van Amburgh made his London debut in 1838 and he continued to perform in the city through the following decade, displaying 'a mighty exhibition of human over animal power'. His portrait with his 'big cats' was painted by Sir Edwin Landseer. (Yale Center for British Art, Paul Mellon Collection)

Above right: 95. Thomas Rowlandson shows a genteel but somewhat grotesque group viewing the paintings at the Royal Academy, around 1815. (Yale Center for British Art, Paul Mellon Collection)

Right: 96. An audience at Drury Lane Theatre, probably in the building designed by Henry Holland and opened in 1794, providing space for 3,600 patrons. Thomas Rowlandson's drawing suggests that the attention of some of the patrons was wandering during the performance. (Yale Center for British Art, Paul Mellon Collection)

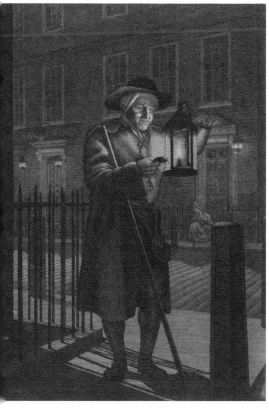

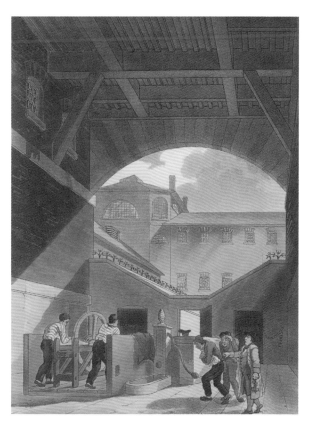

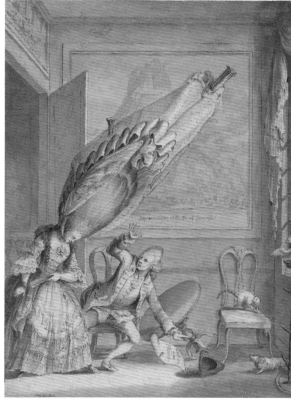

97. A night watchman was a characteristic figure on London's streets for several centuries, with his lantern, staff and watch. In this print by John Bogle of 1776 a woman sits forlornly on the step of the house across the street; the adjoining building sells 'new wines'. (Yale Center for British Art, Paul Mellon Fund)

98. The water engine for male convicts at the Cold-Bath-Field's prison, Clerkenwell, being worked by two prisoners. The building was designed by the prison reformer John Howard and erected in 1794; it was therefore relatively new when Thomas Rowlandson and Augustus Pugin depicted it in 1808. (Yale Center for British Art, Gift of Chauncey Brewster Tinker)

99. Samuel Hieronymus Grimm's caricature of the highly embellished hairstyles for women that were current when he drew this picture around 1771. It was pointedly entitled *The French Lady in London*, for such extravagant fashions were attributed to French influence. Grimm lodged in Covent Garden, which was a centre for the production and sale of satirical prints. (Yale Center for British Art, Paul Mellon Collection)

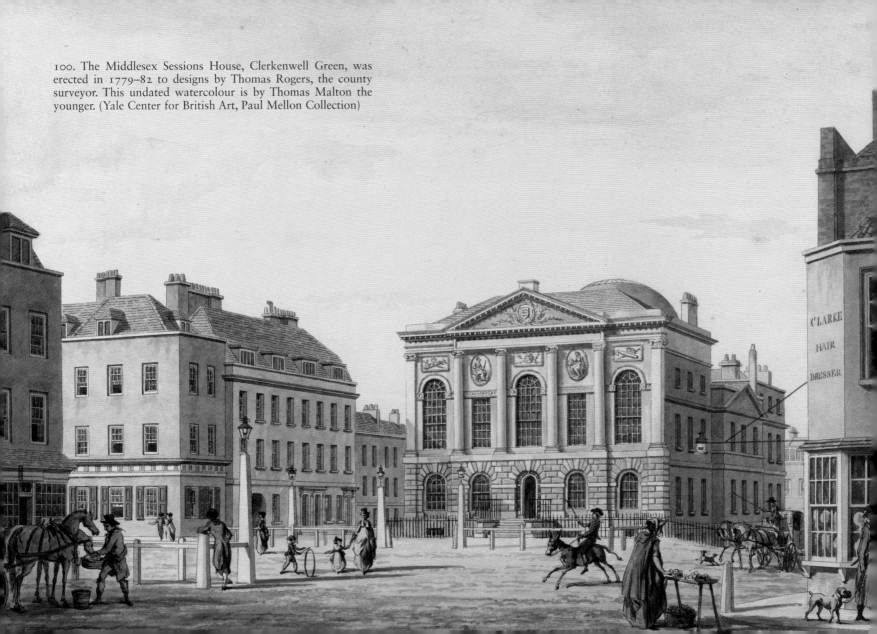

100. The Middlesex Sessions House, Clerkenwell Green, was erected in 1779–82 to designs by Thomas Rogers, the county surveyor. This undated watercolour is by Thomas Malton the younger. (Yale Center for British Art, Paul Mellon Collection)

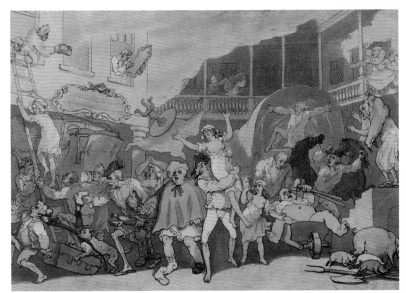

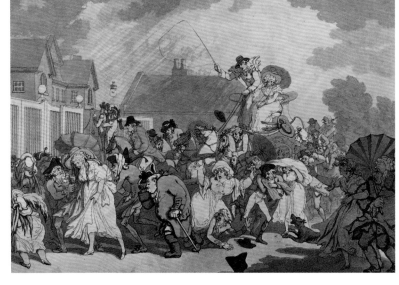

Above left: 101. Inns were a likely source of fires and their yards and stables contained flammable stocks of hay. Thomas Rowlandson shows the confusion caused by such a fire, with the hasty evacuation of the scantily clad occupants and the throwing out of such invaluable items as a mirror, a chamber pot and a table. (National Gallery of Art, Rosenwald Collection, acc. 1945.5.112)

Above right: 102. For those taking their leisure in Hyde Park, a squall of the kind depicted by Thomas Rowlandson in 1791 could be uncomfortable and potentially embarrassing, disordering their sartorial arrangements. (National Gallery of Art, Rosenwald Collection, acc. 1945.5.634)

Right: 103. Fencing was one of the accomplishments expected of young gentlemen and Henry Angelo's Fencing Academy in Bond Street provided the necessary instruction, as illustrated by Thomas Rowlandson; it also contained a shooting gallery and offered boxing lessons. (National Gallery of Art, Rosenwald Collection, acc. 1945.5.632)

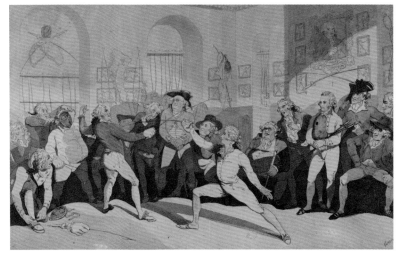

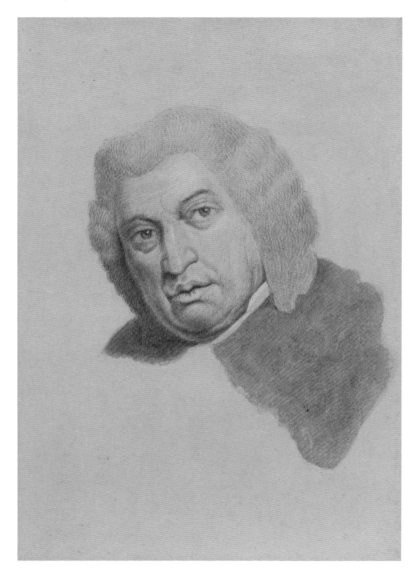

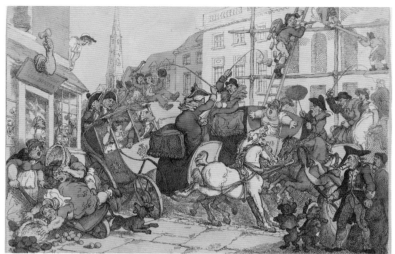

Above: 104. Traffic congestion was one of the *Miseries of London* illustrated by Thomas Rowlandson in 1807. His caption explains that 'in going out to dinner (already too late) your carriage delayed by a jam of coaches – which choak up the whole street and allow you at least an hour or more than you require: to sharpen your wits for table talk'. (National Gallery of Art, Rosenwald Collection, acc. 1945.5.832)

Left: 105. Portrait of Samuel Johnson (1709–84), poet, lexicographer and a leading figure in London's literary world in the eighteenth century. He lived for many years in Gough Square, off Fleet Street. (Yale Center for British Art, Gift of Herman W. Liebert)

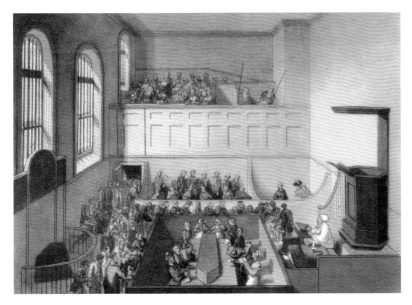

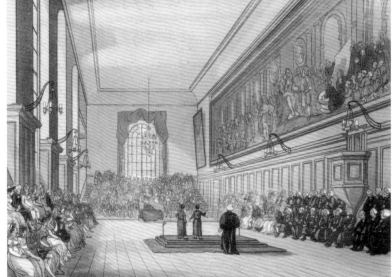

Above left: 106. The chapel inside Newgate prison is shown on a Sunday before an execution, indicated by the coffin on the table, with the condemned sitting around it. Some of the onlookers may have been related to or connected with the prisoners, or were sightseers with a prurient interest in the proceedings. The illustration is by Thomas Rowlandson and A. W. Pugin, around 1808. (Stephen Porter)

Above right: 107. The children at Christ's Hospital, established in 1553, wore a blue outfit, with yellow breeches and stockings, and the institution duly became known as the Blue Coat School. The great hall illustrated by Thomas Rowlandson and Augustus Pugin around 1808 was part of the rebuilding after the Great Fire in 1666; it was replaced by a new range in the 1820s. (Stephen Porter)

Right: 108. St Luke's Hospital in Old Street was founded in 1751 for the care of paupers classified as mentally ill and rebuilt in 1782–84 to the designs of George Dance junior. It was converted in 1917–20 as the Bank of England's printing works and demolished after the Second World War. The stark interior was illustrated around 1808 by Thomas Rowlandson and Augustus Pugin. (Stephen Porter)

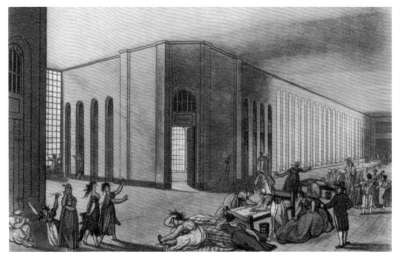

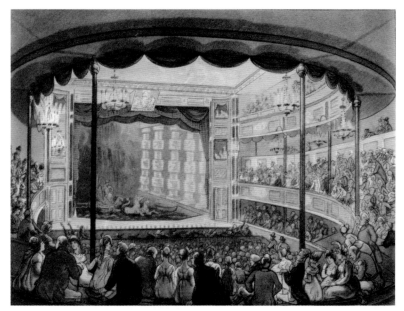

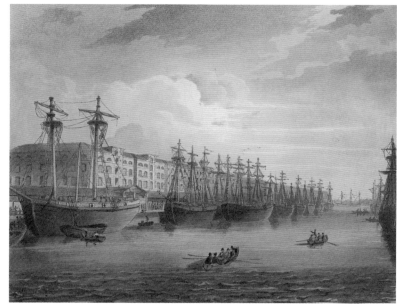

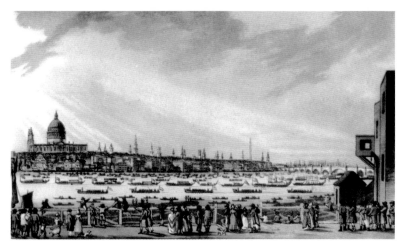

Above right: 109. The West India Docks in 1810 with whaling ships tied up at the dock, and the long run of warehouses behind, by Thomas Rowlandson and Augustus Pugin. (Yale Center for British Art, Gift of Chauncey Brewster Tinker)

Above left: 110. The first Sadler's Wells theatre in Clerkenwell was opened in 1683 by Thomas Sadler. The building illustrated by Thomas Rowlandson and Augustus Pugin, around 1808, was the second on the site. The audience is watching a scene set in a water tank on stage, a characteristic of productions there. (Stephen Porter)

Left: 111. The funeral procession of Lord Nelson passing along the Thames from Greenwich Hospital to Whitehall on 8 January 1806. (Stephen Porter)

Top right: 112. The British Institution for Promoting the Fine Arts in the United Kingdom was founded in 1805. Its Old Master exhibition in the summer of 1832 was depicted by Alfred Joseph Woolmer. (Yale Center for British Art, Paul Mellon Collection)

Bottom right: 113. Thomas Rowlandson's drawing of around 1808 shows the Pass Room in Bridewell, where women vagrants are awaiting removal from the prison, or house of correction, which was designed to punish and correct the inmates, chiefly through whipping or hard labour, not simply to keep them in detention. (Yale Center for British Art, Paul Mellon Collection)

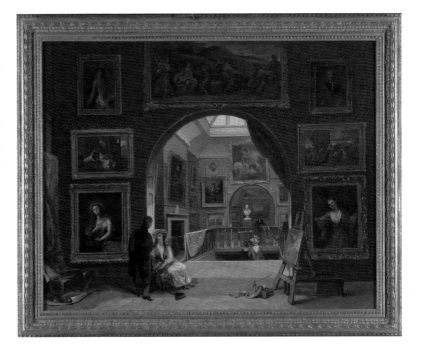

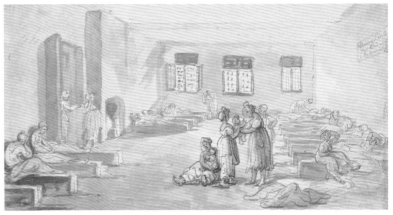

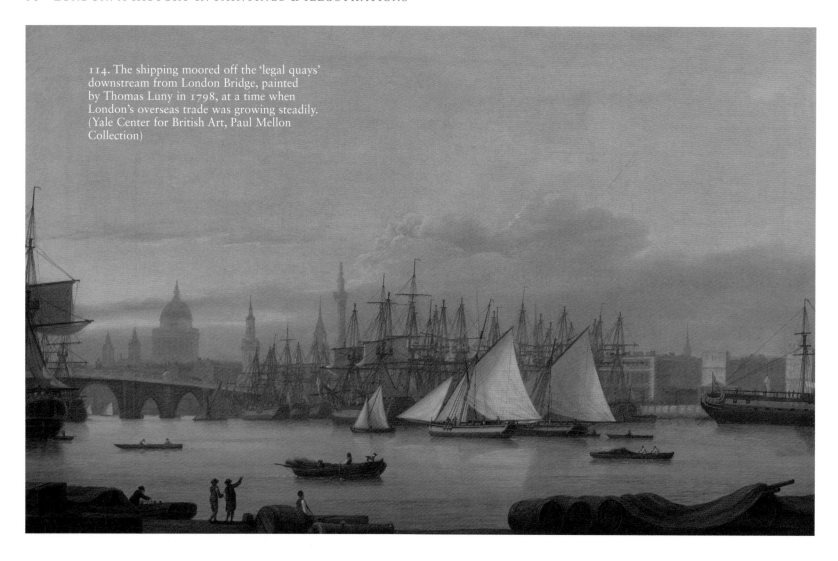

114. The shipping moored off the 'legal quays' downstream from London Bridge, painted by Thomas Luny in 1798, at a time when London's overseas trade was growing steadily. (Yale Center for British Art, Paul Mellon Collection)

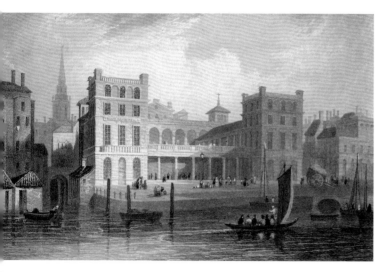

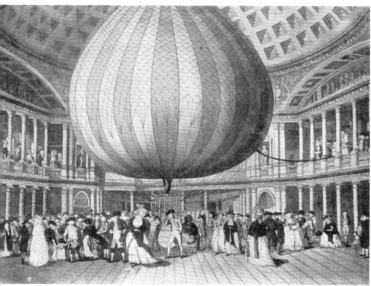

Top left: 115. Charing Cross station stands on the site of Hungerford Market, established there in 1681, and the market hall on the riverside, erected in 1833, which was demolished to make way for the station. (Stephen Porter)

Bottom left: 116. Vicenzo Lunardi, a pioneer Italian balloonist, exhibited his balloon in the large, timber-framed, rotunda of the Pantheon in Oxford Street in 1784. The Pantheon was a grand assembly rooms, built to James Wyatt's designs in 1770–72. It was the most spacious building erected in London since St Paul's Cathedral. (Stephen Porter)

Right: 117. The mackerel seller, one of Francis Wheatley's series *Cries of London*, 1795. (Stephen Porter)

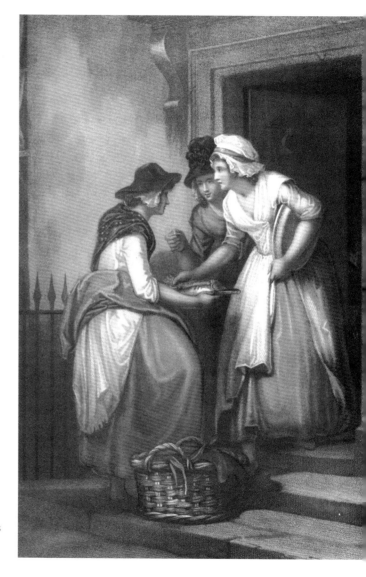

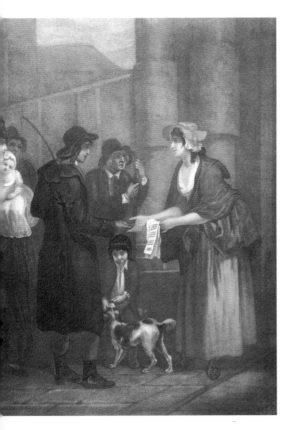

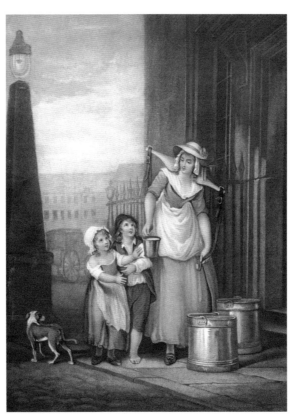

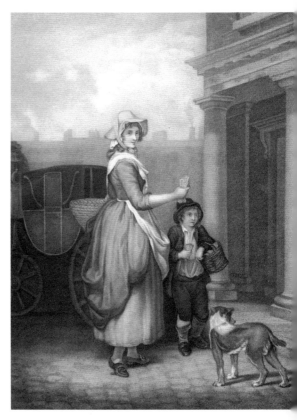

118. The music seller, one of Francis Wheatley's series *Cries of London*, 1796. (Stephen Porter)

119. The milk seller, one of Francis Wheatley's series *Cries of London*, 1793. (Stephen Porter)

120. The match girl, one of Francis Wheatley's series *Cries of London*, 1794. (Stephen Porter)

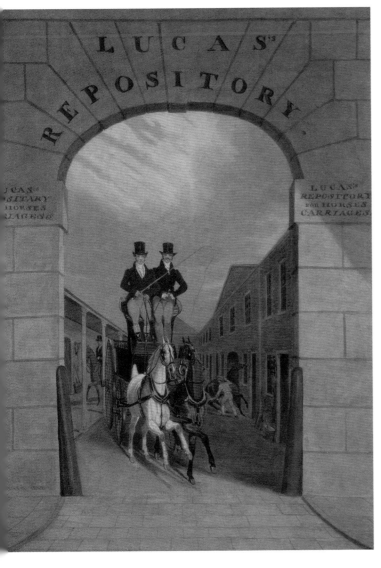

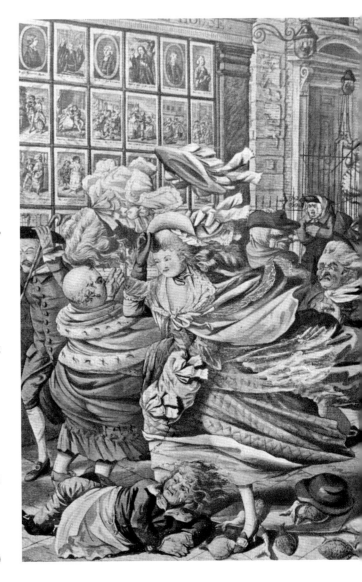

Left: 121. James Pollard's painting of 1818 shows a pair of horses being trained to pull an open vehicle known as a brake at Lucas's yard in Clerkenwell, described as a repository. (Yale Center for British Art, Paul Mellon Collection)

Right: 122. The Bowles family was a dynasty of publishers and booksellers, with a shop in St Paul's churchyard, which is shown here around 1785 by Robert Dighton on a windy day, to the discomfort of passers-by. (Stephen Porter)

Next page: 123. The Long Room in the Custom House, built by Thomas Ripley in 1718–21 and where, according to Daniel Defoe, a 'crowd of people' daily did business. The building was both the custom house for the metropolis and the headquarters of the Board of the Commissioners of Customs. The illustration by J. C. Stadler, in 1808, was made before the building was replaced, in 1813–17. (Stephen Porter)

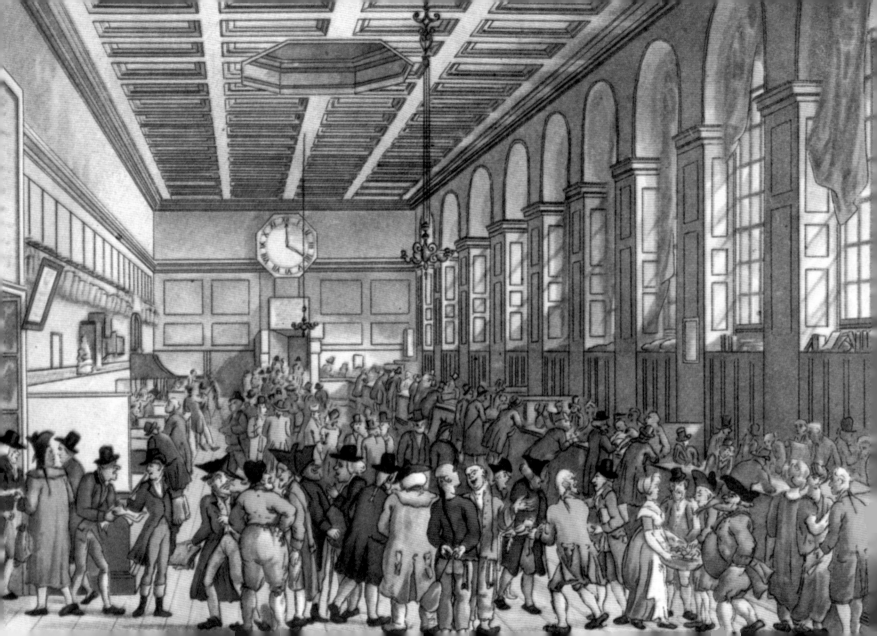

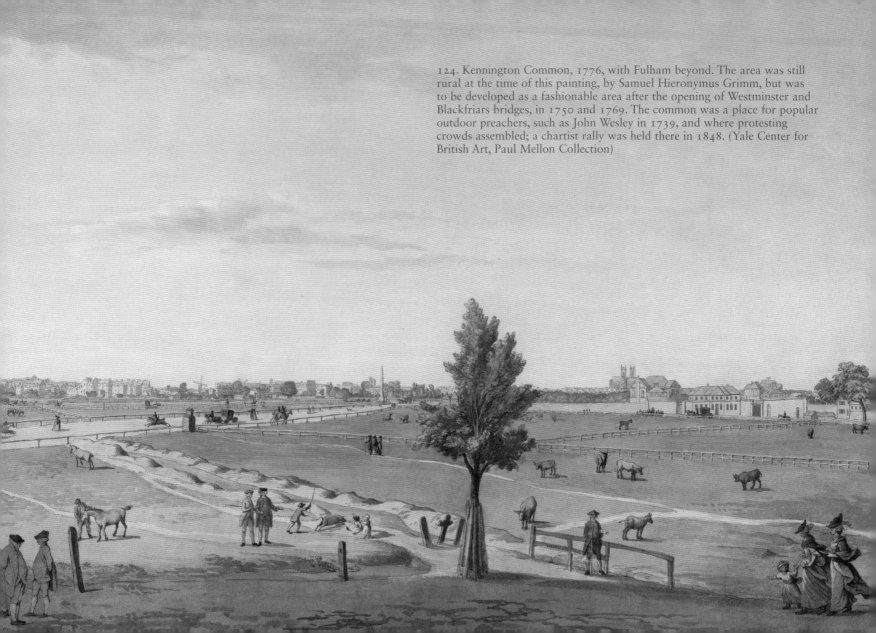

124. Kennington Common, 1776, with Fulham beyond. The area was still rural at the time of this painting, by Samuel Hieronymus Grimm, but was to be developed as a fashionable area after the opening of Westminster and Blackfriars bridges, in 1750 and 1769. The common was a place for popular outdoor preachers, such as John Wesley in 1739, and where protesting crowds assembled; a chartist rally was held there in 1848. (Yale Center for British Art, Paul Mellon Collection)

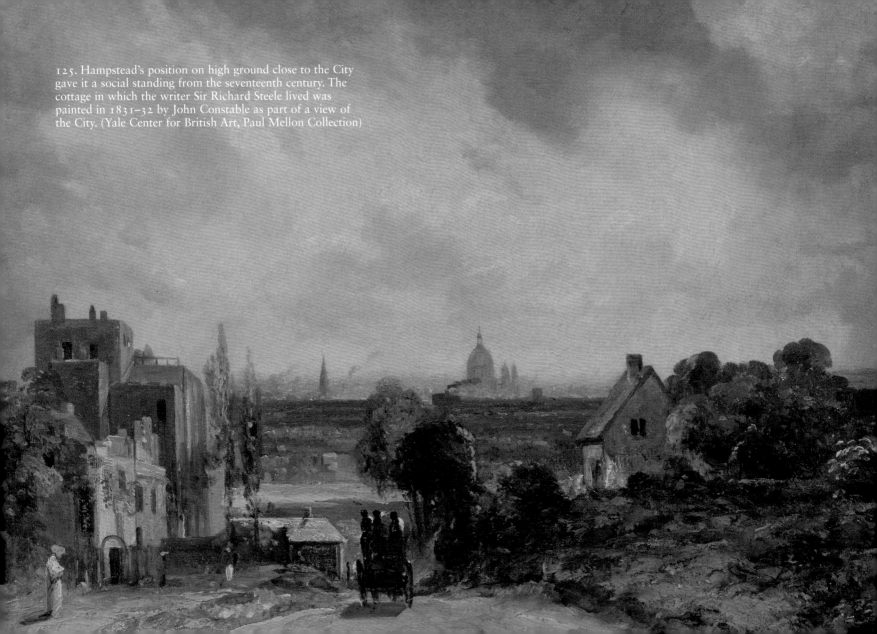

125. Hampstead's position on high ground close to the City gave it a social standing from the seventeenth century. The cottage in which the writer Sir Richard Steele lived was painted in 1831–32 by John Constable as part of a view of the City. (Yale Center for British Art, Paul Mellon Collection)

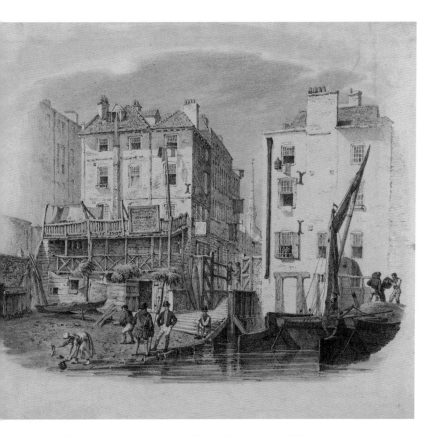

126. This 1822 depiction of Hungerford Stairs, Westminster, by George Harley shows the shabby state of a section of London's riverside in the early nineteenth century. (Yale Center for British Art, Paul Mellon Collection)

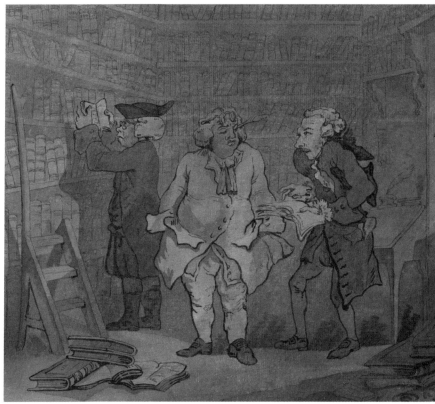

127. *Bookseller and Author, or The Author and his Publisher*, by Thomas Rowlandson, 1784, shows a hopeful author offering a manuscript of his work to a bookseller (booksellers also acted as publishers), but from the reaction, he may be disappointed. The browsing customer seems unaware of the drama being played out behind him. (Yale Center for British Art, Paul Mellon Collection)

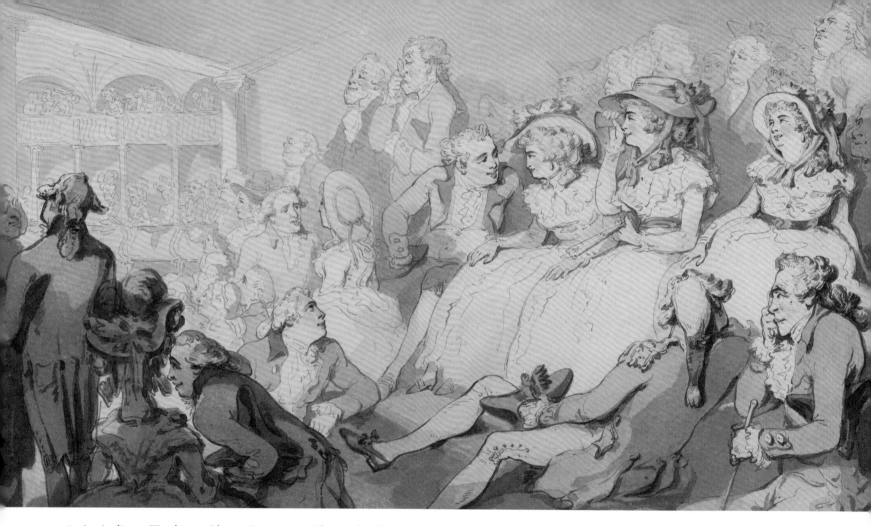

128. *An Audience Watching a Play at Drury Lane Theatre*, by Thomas Rowlandson, around 1785, shows some of the members of the audience to be more interested in the company around them than the action on the stage. Although Rowlandson shows little of the interior, this was the work of Robert Adam, who remodelled the auditorium in 1775–76. (Yale Center for British Art, Paul Mellon Collection)

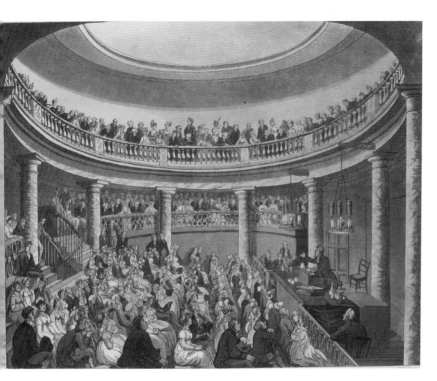

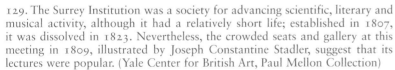

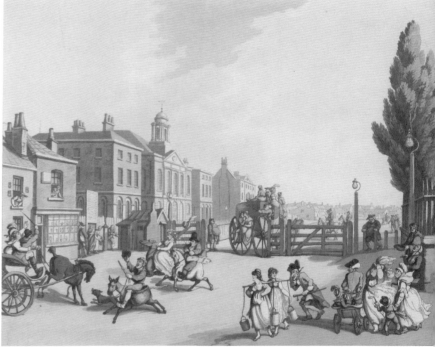

129. The Surrey Institution was a society for advancing scientific, literary and musical activity, although it had a relatively short life; established in 1807, it was dissolved in 1823. Nevertheless, the crowded seats and gallery at this meeting in 1809, illustrated by Joseph Constantine Stadler, suggest that its lectures were popular. (Yale Center for British Art, Paul Mellon Collection)

130. Hampstead Road and the entrance to the Tottenham Court Road turnpike, with St James's chapel, erected to the designs of Thomas Hardwick for the burial ground of St James, Piccadilly, which was established here in 1791. The artist Heinrich Joseph Schutz peopled his illustration of 1798 with some lively and colourful characters. (Yale Center for British Art, Paul Mellon Collection)

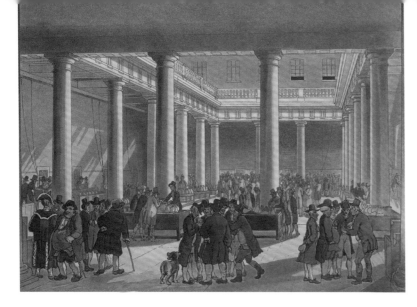

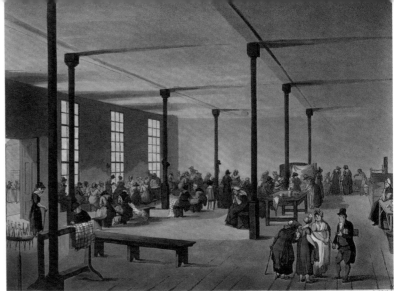

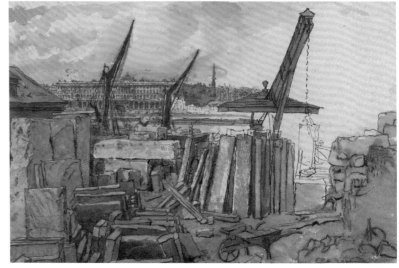

Above left: 131. The Corn Exchange in Mark Lane, 1808, by John Bluck. In 1747 a group of thirty-five corn factors formed a company to build a market for the trade. The building was designed by George Dance the elder and erected in 1747–50, with piazzas on three sides beneath which corn was traded by sample from bins. The exchange quickly became established as the centre of the London grain trade. (Yale Center for British Art, Paul Mellon Collection)

Above right: 132. The women's side of the St James's parish workhouse, with an austere workroom, illustrated around 1808 by Thomas Sunderland, Augustus Pugin and Thomas Rowlandson. (Yale Center for British Art, Gift of Chauncey Brewster Tinker)

Right: 133. The building of Waterloo Bridge, around 1816, with the new Somerset House in the background, by William Henry Hunt; the bridge was opened in 1817. (Yale Center for British Art, Paul Mellon Collection)

Opposite: 134. Like any city, London was prone to fires, many of which were contained before they caused a great deal of damage, but some were destructive. John Constable shows a serious blaze in the City, close to St Paul's, seen from Hampstead around 1826. (Yale Center for British Art, Paul Mellon Collection)

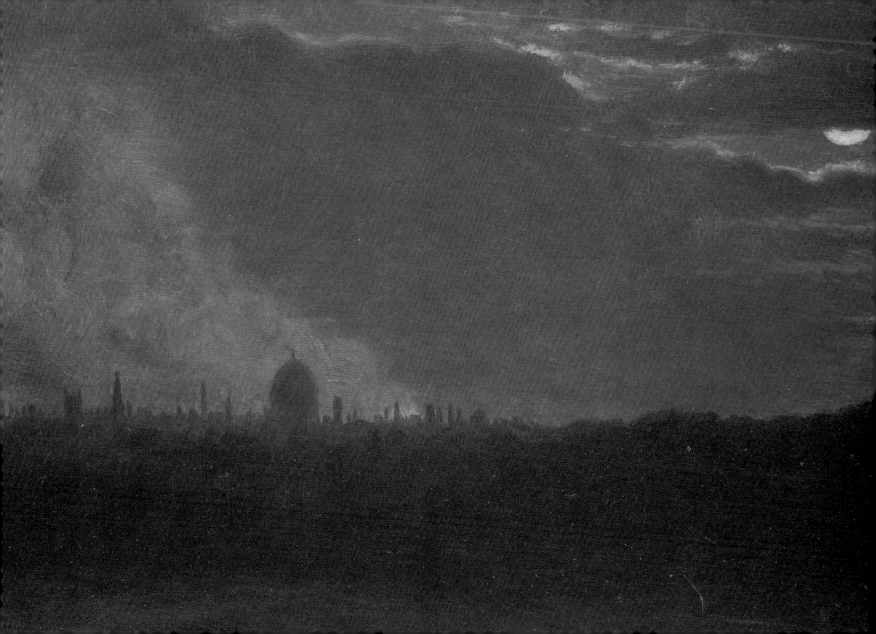

7

VICTORIA'S REIGN

Victorian London expanded dramatically, from a population of 2.239 million in 1841, the year of the first census after the queen's accession in 1837, to 6.586 million in 1901, the year of her death. National population also grew rapidly during the century, as did urbanisation, with the development of an increasing number of large cities, both in the British Isles and Europe. The figures for London suggest a neatness of its boundaries which did not exist in reality. Without an administrative body for the metropolis there was a problem of defining its area, as its suburbs steadily expanded to absorb nearby villages. Paddington's population rose from 1,881 in 1801 to 25,173 in 1841 and 117,846 in 1891, while Hampstead expanded from 4,343 inhabitants in 1801 to 82,329 in 1901. But while the outer areas increased their population, the City's resident population fell, from almost 129,000 in 1801 to 27,000 a century later.

Local government had not kept up with the city's growth, partly because the corporation was resolutely unwilling to extend its authority beyond the City. The first body with responsibility for the metropolis was the Metropolitan Police, established by Sir Robert Peel in 1829; initially its jurisdiction covered an area within four to seven miles of Charing Cross, expanded in 1839 to a radius of fifteen miles but excluding the City. As elsewhere, responsibility for poor relief was transferred from the vestries to district boards of guardians following the Poor Law Amendment Act of 1834, but London was excluded from the other measures of the Whig governments during the 1830s, including the Municipal Corporations Act of 1835.

Pressure for reform came partly because of health hazards resulting from problems of water supply and the discharge of effluent. In 1807 Robert Southey noticed that in the Thames, close to Blackfriars Bridge, 'the common sewers discharge themselves, and blacken the water round about'. The appearance of cholera in 1832 and in subsequent outbreaks caused alarm and led to a campaign for centralised authorities to tackle the issue. The Metropolitan Commission of Sewers was established in 1848, and made some progress by covering open sewers, but met opposition to its plans for a system of main drainage. Cholera returned in 1849, causing 14,000 deaths in London, and again in 1854, and the all too evident foulness of the sewage-laden Thames showed that a stronger body was needed. In 1855 the Metropolitan Board of Works was created, with jurisdiction over much of the built-up area, but again excluding the City. Its plans to eradicate the noxious atmosphere which was believed to cause cholera were not implemented before the aptly named

Great Stink in the hot summer of 1858 emphasised the urgency of the problem. In the following year the board accepted the proposal of its engineer, Joseph Bazalgette, for a system of sewers, with a main sewer along the north bank of the Thames which would intercept the effluent from the branch sewers running down to the river and carry it away from London to an outfall at Beckton. By that time pioneering work by Dr John Snow in Soho had indicated the causes of cholera. An outbreak of the disease in the summer of 1854 had caused several hundred deaths there and, by plotting the location of those cases, Snow traced the source of the outbreak to water from a pump in Broad (now Broadwick) Street. He ordered that the handle of the pump should be removed, to prevent its further use, and the outbreak then came to an end. Further work demonstrated that the disease was carried by polluted water supplies, not miasmic air emanating from insanitary conditions in overcrowded housing, as had been assumed. The final cholera epidemic in London was in 1866 and the sewer system was completed in 1875.

The Metropolitan Board of Works was assigned other functions, including the embankment of the Thames, street improvements and enforcement of building regulations, and in 1866 it took over responsibility for firefighting. But separate bodies were created to administer other matters, including the Metropolitan Asylums Board (1867) and the School Board for London (1870), while the Port of London Sanitary Authority was assigned to the corporation (1872). Plans for local government reform in London were hampered by pressures resisting centralisation. Only with the passing of the Local Government Act of 1888 creating county councils in England and Wales was the impasse broken and the London County Council established, albeit with the boundaries of the Metropolitan Board of Works of thirty-three years earlier. Not until the London Government Act of 1899 were the lower-tier authorities reorganised, with the replacement of the vestries and district boards of works with twenty-eight boroughs. That was done not only as a necessary reform but also to provide local counterbalances to the LCC's centralising force.

Despite the lack of an overall administrative framework and the sluggishness of reform, improvements were carried out. The most striking change to the layout of early nineteenth-century London was initiated by the Prince Regent (from 1811, later George IV, 1820–30) and implemented by his architect John Nash. From the prince's Carlton House in Pall Mall a broad new street, Regent Street, was set out to run north through new foci at Piccadilly Circus and Oxford Circus, on to Portland Place and then to Regent's Park. Nash's scheme envisaged another new street, from the south end of Regent Street, to terminate opposite the façade of St Martin-in-the-Fields church. His plans for a square, or crescent, on that site were prepared in 1826, but not until the 1830s was the newly created space formed and designated Trafalgar Square, with the new National Gallery on its north side opened in 1838 and the column carrying Nelson's statue completed in 1843.

To the south of Trafalgar Square, Whitehall had already undergone some changes since the destruction of the palace, with the erection of the Admiralty building (1726) and the Horse Guards (1760). It developed as the government's quarter, housing the Civil Service, which grew as government took on a greater range of functions domestically and as the

British Empire expanded. The controversy over the choice of architectural styles for the new blocks south of Downing Street in the mid-nineteenth century was so fierce that it became known as the battle of the styles. An Italianate classical design was eventually preferred to a rival Gothic one. Yet the Gothic Revival plans of Sir Charles Barry and A. W. N. Pugin had been chosen for the new Palace of Westminster, to replace the Houses of Parliament, burnt down in October 1834. The palace was begun in 1840 and largely completed in 1860, with an impressive façade to the river and two tall and distinctive towers. Parliament Square was laid out in 1868.

Gothic became the fashionable style of Victorian London, preferred for a range of buildings, from purpose-built banks and offices to public houses, and also for the other large-scale government building of the reign, the Royal Courts of Justice, erected between the Strand and Carey Street to G. E. Street's design and completed in 1882. It was also chosen for the buildings of Albertopolis in South Kensington, erected on the initiative of Albert, the prince consort, from the profits of the Great Exhibition, which was held in Hyde Park in 1851. They included the Victoria and Albert Museum, the Natural History Museum and Imperial College.

The centre of the city, too, was transformed, by street improvements, to ease traffic congestion and clear slum districts, and the erection of larger and more imposing edifices. King William Street was laid out to connect the Bank with the new London Bridge and cut across existing streets, with a section running southwards to the bridge which was carried on a viaduct. Commercial Street was set out in 1845–46 to connect Whitechapel High Street with Shoreditch, cutting through the existing streets and courts and displacing 1,300 people. Clearance of the poor areas of St Giles-in-the-Fields began when New Oxford Street was driven through slums north of the High Street between 1842 and 1847. Further demolition followed in the 1880s when Charing Cross Road and Shaftesbury Avenue were built by the Metropolitan Board of Works, destroying much bad housing there, which was all cleared by the end of the century.

Victoria Street was set out in 1851, described by the American author Nathaniel Hawthorne as 'penetrating through what was recently one of the worst parts of the town, and now bordered with large blocks of buildings'. On the south side of the street London's first mansion flats were erected in 1853–54 in Ashley Place, with accommodation which Hawthorne described as 'a handsome suite of apartments, arranged on the new system of flats, each story constituting a separate tenement, and the various families having an entrance hall in common. The plan is borrowed from the Continent, and seems rather alien to the traditional habits of the English.' That may have been so, but it became a popular type of accommodation in London, with many such blocks erected in the late nineteenth and early twentieth centuries.

The corporation constructed the Holborn Viaduct, in 1869, spanning Farringdon Road, which had been a traffic bottleneck, and created Holborn Circus as part of the scheme. It was also responsible for Cannon Street and Farringdon Road, and Queen Victoria Street between Blackfriars Bridge and Mansion House, opened in 1869–71, cutting across the street plan of Saxon

London. With the Victoria Embankment, built in the 1860s, the new street formed part of a route relieving traffic congestion along the Strand, Fleet Street, Ludgate Hill and Cheapside. As well as Shaftesbury Avenue and Charing Cross Road, the Metropolitan Board of Works set out Clerkenwell Road, Great Eastern Street and Hyde Park Corner. Other streets were widened, to improve the flow of traffic, and so providing sites for new buildings.

Although such improvements eased traffic congestion, it could not be eradicated. However, travel was also improved by the steamboat services and the coming of the railways from the late 1830s and underground lines from the 1860s. The railways provided long-distance travel at hitherto unknown speeds between London and much of the rest of the country, as well as suburban services for commuting, which became an increasingly common practice after the middle of the century. Those markets supplied by the railways were also improved. By the early 1840s, 210,377 cattle and 1,650,448 sheep were sold annually at Smithfield, but in 1855 the livestock market was closed, greatly reducing the numbers of animals driven along the city's streets. Most railway lines ran to termini, of varying size and grandeur, around the fringe of the centre, but in 1866 the Southern Railway was extended across the river at Blackfriars and then to Farringdon, and the Metropolitan line had been continued to Moorgate, allowing meat to be brought to Smithfield, where the Central London Meat Market was built in 1867–68. The corporation also rebuilt Leadenhall Market, in 1880–81, which was 'the largest and best poultry market in London', while Covent Garden specialised in market garden produce, which could now be brought in from a wider area. But Hungerford Market, established in 1681, was suppressed when Charing Cross station was built on its site in 1864. Outside the station, in 1863 a replica Eleanor Cross was erected about 200 yards from the site of the original, built in 1291–94 and demolished in 1647.

The last railway terminus to be built, at Marylebone (1899), destroyed Blandford Square and Harewood Square, but many of the estimated 100,000 people displaced for railway construction between 1850 and 1900 had occupied poor housing. On the other hand, the improved communications provided by the suburban railways encouraged developers to build thousands of houses, mostly in straight, and often monotonously long, streets. The newly built areas contained a scattering of churches and chapels, including Roman Catholic ones. The Victorians were very sensitive to the nuances of the social hierarchy and the appearance of the houses reflected the status of those for whom they were intended. They ranged from detached and semi-detached villas with bay windows, some detailing and accommodation for at least one domestic servant, which were aimed at the professional classes, through the smaller semi-detached houses for the growing number of white-collar workers and the better-off artisans, to the plain-fronted terraces built for the 'lower classes'. The novelist Arthur Conan Doyle sent his characters on a journey from Vauxhall Bridge through Stockwell to Brixton in 1890: 'Long lines of dull brick houses were only relieved by the coarse glare and tawdry brilliancy of public-houses at the corner. Then came rows of two-storeyed villas, each with a fronting of miniature garden, and then again interminable lines of new, staring brick buildings – the monster tentacles which the giant city was throwing out into the country.'

When Charles Booth, a wealthy businessman, carried out a survey of London, beginning in 1886, he classified housing according to the perceived status of the occupants, in seven categories ranging from the 'Upper-middle and Upper classes. Wealthy', through those who were 'Fairly comfortable. Good ordinary earnings', to the 'Very poor, casual. Chronic want', and then those described as 'Vicious, semi-criminal'. His results and interpretative essays were published as *Life and Labour of the People in London*, which in the second edition filled nine volumes. One finding of Booth's work which surprised him was the extent of poverty in the metropolis; he calculated that 30 per cent of Londoners lived on or below his 'poverty line'.

Slum clearance became a policy objective, supported by the collection of statistics in social and public health investigations, which detailed the buildings and their occupants. They provided some shocking figures. For example, the rookery left behind by the clearance for New Oxford Street had ninety-five houses standing on a little over one acre, housing 2,850 people, a density of thirty people per house. Multiple occupation was common in such areas. Between 1866 and 1868 the site of the Royal Courts of Justice was cleared by the removal of 400 buildings with a population of 4,125 in thirty-three streets, courts and alleys. A writer in *The Times* was not unsympathetic to those expelled but was puzzled by the nature of this district, only a few hundred yards from the paper's offices, reporting that its occupants were 'human swarms whose modes of existence are among the unsolved social mysteries'.

Not all of the areas which attracted attention were close to the centre, or the result of gradual overcrowding. The Potteries area in North Kensington contained 595 rooms in 214 houses, with a population of 1,147, and the district was also home to 1,041 pigs. The Wells Street area of Poplar was developed after the construction of the nearby West and East India docks and the builders took the opportunity to simultaneously build small houses fronting the streets and even smaller ones in courts to their rear. They thereby created an instant slum, for demand was such that all the houses were filled. After the passing of the Artisans' and Labourers' Dwellings Improvement Act in 1875 (known as the Cross Act after Richard Cross, the Home Secretary), the district was one of the priorities for clearance; of the 208 houses affected by the scheme, eighty-one were categorised as unfit for human habitation.

To replace the slums, model housing was constructed, typically blocks of flats. The American banker George Peabody established a model dwellings company, and its first block of dwellings, in Commercial Street, Spitalfields, was opened in 1864. By 1882 some 14,600 people were living in Peabody housing. But the philanthropic housing societies could not afford to build in districts where property values and rents were high, such as Poplar, and so after the Housing of the Poor Act was passed in 1890 the new LCC began building model dwellings. That was the beginning of a policy of providing public housing, in those areas and elsewhere, which both the county and the borough councils were to develop enormously in the twentieth century.

As well as efforts to eradicate the worst housing, there was growing awareness of the predicament of the abject and homeless poor, whose plight could no longer be ignored, especially after the publication in 1883 of Andrew Mearns's

The Bitter Cry of Outcast London. For the homeless, soup kitchens and night shelters were provided by missionary movements, the most famous of which was the Salvation Army, founded in 1865 by William Booth. Despite its worthy aims, the Salvation Army was unpopular with brewers and pub landlords because of its emphasis on temperance, and also with the Church of England and among the residents of the East End, who sometimes even attacked its workers. The Victorians linked charity with moral improvement, a connection that was not always popular on London's streets.

By the Poor Law Amendment Act of 1834 the Poor Law was administered by Poor Law Unions run by Boards of Guardians. Some London parishes were large enough to constitute a union, and others were not drawn into the system until another Act of Parliament, in 1867. Under the arrangements, the workhouse system was greatly expanded. The objective was to keep the cost to the ratepayer as low as possible, by creating unpleasant and degrading conditions which would deter those able and fit to work from claiming poor relief. Work of a harsh and monotonous kind was provided, for nothing could be produced which would compete with the output of commercial businesses. The forty union workhouses in London contained mostly children, the infirm and the elderly; their inmates were segregated by sex and so families were divided.

In practice, the workhouse system was cruel, demeaning and socially divisive and was strongly criticised by reformers, including Charles Dickens, who mentioned workhouses disparagingly in almost all of his novels, as well as in many of his other writings. Yet it had its supporters, for keeping the costs of poor relief down, and perhaps, too, for putting the poorest members of society out of sight, behind the plain walls of the workhouses. But some aspects could not be ignored or condoned, and in the 1860s the deplorable state of workhouse infirmaries and pauper schools, in which thousands of orphans were educated, was exposed. The death rates within them were unacceptable and, following the establishment of the Metropolitan Asylums Board, the workhouse infirmaries were to develop as general hospitals. The nineteenth century also saw the establishment of specialist dispensaries and hospitals for infectious diseases, at least sixty-six of which had been founded by the 1860s. With the provision of hospitals, advances in medicine, cleaner water supplies and the solution to the earlier problem of sewage disposal, the death rate in London by the end of the century was only slightly higher than the average for other urban areas. The treatment of orphans had improved, with the Poor Law unions generally sending them to local schools, which were rapidly erected across London by the School Board, in a rather appealing Queen Anne style.

The late Georgian period had seen growing pressure from reformers, especially John Howard and Elizabeth Fry, for improvements to conditions in prisons, and those efforts were successful. New prisons were built away from the centre of London and those within it were closed, including all the debtors' prisons. Wormwood Scrubs, Holloway, Pentonville and Brixton were built between 1820 and 1890, while ten prisons were closed during the same period, including those in Southwark. The Millbank Penitentiary was built in 1816 and closed in 1890 (the Tate Gallery was built on its site) and Tothill Fields was demolished in 1885 and replaced by the Roman Catholic Westminster Cathedral.

The Chartist campaigner Ernest Jones was incarcerated in solitary confinement in the Tothill Fields prison in 1848, when fear of insurrection was running high because of revolutions and protests on the Continent. In early March a crowd of about 10,000 took over Trafalgar Square and for two days resisted police efforts to expel them, and, although a Chartist rally in April on Kennington Common was not as well attended as expected, on 29 May a much larger crowd of demonstrators marched through the city to the square. Thereafter Chartism declined as a mass movement, but working-class radicalism continued. The First International Working Men's Association was formed in London in 1864 and the city contained more than 100 working men's clubs. The Chartist demonstrations had shown that by creating Trafalgar Square the government had provided an ideal place for crowds to assemble, close to Whitehall and Westminster. Attempts to prevent assemblies there did not always succeed. On 30 July 1871 one of the largest crowds ever to gather in the square assembled there, despite a ban, to hear the leading republican MP Charles Bradlaugh speak critically of the monarchy, at a time when the queen was very unpopular. Popular orators were predicting the end of the monarchy after the queen's death, which caused alarm among the upper and middle classes, and their perturbation was increased by the events of the Paris commune and 'the outbreak', as the Earl of Derby put it, of the Socialist Party there, which had helped to increase republican support in Britain.

During the mid-1880s an economic recession caused much hardship and a protest rally of the unemployed was held in Trafalgar Square in February 1886. Things turned ugly when a section of the crowd broke away and rampaged through St James's, taking the opportunity to hurl stones at the windows of the gentlemen's clubs in the neighbourhood. The staff responded by throwing such items as shoes, nail brushes, crusts of bread and matchboxes. After a while the crowd surged on into Piccadilly, alarming the shoppers there, and eventually was dispersed in Mayfair. The incident, designated 'the Pall Mall riot', shook the complacency and confidence of wealthy and respectable Londoners. Consequently, the government of the day was determined to prevent the square being used again as a focus by demonstrators and in November 1887 the Home Office banned all meetings there. In protest at this curb on freedom of assembly, a demonstration was arranged for 13 November and a crowd of about 40,000 managed to gather in the square, where it was confronted by 5,000 police, 200 Life Guards and a battalion of Grenadier Guards. They used strong methods, including fixed bayonets, to drive the crowd out of the square, causing two deaths and hundreds of injuries on what came to be known as Bloody Sunday. The ban on public meetings in the square was not lifted until 1892. But it did not require demonstrations to draw attention to the economic hardship, for many unemployed and homeless hung around the square, the most conspicuous location in London.

Working-class protests were also expressed through strikes, two of which, in 1889, attracted much attention and support. The first was by 700 women employed at Bryant & May's match factory at Bow, which was skilfully organised by Annie Besant, and the second was by dockworkers, in support of a claim for a 6d per hour wage increase, which became known as the 'Docker's

Tanner'. London continued to have a wide international trade and the number of ships entering the port roughly doubled between the mid-1790s and the early 1860s, although its share of Britain's trade declined as ports serving the industrial areas grew, notably Liverpool. Despite that relative decline, it still had 30 per cent of the country's overseas trade by value in 1913.

London was also an industrial centre, containing 15 per cent of the manufacturing jobs in England and Wales, both craft-based work in relatively small units and heavy industries on a factory scale. Clothing remained its largest industry and it expanded following the invention of the sewing machine in 1846 and the band-saw (which made it possible to cut many cloths simultaneously) in 1858. It employed 30 per cent of the city's manufacturing workforce, while shoemaking employed 10 per cent. No one trade was dominant across the city, but some districts developed specialities, such as furniture making in Shoreditch and leather trades in Bermondsey, which accounted for 'the unpleasantness of the compound of horrible smells which pervade the whole neighbourhood', according to Charles Dickens the younger.

The city also contained the financial businesses to service the trade and industrial sectors, including the raising of the large amounts of capital required to build the railways. That was made easier by the repeal in 1825 of the Bubble Act of 1720, passed in the aftermath of the South Sea Bubble and requiring joint-stock companies to obtain a royal charter. The removal of that constraint on business was balanced by regulation contained in successive company Acts and bankruptcy Acts. The accountancy business developed in parallel with the growth of the financial sector, from twenty-four accounting firms in London in 1811 to 840 by 1883. Yet the wealth generated by the financial district of the City was not readily apparent beyond the central area around the bank. Bradshaw's *Guide through London* of 1862 commented that its 'enormous wealth and splendour are but poorly evidenced by dingy warehouses, dark alleys, and retired counting-houses'. Nor was its prosperity apparent from the riverside. In 1855 Nathaniel Hawthorne took a steamer downriver, 'passing the Custom House and the Tower, the only prominent objects rising out of the dreary range of shabbiness which stretches along close to the water's edge'.

Although broadly based, the city's economy was subject to trade fluctuations and periodic financial crises, such as those in 1847–48 and in the 1860s. The financial crisis of 1867 more or less sealed the fate of London's long-standing shipbuilding industry, the greatest achievement of which had been the building of Isambard Kingdom Brunel's prodigious *Great Eastern* at Millwall as recently as 1854–59. Shipbuilding and marine engineering on the Thames employed 6,000 men in 1851 and 27,000 by 1865, but the number fell to 9,000 by 1871 and to 6,000 by 1891. New employment was provided on the river by the opening of further docks, the Victoria in 1855 and the Albert in 1880, serving the newly developed industrial districts of Canning Town, Silvertown and Beckton, and the Millwall Docks, opened on the Isle of Dogs in 1868. As with industry, trade fluctuations caused variations in business and so sharp competition among the dock and warehouse companies.

As industry expanded, especially along the Thames and in the East End, so social zoning was accentuated, with east

London developing as a predominantly, although by no means exclusively, working-class and industrial area. Indeed, it became something of a fascination to Londoners from other parts of the capital, with a reputation for being poor, rough, unhealthy and unruly. In 1888 the barbarous Whitechapel Murders were committed. Six women were killed and mutilated by 'Jack the Ripper', the name appended to letters sent to the police. The crimes shocked late Victorian England and contributed to the area's reputation, although at the same time they gave those working to alleviate the poverty there the opportunity to publicise the real situation. The East End's character was modified by the arrival in the last two decades of the century of Jewish immigrants from eastern Europe, fleeing from persecution. Ireland had been the most common source of migrants to London in the early part of the reign and 5 per cent of London's population was of Irish origin by 1851; the Jews were the most numerous group in its later decades. The Jewish population of London rose from around 46,000 in 1881 to around 140,000 in 1905. They settled mainly in the East End, where many were engaged in the clothing trades. By 1901 roughly a third of the eastern European Jews in London worked in the industry, mostly in the local sweatshops, although there was also a strong domestic industry based on the putting-out system, in which workers took the articles or pieces home or to their own workshops.

London's housing and social problems were offset by growing prosperity and greater leisure, with increasing numbers of theatres, the emergence during the mid-century of the music hall and the opening of concert halls in Langham Place in 1893 and Wigmore Street in 1901. More buildings connected with national history, housing collections of art and sculpture, or having a literary association were opened to the public, and new museums were established. This was largely in response to increasing demands for such buildings to be accessible to all, preferably free of charge, so that the growing educated working classes would not be deterred from visiting them.

Victoria's reign also saw an upsurge in popular spectator sports. Lord's cricket ground was established in St John's Wood in 1814 and the pavilion dates from 1890; the Oval was opened as a cricket ground in 1846 and its pavilion was completed in 1897. Football clubs were formed in increasing numbers from the 1860s, including the Wanderers, founded in 1864 and based at the Oval. The first FA Cup final was played there in 1871, with the Wanderers the winners in front of a crowd of almost 2,000, and it staged the final annually until it was transferred to Crystal Palace in 1895. For exhibitions, the Royal Agricultural Hall in Islington was opened in 1862 and the exhibition hall at Olympia in 1886. As the Great Exhibition had celebrated Britain's achievements in the mid-century, so Queen Victoria's Golden and Diamond Jubilees, in 1887 and 1897, when her earlier popularity had been regained, provided the opportunity for celebrations, with London playing a prominent role. During her long reign it had become the capital of a worldwide empire that covered a quarter of the globe.

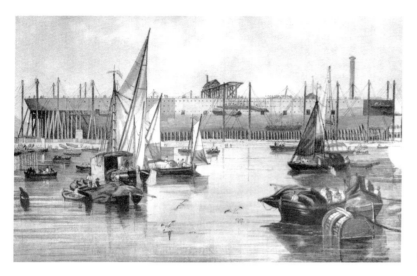

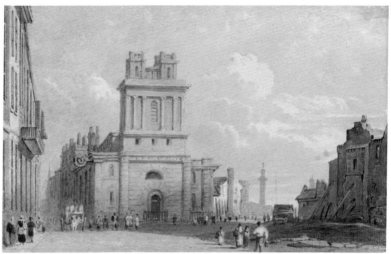

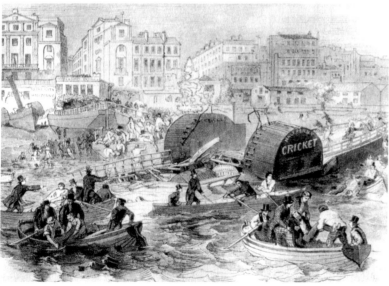

Above right: 135. The making of King William Street, laid out to connect the Bank with the new London Bridge, which was opened in 1831. The church is St Mary Woolnoth, designed by Nicholas Hawksmoor and built in 1716–27. The painting is by John Varley. (Yale Center for British Art, Paul Mellon Collection)

Above left: 136. The size of Brunel's *Great Eastern* is conveyed in this illustration of its construction on the west side of the Isle of Dogs in 1857. (Stephen Porter)

Left: 137. Steamboats operated frequent services along the river in the nineteenth century. On 27 August 1847 the boiler of the *Cricket* exploded as the vessel was about to leave the Adelphi pier. It was crowded with passengers, many of whom were killed. (Stephen Porter)

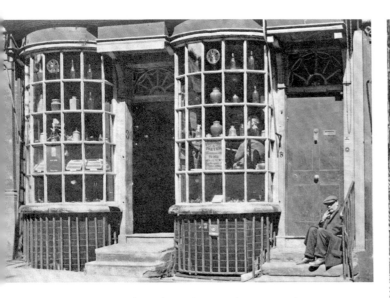

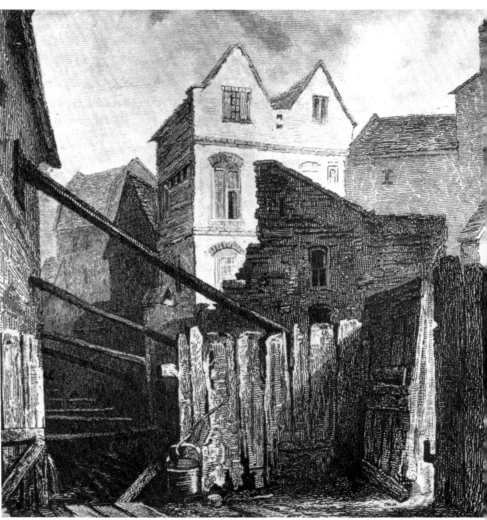

Above: 138. The eighteenth- or early nineteenth-century shopfront of Messrs Fribourg & Treyer, Haymarket, photographed by Donald M'Leish around 1930. (Stephen Porter)

Right: 139. The decayed buildings of the Field Lane rookery adjoining the Fleet Ditch, which was cleared in 1844. (Stephen Porter)

Opposite: 140. This watercolour by Joseph Nash shows the opening of the Great Exhibition by Queen Victoria on 1 May 1851. The exhibition celebrated the nations' technological achievements, and Nash's painting emphasises the scale and lightness of Joseph Paxton's specially designed and innovative building in Hyde Park. (Stephen Porter)

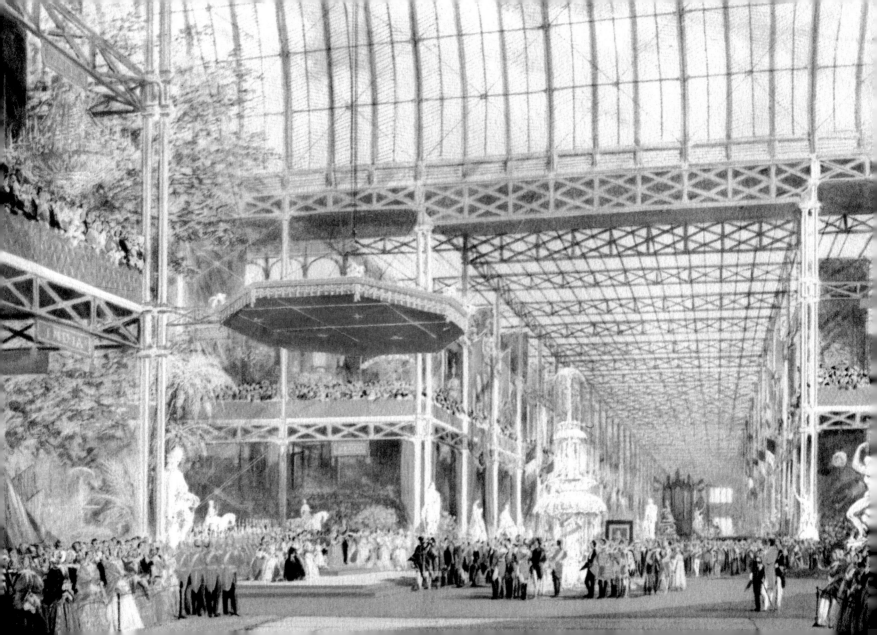

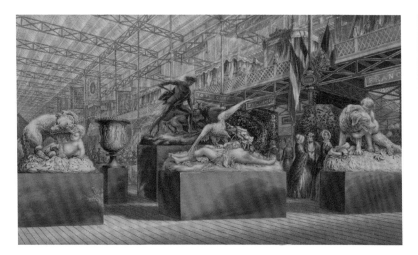

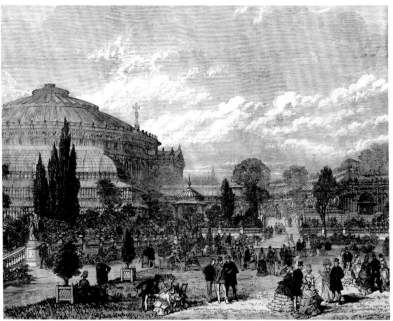

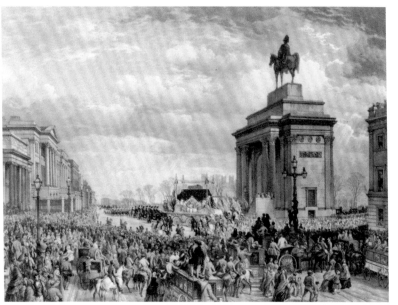

Above right: 141. The Royal Albert Hall, erected in 1867–71, and the Horticultural Society's gardens to the south. (The Governors of Sutton's Hospital)

Above left: 142. The stands in the Great Exhibition of 1851 were arranged by country, as shown in George Baxter's print. (Yale Center for British Art, Paul Mellon Collection)

Left: 143. The long and slow funeral procession of the Duke of Wellington in 1852 was depicted by Louis Haghe, who showed the funeral car passing the Wellington Arch at the end of Piccadilly, surmounted by the equestrian statue of the duke which was removed in 1910. (Stephen Porter)

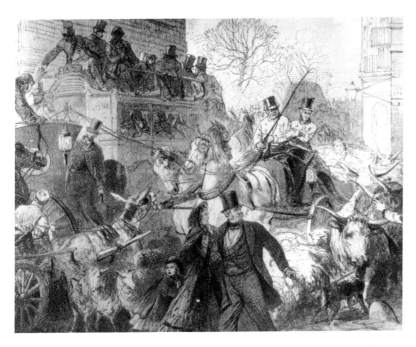

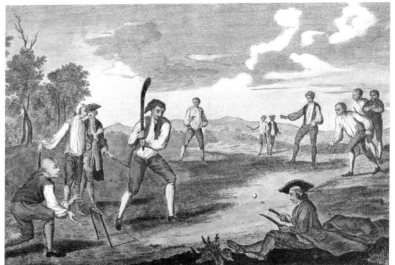

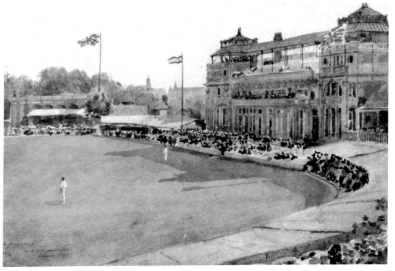

Above left: 144. Congestion and confusion in Park Lane in 1864, as vehicles, pedestrians and livestock being driven to market are all crowded together. (Stephen Porter)

Above right: 145. Cricket was a popular form of recreation and Francis Hayman depicts here an informal game played with a curved bat on an uneven surface in the Artillery Ground in 1785. (Stephen Porter)

Right: 146. Lord's cricket ground, named after its founder the professional cricketer Thomas Lord (1755–1832), was moved to St John's Wood in 1814 and became the 'home of cricket'. Herbert Marshall shows a match there around 1915 and the pavilion, which was erected in 1890. (Stephen Porter)

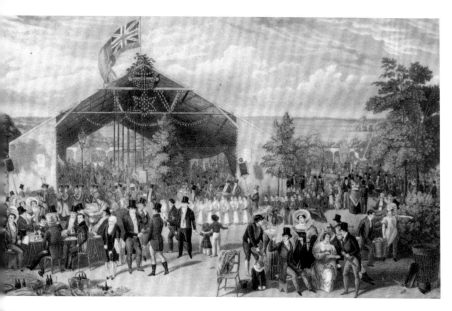

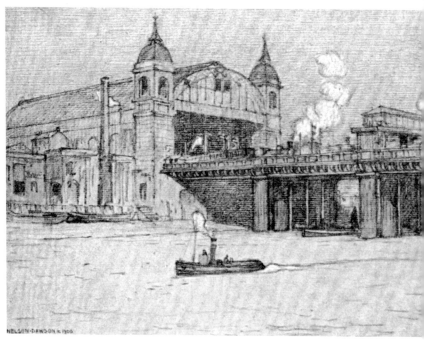

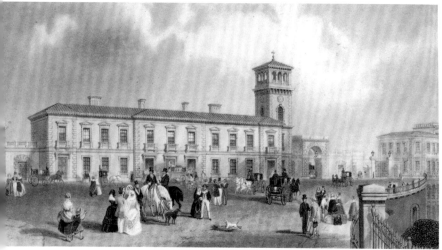

Above right: 147. Cannon Street station was built in 1865–66 for the South Eastern Railway, on the site of the Steelyard. Its distinctive features are the tall, square towers with domes and spires facing the river and the impressive iron arch spanning the station, 680 feet long and 106 feet high. The view from the river was painted by Nelson Dawson around 1900. (Stephen Porter)

Above left: 148. Londoners enjoyed going to the surrounding villages for their entertainment. Here the Licensed Victuallers hold a dinner in a large marquee at Hackney, in 1846, depicted by George Gunt. (Stephen Porter)

Left: 149. London Bridge station in Southwark was the first of London's stations, opened in 1836 as the terminus of the London and Greenwich Railway. (Stephen Porter)

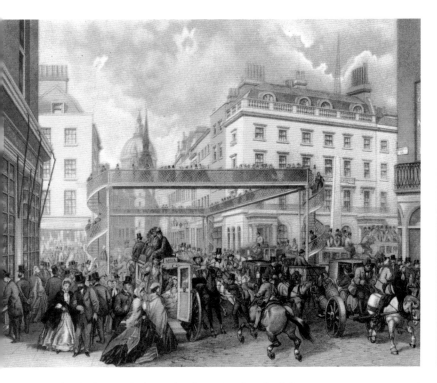

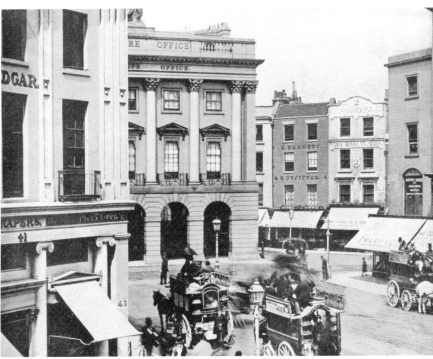

150. A solution to the hazards of crossing London's busy streets was suggested in this ingenious multiple footbridge to span the roadways at Ludgate Circus, designed around 1865 but not built. (Stephen Porter)

151. The junction of Piccadilly and Regent Street seen in a photograph of around 1870. (Stephen Porter)

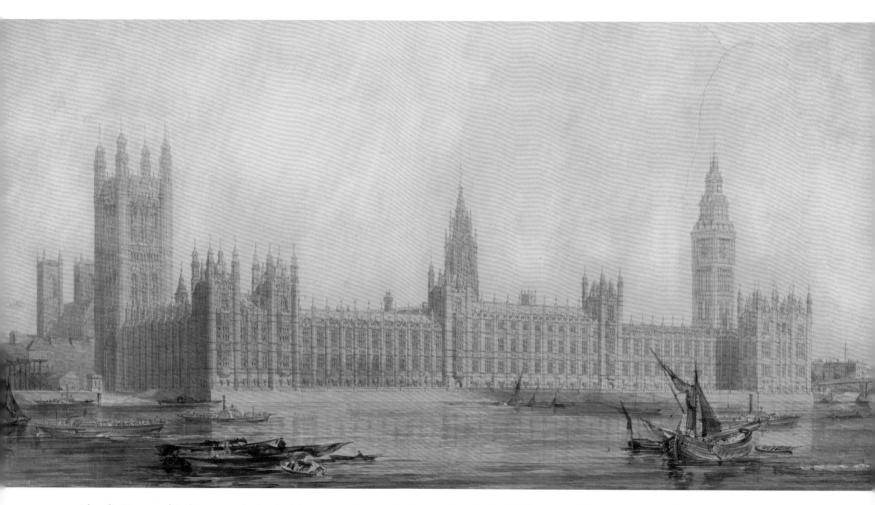

152. After the Houses of Parliament and other buildings were destroyed by fire in 1834, Sir Charles Barry won the competition to design a new Palace of Westminster; he was assisted by Augustus Welby Pugin. This is Barry's drawing of the proposed front to the Thames. (Yale Center for British Art, Paul Mellon Collection)

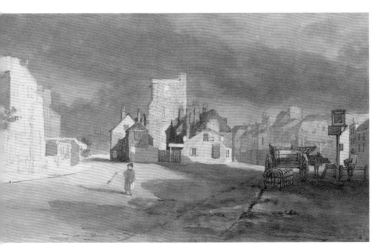

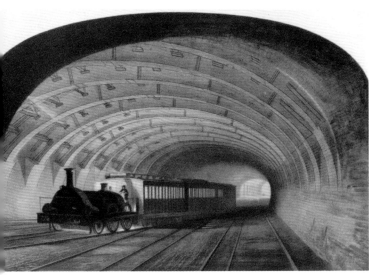

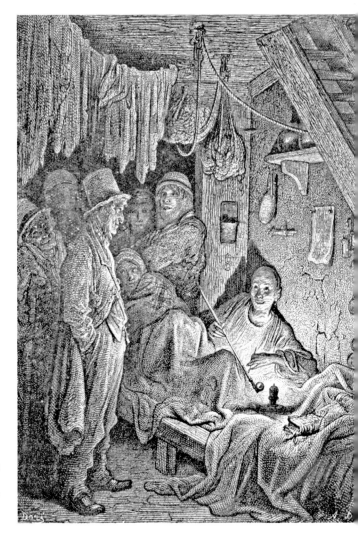

Top left: 153. Among the villages absorbed by the growing metropolis was Stratford by Bow, which was still essentially rural in character when it was painted by Thomas Shotter Boys in the mid-nineteenth century. (Yale Center for British Art, Paul Mellon Collection)

Bottom left: 154. A train on the Metropolitan Railway, the first underground line, near Paddington in 1863, the year in which the line opened. The trains were hauled by steam locomotives. Nearly 10 million passengers were carried in the first year. (Stephen Porter)

Right: 155. An opium den in one of the riverside districts of the East End, depicted by Gustave Doré in *London: A Pilgrimage* (1872). (Stephen Porter)

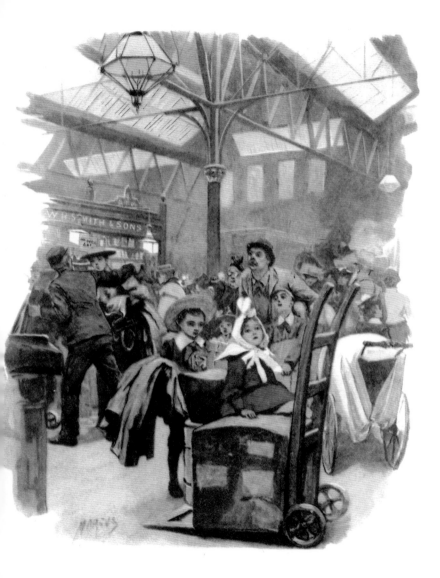

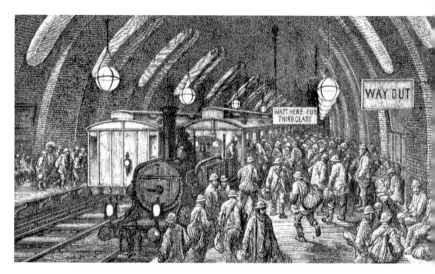

Above: 156. A crowded station on the Metropolitan Railway, 1872, with the sign marking the spot where third-class passengers should wait for their carriage. By Gustave Doré and Blanchard Jerrold. (Stephen Porter)

Left: 157. Cannon Street station around 1900. In the background is a bookstall of W. H. Smith & Sons; the company opened its first station bookstall at Euston in 1848 and they quickly became a feature of railways stations. (Stephen Porter)

8

THE TWENTIETH CENTURY

Following Queen Victoria's death in 1901, a plan was prepared by the architect Sir Aston Webb for improvements to commemorate her reign. A large memorial was erected outside Buckingham Palace, where the layout was changed so that it stood in the centre of a circular roadway. The Mall was set out as a wide thoroughfare on a new alignment and at its eastern end Admiralty Arch was built, opening into Trafalgar Square. Buckingham Palace had been gradually enlarged since the construction of the original house in Queen Anne's reign, with a new wing closing the courtyard that faced St James's Park added by Edward Blore in the 1840s; that was now refaced by Webb. The work was largely completed by 1911, when the memorial was unveiled by George V. Admiralty Arch was both part of Victoria's memorial and an addition to the new government offices around Whitehall, which were built in the early years of the century: the War Office and the Office of Woods and Forests in Whitehall and a large office block in Parliament Street.

Street improvements continued to be implemented, with the setting out by the LCC of the Aldwych and Kingsway, which cleared away several streets, widened the eastern section of the Strand and opened a new route northwards from Waterloo Bridge. But not until the completion of Bush House in 1935 were all of the new frontages occupied, in a range of styles.

Such improvements were justified by the need to ease traffic congestion. The nature of that traffic was altered by a major and remarkably swift change, as vehicles powered by the internal combustion engine replaced those drawn by horses. The removal of horse dung from the streets and stables ceased to be a problem and the provision of large quantities of hay was replaced by the need to make petrol supplies available. The first motor buses came into service in October 1899 and the number on the streets increased rapidly after the middle of the first decade of the century, from 241 in 1906 to almost 3,000 by the end of 1912. The number of horse-drawn buses declined as motor buses replaced them, and the last one was withdrawn in August 1914. But congestion was not reduced by the change, as cabs, vans, lorries and cars increasingly came into use. The decade also saw the adoption of electric power for transport, with electric trams brought into service, especially after they were promoted by the LCC from 1903. They were ultimately to lose out to the buses, but the use of electric power on the underground system began with the opening of the Central Line in 1900, and electrification was completed by 1906. The extension of the network continued, with lines constructed beyond the central area.

Transport was just one of many aspects of London life to which the LCC was making a vigorous contribution. Its profile was further raised by the building of its new headquarters, County Hall, on the South Bank, begun in 1908. The smooth running of the city was nevertheless punctuated by dramatic events from time to time. In January 1911 Londoners' attention was briefly focused on Sidney Street, in the East End, where the police cornered members of a group of Latvian anarchists in a house. The gang exchanged fire with armed police and a detachment of Scots Guards from the Tower until the siege ended when the house caught fire and eventually collapsed. Inside were the bodies of two of the anarchists, but the rest of the gang escaped. The incident attracted much attention, because the offenders were political refugees, they and the police used firearms, troops were deployed and the Home Secretary, Winston Churchill, had gone there during the siege.

Political agitation on London's streets in the years before the First World War was dominated by the campaigns of the Women's Social and Political Union, which became the Militant Suffrage Society, to obtain equal political rights for women. In 1906 the suffragettes switched their centre of operations from Manchester to London and began a series of protests, which included invading the House of Commons, a large gathering in Hyde Park in 1908 (which was supervised by no less than 600 police), probably the first leaflet raid when a suffragette drifted over the Houses of Parliament in an airship painted with the words 'Votes for Women', the disruption of political meetings and breaking of the windows of stores, offices and the houses of their opponents, including 10 Downing Street. The

Conciliation Bill in 1909 brought a respite, but when it was not passed suffragettes again went to the House of Commons and in the ensuing melee the prime minister, Herbert Asquith, was showered with glass and a colleague's hat was kicked to pieces. A forceful phase of protests began in 1913 that included further marches and window-breaking raids on the West End, hunger strikes, vandalising government property, setting fire to pillar boxes, arson and disfiguring works of art. Letter bombs were sent to the prime minister and Chancellor of the Exchequer and part of Lloyd George's house under construction at Walton Heath was blown up, even though he was known to support votes for women. In May 1914 an attempt to present a petition to the king at Buckingham Palace was thwarted by the police. The campaign was suspended after the outbreak of the First World War in August, as the movement switched its energies to support the war effort.

London generally prospered during the war, for the great increase in government spending created many new jobs. With virtually full employment, the economy flourished and rationing was not introduced until 1918. Military purchasers replaced civilian ones, with a decline in demand for consumer goods and a fall in shipping using the docks but a substantial rise in the output of clothing and leather goods, for example, to meet military requirements. Women replaced men who had joined the forces in places like the postal service, and many took jobs in the greatly expanded munitions industry, which generated thousands of new jobs. Although those were not continued after the end of the conflict in 1918, by 1921 there were 950,000 women in the workforce. The adverse effects of the war were the loss of life among the forces, with approximately 124,000 Londoners killed on active service, and among civilians in air raids. Zeppelins launched eleven raids on the city, all of them at night, with the worst raid, in June 1917, killing 160 people. As larger aeroplanes were developed, the Germans came to prefer them to the Zeppelins and those raids continued until May 1918. In total, 670 people were killed and 1,960 injured in the raids, which had scarcely any effect on the city's economy but made a strong impression on the citizens; this new form of warfare, striking a civilian population apparently at random, proved unsettling. And, just as the war was coming to a close, the worldwide influenza outbreak reached the city and killed 18,000 Londoners during the autumn and winter of 1918–19.

The post-war period was one of readjustment, as economy and society adapted after the changes imposed by war and integrated the large numbers of returning service personnel. Women were politically enfranchised at last. Economically, a boom in 1919 was followed by a slump in the following year, and problems of poor relief again came to the fore. To maintain their obligations to those in their borough requiring outdoor relief, the councillors at Poplar defied the government and refused to follow the procedure whereby the borough councils collected the rates for other authorities, including the LCC. Some of the councillors were imprisoned for a time, but in 1924 their case, which was labelled Poplarism, was upheld in the courts.

One of the major challenges was the continuing problem of slum clearance and the provision of good housing. Garden estates were built by the boroughs in the immediate aftermath of the war, known as Homes Fit for Heroes, and much larger schemes followed. The LCC had been granted powers to acquire land for building outside the county's boundaries in 1900. It now took full advantage of this and erected housing estates beyond the city, the largest being at Becontree and Dagenham, in Essex. In the 1930s it adapted its policy and also built houses and blocks of flats within the county. The boroughs, too, expanded their housebuilding programmes and continued to clear slums. Despite those efforts, overcrowded housing, multiple occupation and deficient sanitation remained problems in some districts into the second half of the century. The local authorities provided roughly 20 per cent of the housing erected in the twenty years after the First World War and private builders contributed the remainder of the 771,759 houses and flats built in and around the city. The term Greater London came into use to describe the expanded area of the metropolis. Extension of the tube lines encouraged that growth; the area of north-west London served by the Metropolitan Line from Baker Street was later dubbed Metro-Land. Streets of semi-detached houses predominated in the newly built areas, punctuated by parades of shops and a cinema. The number of cinemas in the county of London rose from ninety-four in 1911 to 258 in 1930 and continued to increase, compared with a fairly steady number of fewer than 100 theatres and music halls.

As the outer areas grew, so the population of inner London declined, as older houses were cleared and replaced by other buildings. The population of the City fell by two-thirds between 1919 and 1939. In Cripplegate housing was replaced by warehousing, and the area around Mark Lane and Mincing Lane became 'honeycombed with vaults', according to the writer

Harold Clunn. He commented that the merchants and clerks formed a community of their own in the 'maze of corridors' running between the blocks of offices, with 'various restaurants, tea-shops, tobacconists, and hairdressers' establishments, the existence of which must be quite unknown to the outside world'. Commercial pressures in the City and its falling population had seen the demolition between 1860 and 1897 of twelve of the Wren churches erected after the Great Fire, and three more were knocked down before 1940. They included All Hallows Lombard Street, where Clunn contributed to the debate on whether it should be retained with the comment that the church was 'occupying ground obviously better suited in our own day to business requirements' and that its retention was to 'sacrifice good money which might well suffice to build a dozen churches in the suburbs'. Warming to his theme, he asked, 'If every building with a claim to antiquity is to be suffered to exist for perpetuity, where is the space to be found in course of time to allow for any future progress in the world?' This was an issue which was to continue throughout the century, as the conservation movement gathered momentum.

A part of the reason for the development of the outer areas from the mid-1930s was the dispersal of industries, particularly strategic ones, in anticipation of a war with Germany and the likelihood of devastating aerial bombardments. National Socialism made an impression in London in those years through the activities of Sir Oswald Mosley's British Union of Fascists, which engaged in anti-Semitic harassment. The most serious incident was its attempt to march through the East End on 4 October 1936, in a provocative demonstration directed at the Jewish communities there. Some 3,000 of Mosley's blackshirts formed up, with 7,000 police in attendance. A large crowd gathered to prevent them advancing further into the East End and hastily constructed a barricade in Cable Street. The police used baton charges to try to clear a passage for the marchers, but were resisted and pelted with objects thrown from the crowd and the upper windows of buildings. The violence, the construction of further barricades, the determination of those opposing the march and their numbers, estimated at 100,000, convinced the Metropolitan Police Commissioner, Sir Phillip Game, that persisting with the police's strategy could only result in prolonged rioting and bloodshed, and so he ordered the blackshirts to turn around and march away, which they did. The clashes on that day became known as the Battle of Cable Street. The Public Order Act passed in the following December did much to prevent such provocative marches in future.

The Second World War began in September 1939 and continued for almost six years. Londoners had been prepared for war and its possible consequences, with a range of air-raid precautions put in place in anticipation of an aerial bombardment. The raids did not begin for a year, but the first one, on 7 September 1940, was followed by fifty-seven consecutive nights of bombing, and then a series of intensive raids until May 1941. After that period, known as 'the Blitz', there were intermittent alarms until attacks by V-1 flying bombs began in June 1944, followed by V-2 rocket attacks in September, which continued until March 1945. In all, the city endured 354 raids by aircraft and 2,937 hits by pilotless bombs, with 29,890 people killed, 8,938 of them by the pilotless bombs, and 50,000 injured. The combined figure for those killed and injured was 54 per cent of the national total in air raids. In Greater London, 116,000 houses were destroyed and 288,000 were seriously damaged, with the East End suffering particularly badly. Significant historic buildings were lost, including eighteen City churches, seventeen livery company halls and parts of the Inns of Court, and among those badly damaged were the Houses of Parliament and the Charterhouse. The impact of the war was immense, not only because of the raids and their effects, including homelessness and overcrowding, but also the evacuation of children, disruption of schooling, the redeployment of labour and the demands of the armed services, interruptions to supplies and hence shortages of food and materials, and a significant fall in population. Not all industries recovered, and the replacement of factories, workshops and housing took time, although the housing shortage was ameliorated temporarily by the erection of prefabricated houses, affectionately known as prefabs.

Despite the problems of adjustment and shortages of materials and food, which continued for some years, the immediate post-war period was one of expanding trade and economic recovery. The optimism and aspirations of the post-war period were expressed in the Festival of Britain, held on the South Bank in 1951 to mark the centenary of the Great Exhibition. The Royal Festival Hall was completed for the Festival and its construction marked the beginning of the long process of regenerating the South Bank.

One of the post-war measures was the Clean Air Act of 1956. Air pollution had a harmful impact during the centuries when coal was the predominant fuel, not least by causing intermittent dense and deadly fogs, and exacerbating respiratory diseases. Unhealthy and unpleasant, the pollution nevertheless had an aesthetic benefit, as an employee at County Hall later recalled, remembering the 'exceptional beauty of the sunsets, on occasion, behind Big Ben, going down in a haze of mauve, purple, indigo'. Although it was some years before the Act took full effect, its implementation, with the steady replacement of coal as a fuel by electricity, oil and gas, slowly removed the worst pollution. The grimy layers of sooty accretions on buildings could then be removed, so that they could at last be seen as their builders had seen them.

These improvements were made against a background of the considerable challenges which the metropolis faced during the second half of the twentieth century. Its role as imperial capital and centre of world trade was swiftly lost as the United Kingdom's influence and the dominance of its currency waned and as, within barely twenty years, the countries of the empire rapidly gained independence. This coincided with a period during which a new spirit of economic and political cooperation on the Continent saw the creation and subsequent expansion of the Common Market. Britain's failure to join the original organisation gave other European cities the chance to get ahead as business centres, while London lost trade to such ports as Rotterdam and Dunkirk and, domestically, to Tilbury, Felixstowe and Dover. The closure of the docks along the Thames in the 1960s and 1970s signified the loss of the capital's seaborne trade, a key element in its economy for so much of its existence, and those years also saw a steep decline in its manufacturing industry, with the number of jobs in the sector falling by 80 per cent between 1961 and 1993.

Intervention by central government during the second half of the century included changes to London's local government. In 1964 the LCC was replaced by the Greater London Council, created as a strategic planning authority, also taking over the LCC's functions, but covering a much larger area intended to include the whole of the metropolis. At the same time, the boroughs created in 1899 were replaced by thirty-two new ones. But the GLC was abolished in 1986 and not replaced by a London-wide body. The Inner London Education Authority was retained in 1964, within its existing boundaries, which were those of the LCC, but was abolished with the GLC.

Government also intervened in the economic planning process. As in the first Elizabethan age, London's growth and predominance were perceived to be inimical to the country's economy and society, and steps were taken to reduce them. Action included vigorous attempts to decentralise jobs, in both the Civil Service and the private sector. The Location of Office Bureau was created in 1963 to facilitate the movement of office jobs out of the capital, and it operated for almost twenty years. But Greater London's population was falling steadily and declined from more than 8 million to 6.8 million between the end of the Second World War and the mid-1980s, so that the planners were compelled to reconsider their approach.

Recognition of the deleterious effects of the changes in the dock areas along the river prompted the government to establish the London Dockland Development Corporation, in 1981, with oversight of all planning matters and the powers to acquire and dispose of land. Over the following years much of the area within its jurisdiction was redeveloped, along the north side of the Thames as far downstream as the royal docks and including the Surrey Docks on the south side. The most spectacular new development was at Canary Wharf on the northern part of the Isle of Dogs, which included a fifty-storey tower, completed in 1991; two further tall towers were built there ten years later. Canary Wharf was seen as a potential rival to the City, as it developed into a major financial centre. The City's response was to relax its planning controls on high buildings and over the following years a number of tall structures were erected, giving central London a new and varied skyline.

In the mid-1980s the prospects did not look good, but London proved to be adaptable and recovered, with the development of the City's financial services in particular, to meet the needs of the global economy, as well as other fields, such as communications, music, fashion, design, publishing and tourism. Districts which seemed to have been in irreversible decline were regenerated. London's economic supremacy within the United Kingdom was strengthened and it retained its political and cultural dominance. Its population decline was reversed before the end of the century, as it continued to attract and integrate newcomers, from the United Kingdom and overseas. When the Romans chose the site of Londinium they chose wisely and well, and their settlement on the north bank of the Thames grew to be one of the world's greatest and most resilient cities.

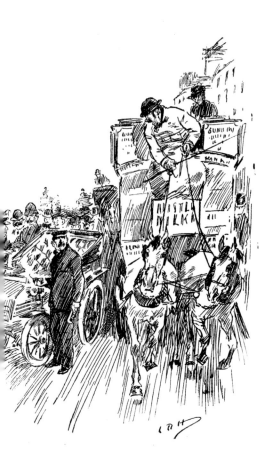

158. Motor vehicles rapidly replaced horse-drawn ones during the early years of the twentieth century. As the *Punch* illustrator shows, the process was not without the occasional dispute. (Stephen Porter)

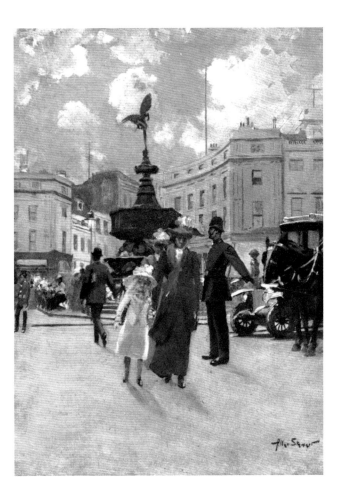

159. A London policeman shows pedestrians across the street at Piccadilly Circus, 'the centre of amusement and pleasure in London', ahead of a motor car and a horse-drawn vehicle, in a painting by Allan Stewart around 1915. (Stephen Porter)

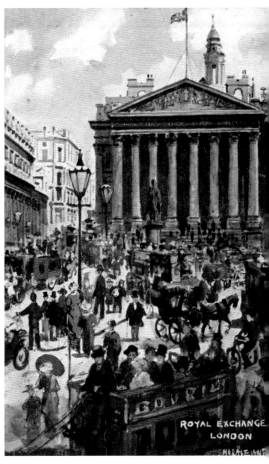

160. The throng of people and traffic in front of the Royal Exchange, around 1913. (Stephen Porter)

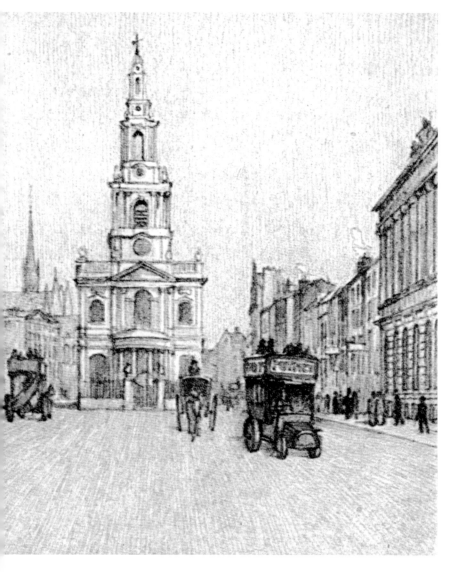

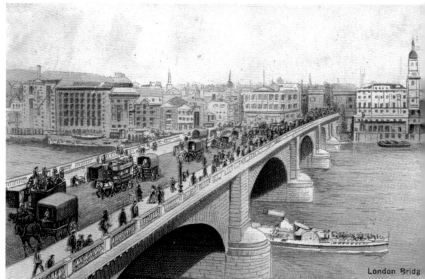

Above: 161. London Bridge around 1900, before the advent of motor vehicles. (Stephen Porter)

Left: 162. The church of St Mary le Strand, painted in the early twentieth century by Nelson Dawson. (Stephen Porter)

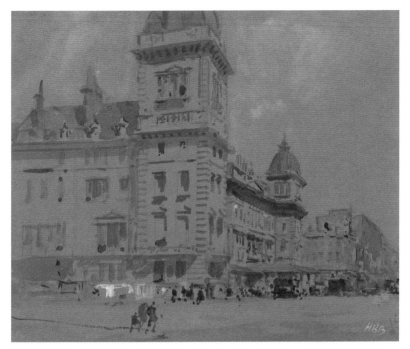

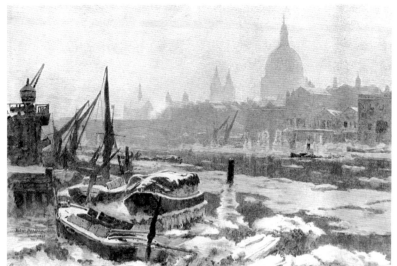

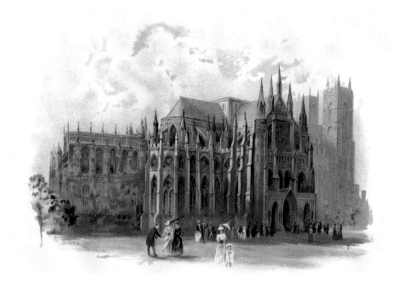

Above left: 163. Paddington Station was designed by Isambard Kingdom Brunel as the London terminus of the Great Western Railway; the illustration is by Hercules Brabazon Brabazon (1821–1906). (Yale Center for British Art, Bequest of Joseph F. McCrindle)

Above right: 164. The Thames in London has not frozen over since the early nineteenth century, but this painting of 1905 by Herbert Menzies Marshall, looking across to St Paul's, conveys the effect of a severe winter. (Stephen Porter)

Right: 165. Westminster Abbey from the north-east around 1904, by Charles Wilkinson. (Stephen Porter)

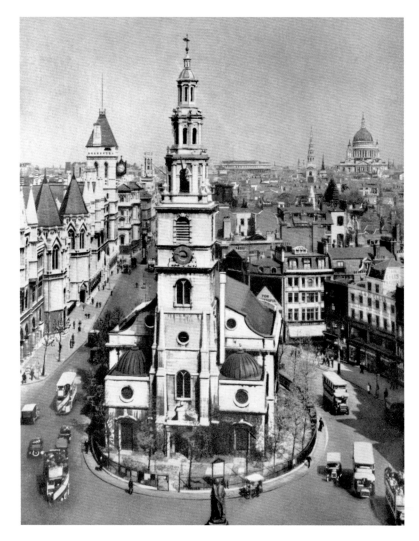

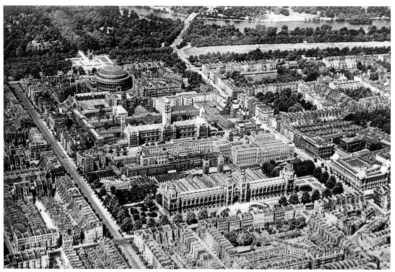

Above: 166. The museums area of South Kensington, around 1930, with Hyde Park and the Albert Hall at the top of the photograph, and the Science Museum prominent towards the bottom. (Stephen Porter)

Left: 167. St Clement Danes church in the Strand escaped the Great Fire but was demolished in 1680. A new church was built to Sir Christopher Wren's designs and completed in 1682. Wren cased the tower in Portland stone and in 1719 James Gibbs added the spire. Photograph looking east to the Royal Courts of Justice, probably taken in the 1920s. (Stephen Porter)

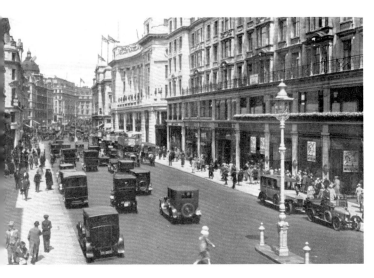

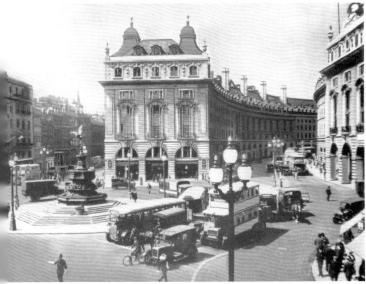

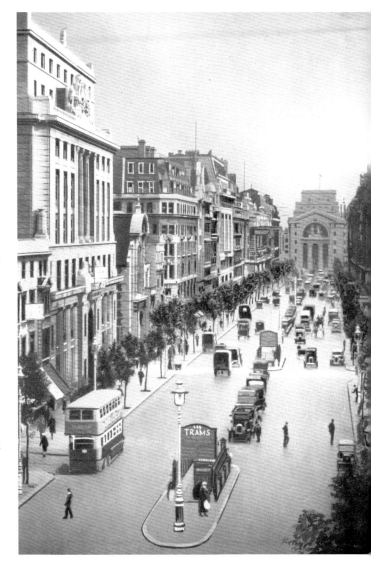

Top left: 168. A photograph of the 1920s shows New Regent Street busy with both traffic and pedestrians. (Stephen Porter)

Bottom left: 169. Piccadilly Circus, photographed in the 1920s. Traffic then passed around the monument to the 7th Earl of Shaftesbury, the philanthropist, of 1886–93, which is topped by a statue of Eros in aluminium, by Alfred Gilbert. (Stephen Porter)

Right: 170. Kingsway looking south in a photograph of the 1920s. (Stephen Porter)

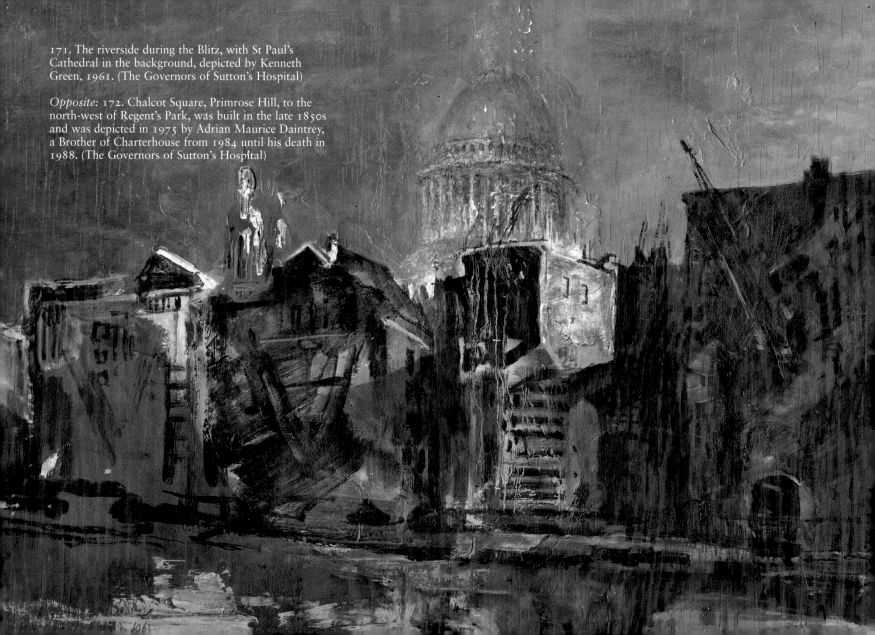

171. The riverside during the Blitz, with St Paul's Cathedral in the background, depicted by Kenneth Green, 1961. (The Governors of Sutton's Hospital)

Opposite: 172. Chalcot Square, Primrose Hill, to the north-west of Regent's Park, was built in the late 1850s and was depicted in 1975 by Adrian Maurice Daintrey, a Brother of Charterhouse from 1984 until his death in 1988. (The Governors of Sutton's Hospital)

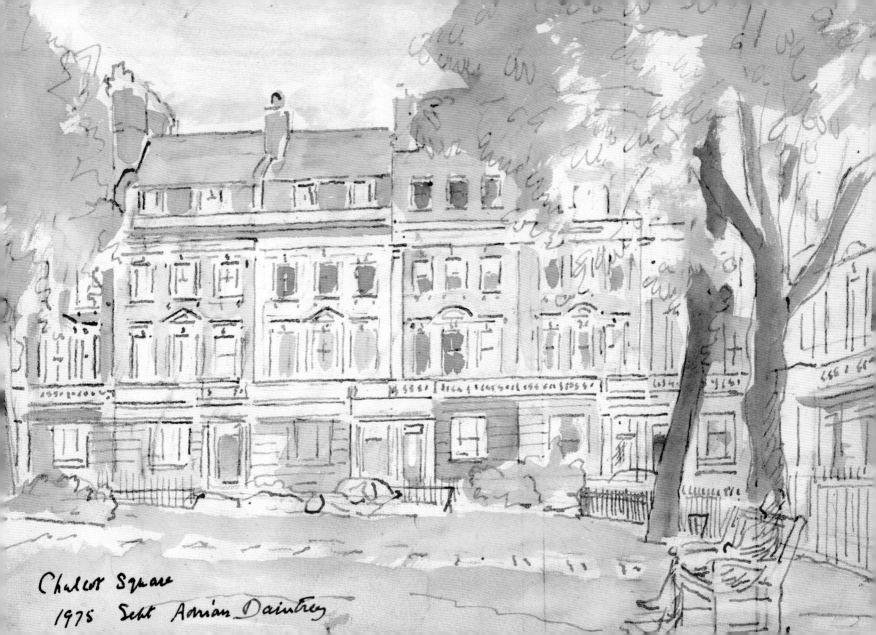

Chalcot Square
1975 Seht Adrian Daintrey

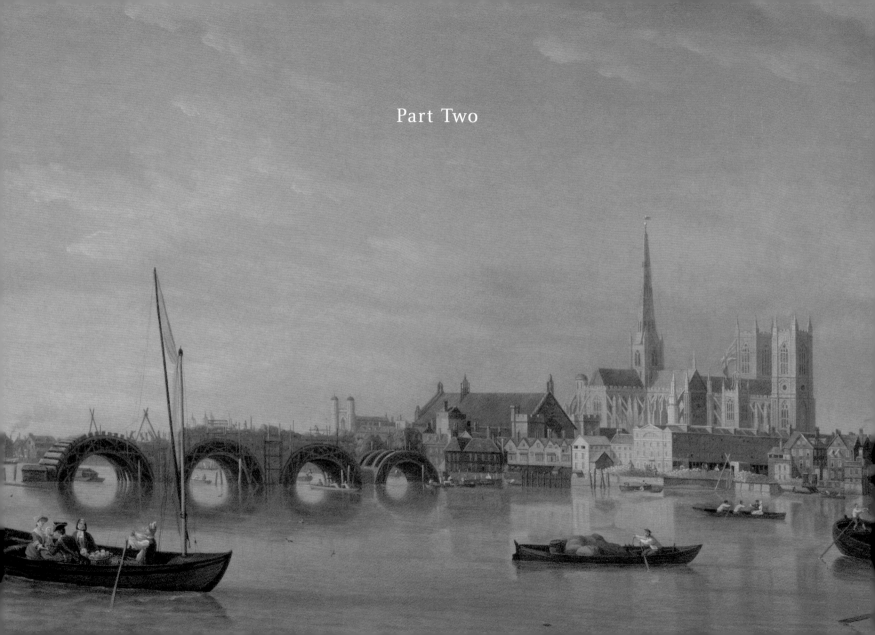

Part Two

9

THE CITY

The City is a term applied to the area administered by the corporation and the smaller financial district within it, also denoted as 'the square mile'. The administrative area is larger than that enclosed by the Roman walls, particularly on the west side, where it includes Smithfield and extends along Holborn to Gray's Inn Road and incorporates Fleet Street, up to the site of Temple Bar. On the east side, the City includes Spitalfields and Portsoken Ward, outside the walls, but excludes the Tower, within them.

Its administration is based at Guildhall, on the east side of Aldermanbury, the name of which was recorded around 1124. The Old English word 'ealdormann' became alderman, the chief officer of each of the City's twenty-four wards, which became twenty-five in 1394 and twenty-six in 1550, when Southwark was incorporated into the City. A guildhall was referred to in 1128 and a hall for public meetings was in existence before the end of the twelfth century. The guildhall was probably rebuilt between 1270 and 1290 and was replaced by a new building between 1411 and around 1430. The rebuilding of the chapel and college was authorised in 1429–30; on its south side was a library, established by Richard Whittington's executors and built in 1423–25.

The whole Guildhall complex was gutted by the Great Fire. The stone structure resisted the flames and the building was restored, with a new roof and gallery, and the council chamber, lord mayor's court, sheriff's court and offices were rebuilt. The opportunity was taken to construct a direct route to the Thames along the new streets of King Street and Queen Street. The rebuilding after the fire included raising the walls, creating a clerestory and installing a ceiling, rather than reproducing the original open-timber roof. The ceiling was replaced with a hammerbeam roof in 1864–68. That was destroyed in an air raid in the Second World War and a new open-timber roof was built in 1953–54.

To the south of the Guildhall is Cheapside, a market and shopping street that effectively was the City's high street. At the west end of Cheapside is the ecclesiastical enclave of St Paul's, from which Ludgate Hill runs down to the valley of the River Fleet. Beyond the valley, Fleet Street runs westwards to the City's boundary; the street became a centre of printing and publishing and the national focus for the newspaper industry, and also contained banking and insurance businesses, a speciality that continued beyond Temple Bar into the Strand. From the Thames northwards to beyond Holborn and straddling the City's western boundary is London's legal quarter, containing the Inns of Court, the Royal Courts of Justice and, formerly, the Inns of Chancery.

On the riverside, east of the Temple, the royal palace of Bridewell was built for Henry VIII in 1515–23. A wooden gallery was constructed to connect it with the Dominican priory of Blackfriars when the court lodged here for the visit of Emperor Charles V in 1522. The court was there again in 1528 for the hearings for Henry's divorce from his queen, Katherine of Aragon. The priory was dissolved in 1538 and the palace, disliked by Henry VIII and Edward VI because of its low-lying position, was granted to the City in 1553 and used as a prison and workhouse, and a school for orphans and young criminals. It was closed in 1855 and demolished in 1863.

Alongside Dowgate, between Blackfriars and London Bridge, was the Steelyard, the London base of the merchants of the Hanseatic League and the only privileged enclave for foreign traders in England, apart from the much smaller Hanseatic depot at King's Lynn. The merchants of Hamburg, Lübeck and Cologne had their own trading stations until they merged in 1282 to form the Steelyard, or Stahlhof. By the late fifteenth century this sample yard covered three acres and was occupied by up to twenty Hanse merchants, leading separate lives from the Londoners and following their own rules. Their trading privileges included lower duties on cloth exports; in return London's connection with the Hanse network brought benefits, especially the goods imported from the Baltic, including grain, flax, linen cloth and steel, and naval supplies, such as hemp, timber and tar. But by the late sixteenth century the Hanse's economic power was on the wane, undermined by direct Dutch and English trade with

the Baltic. In 1598 Elizabeth I both withdrew the merchants' privileges and expelled them from the Steelyard. James I allowed them to return, but did not restore their privileges. The German merchants finally left in 1853 and the site was taken for Cannon Street station, built in 1865–66.

Thames Street ran parallel to the river from Blackfriars as far as the Tower, connecting the premises standing on the wharves and stairs, and the landing places at Queenhithe and Billingsgate. John Stow wrote, in 1598, that the street contained 'many fair houses large for stowage, built for merchants'. The market at Billingsgate developed as London's principal fish market and did much to give the narrow street a smelly and congested character, which produced differing reactions. In 1801 Francis Witts found it to be 'a wonderful scene of noise & Commerce', while to the American novelist Nathaniel Hawthorne, in 1857, it was 'a dirty, evil-smelling, crowded precinct, thronged with people carrying fish on their heads, and lined with fish-shops and fish-stalls, and pervaded with a fishy odor … though we heard none of the foul language of which it is supposed to be the fountain-head'. That colourful language was notorious by the sixteenth century and became a term used more widely to describe a lively vocabulary. George Jeffreys, Lord Chancellor under James II, even when he was in court 'talked fluently, and with spirit; and in such Billingsgate language, as should not come out of the mouth of any man'.

In contrast to the riverine character of Thames Street, the more staid business district developed in and around Lombard Street, Threadneedle Street and Cornhill. Lombard Street took its name, in the early fourteenth century, from the merchants from Lombardy and elsewhere who had settled there. The word Lombard came to be applied to places where money transactions took place, which developed into banks, or pawnshops.

Disputes between England and Flanders in the mid-thirteenth century had weakened the Flemish merchants' earlier dominance in English trade, especially the export of wool to the Flemish clothmakers. The Italian merchants had a toehold in the English economy as the collectors of papal taxes and began to exploit the openings left by the Flemish, both in wool exports and the import of luxury items such as spices and expensive textiles. Members of the royal court were profitable customers, and in the mid-fourteenth century the king's Great Wardrobe was in Lombard Street. The king's exchange, where foreign currency and gold were converted into English coin, was also there from the 1370s until the fifteenth century. As the English cloth industry developed, the Italian merchants handled its exports and supplied the clothmakers with alum, dyes and soap. By the fifteenth century a quarter of English trade was in the hands of a group of about seventy Italian merchants, most of them operating from London, who also acted as bankers and transacted life assurance business.

The merchants met in Lombard Street twice daily. From 1527 a chain was drawn across it during the hours when they were meeting, to prevent vehicles from passing along the street. In 1568 the Royal Exchange was built, where the merchants could congregate, rather than in the open street. They set the currency rates and settled bills of exchange. The Exchange's presence thereafter, as the hub of trade of a worldwide empire, inevitably affected the nature of the businesses carried on in the area.

Although it was destroyed in the Great Fire, during the seventeenth century the district's importance as London's financial centre was strengthened by the gradual influx of goldsmiths, mostly from Cheapside. By 1677 there were twenty-eight goldsmiths in Lombard Street who were issuing notes, and only three in Cheapside. It also developed as the centre of banking and insurance, and as a focus of business information, with news exchanged at the local coffee houses. Partly because of the exchange of news in and around Cornhill, the area became a centre for the publishing, printing and bookselling trades, which had their origins here in the late fifteenth century. The Cornhill publishers issued a range of titles, including travel books, maps and atlases, and those connected with business, such as books on shorthand and commercial directories.

The Bank of England was established in 1694 and from 1734 occupied a site in Threadneedle Street, and the Stock Exchange evolved from meetings of stockbrokers at coffee houses in and around Exchange Alley, until eventually it was established in 1773 in its own building, also in Threadneedle Street. The headquarters of the South Sea Company was built in the street in 1724–25 and after the company was wound up, South Sea House was occupied from 1857 until 1900 by the Baltic Exchange. It was then demolished and replaced by the British Linen Company Bank building of 1902–3.

Despite the dominance of the financial and mercantile businesses, other trades had a presence in the district. The most numerous tradesmen in Lombard Street from the eighteenth century were the goldsmiths and merchants, followed by factors and scriveners, with luxury trades represented by silversmiths, jewellers and engravers. The street also attracted booksellers, including Thomas Guy, the founder of the hospital which bears his name. Linen drapers, in particular, had shops in Cornhill and so, increasingly, did those engaged in the luxury trades. Indeed, it contained a range of retail and wholesale businesses well into the nineteenth century.

The quarter continued to develop as the leading district for banking and insurance, with a worldwide reach. In 1873 Lombard Street had nine clearing banks, both joint-stock and private, and there were thirteen others within the City's financial district around the Bank of England. The Bankers' Clearing House was established in Post Office Court, off Lombard Street, to settle daily payments. By 1900, between 70,000 and 100,000 cheques were handled there daily, and in the 1950s it was handling more than a million items a day. Threadneedle Street was also a banking street, although the most numerous businesses there were those of stockbrokers and jobbers.

The resident population gradually moved away from the financial district, and from the mid-nineteenth century tall, purpose-built commercial premises steadily replaced the brick buildings of the late seventeenth and eighteenth centuries. Many of them were built directly on to the pavement, giving Lombard Street, a narrow and winding thoroughfare, a particularly enclosed atmosphere.

As well as the districts dominated by the financial, legal or publishing businesses, the City contained quarters where the tradesmen were engaged in quite different occupations. They included the textile workers in Cripplegate and the brass founders in Lothbury, whose specialities included, from the mid-seventeenth century, the manufacture of fire engines. Nor did the increasing pace of commercial development and depopulation in the nineteenth century change the character of all areas within the City. In the late 1860s the lawyer and poet Arthur Munby found that in Cripplegate on a Sunday 'these old 17th and 18th century streets and alleys, these deserted old churches, bring back something of the interest and delight with which one wanders through a medieval town abroad'. He was equally struck by the character of the district near Queenhithe, with its 'many quiet unmolested old houses, many silent unfrequented passages and little yards, with an old water tub at the far end, an old hooded doorway and mullioned kitchen window, an old whitecapped woman sitting peacefully before the fire within: places that are like rural England, that are hundreds of miles away from common London life'. But commercial pressures, the replacement of ageing buildings and destruction during air raids in the Second World War gradually transformed even those pockets of the earlier City.

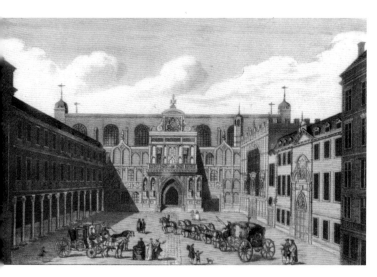

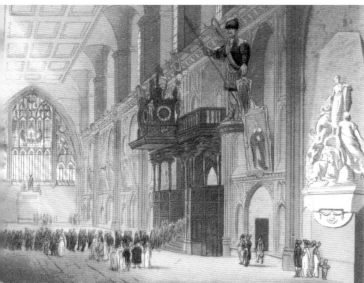

Top left: 173. The Guildhall, the centre of the City's administration, completed around 1430, and restored after the Great Fire. (Stephen Porter)

Bottom left: 174. The interior of the Guildhall, around 1808, by Thomas Rowlandson and Augustus Pugin. The large wooden figure is one of a pair carved in 1708 representing Gog and Magog, associated in legend with the Guildhall site; the monument is to William Pitt the Elder, prime minister, who died in 1778. (Stephen Porter)

Right: 175. St Olave's, Hart Street, was Samuel Pepys's church and the mural monument to his wife Elizabeth, which he commissioned from the sculptor John Bushnell after her death in 1669, was placed above the chancel and is a prominent feature in E. W. Haslehust's painting of around 1924. (Stephen Porter)

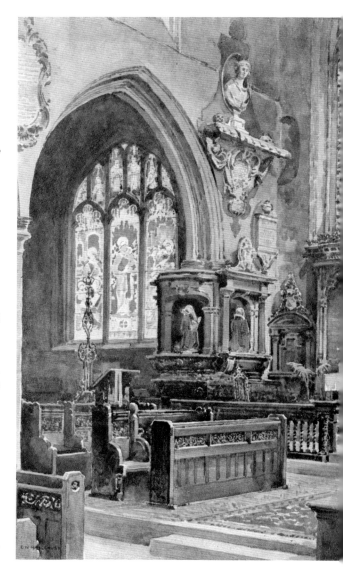

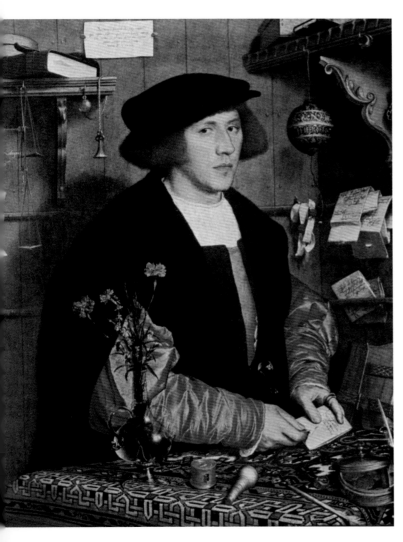

Left: 176. George Gisse, merchant of the Steelyard, the Hanseatic League's site alongside the Thames in London. The portrait, by Hans Holbein, is dated 1532. Gisse holds a letter addressed 'to the excellent Gisze, in London, England', and there are other letters behind him, as well as a set of scales. (Stephen Porter)

Right: 177. The East India Company was formed in 1600 and took a lease of Lord Craven's house in Leadenhall Street in 1648. Daniel Defoe described it in 1722 as 'an old, but spacious building; very convenient, though not beautiful'. (Stephen Porter)

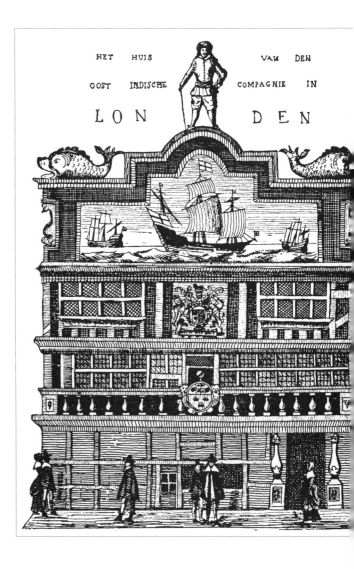

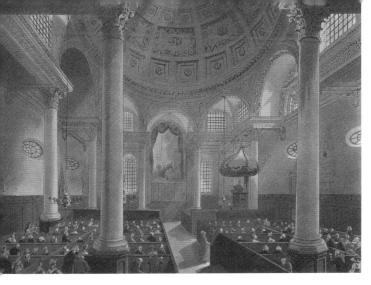

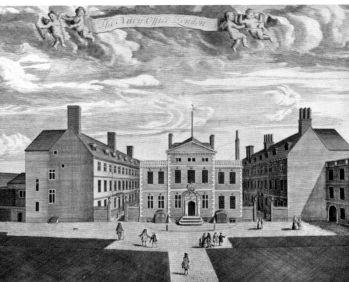

Top left: 178. Saint Stephen's, Walbrook, in 1809. One of the finest of Wren's City churches, it was begun in 1672 and completed in 1680. The box pews shown here by Thomas Rowlandson and Augustus Pugin were removed in 1888. (Yale Center for British Art, Gift of Chauncey Brewster Tinker)

Bottom left: 179. The Navy Office in Crutched Friars by Thomas Taylor, 1717. The building was described as 'extremely neat, regular, and plain. It stands in the Center of a handsome little pav'd Square, and looks like an Eminent Mathematician with all his Apparatus about him; every Side of the Square being furnish'd with Buildings appertaining thereto.' (Stephen Porter)

Right: 180. The City was peppered with the halls of the various livery companies; the Painter Stainers' Hall in Little Trinity Lane was destroyed by the Great Fire and its replacement, with its elaborate doorway, was built by 1670. It was depicted by Charles Tomkins in 1799. (Yale Center for British Art, Paul Mellon Collection)

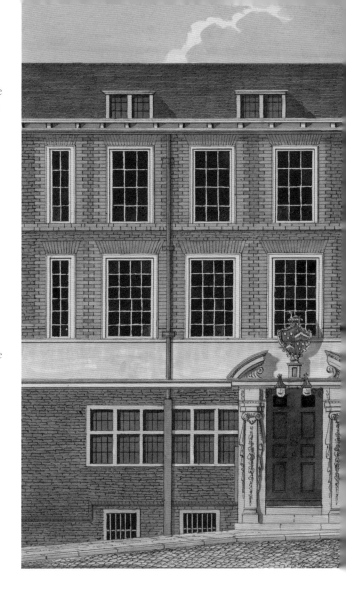

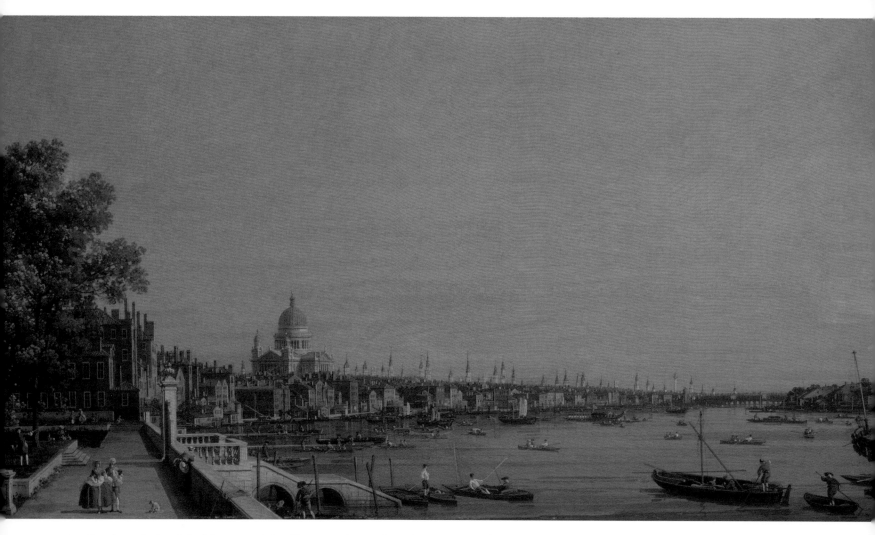

181. Canaletto depicted the Thames and the City around 1750 from the viewpoint of the terrace of Somerset House, with St Paul's and the array of towers, steeples and spires of the City's churches visible on the skyline, and the river busy with boats. (Yale Center for British Art, Paul Mellon Collection)

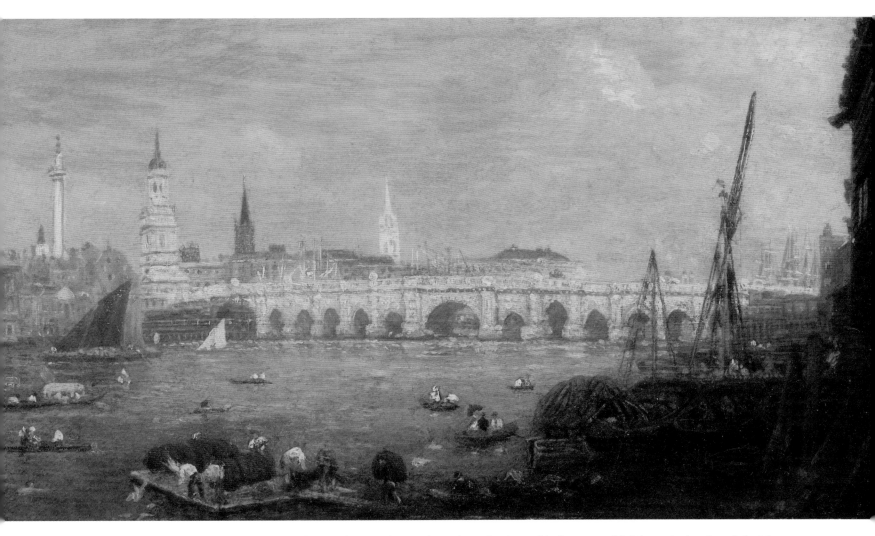

182. A view across the Thames at London Bridge around 1825 shows a cluster of vessels on the river, with the tower of St Magnus's church and the Monument prominent in the cityscape; painted by Frederick Nash. (Yale Center for British Art, Paul Mellon Collection)

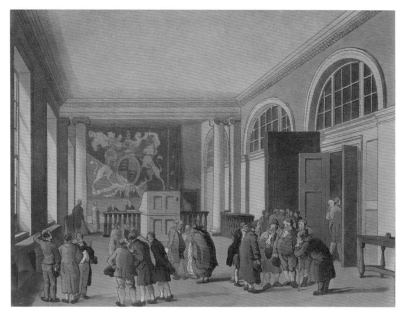

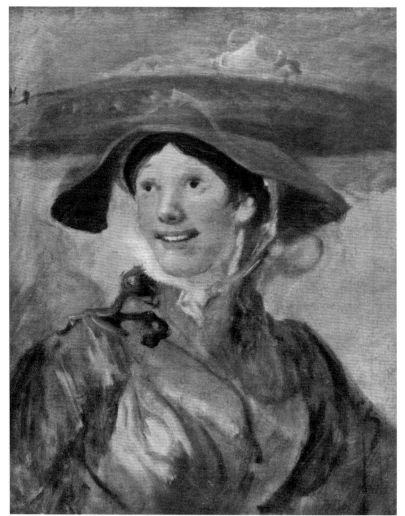

Above: 183. The Excise Office in Old Broad Street, in 1810. This had been built in 1769–75 to the designs of William Robinson, with four ranges around two courtyards housing the commissioners and their clerks, who were responsible for receiving the excise imposed on a range of goods, from beer and ale to wheeled carriages. (Yale Center for British Art, Gift of Chauncey Brewster Tinker)

Right: 184. *The Shrimp Girl*, by William Hogarth. Fish landed at Billingsgate were sold around the streets, as illustrated by Hogarth's painting of the 1740s. (Stephen Porter)

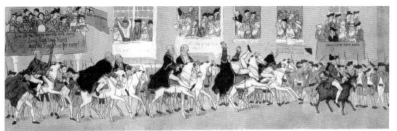

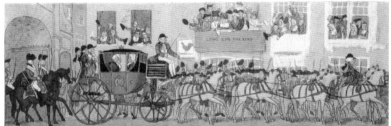

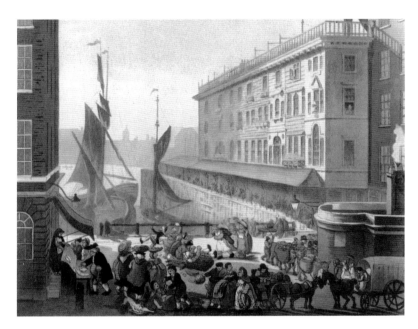

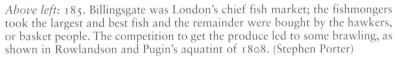

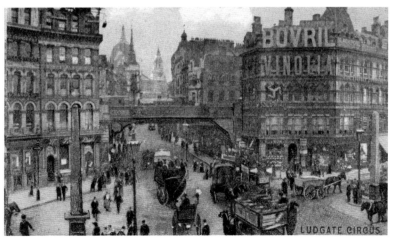

Above left: 185. Billingsgate was London's chief fish market; the fishmongers took the largest and best fish and the remainder were bought by the hawkers, or basket people. The competition to get the produce led to some brawling, as shown in Rowlandson and Pugin's aquatint of 1808. (Stephen Porter)

Above right: 186. The Grand Procession to St Paul's on St George's Day in 1789, during the crisis preceding the French Revolution, prompted an outpouring of loyalty to the monarch, with banners proclaiming 'Long live the King' and 'May the King live for ever' hung out of the windows; by Thomas Rowlandson. (Stephen Porter)

Right: 187. Ludgate Circus in the early twentieth century, looking east. (Stephen Porter)

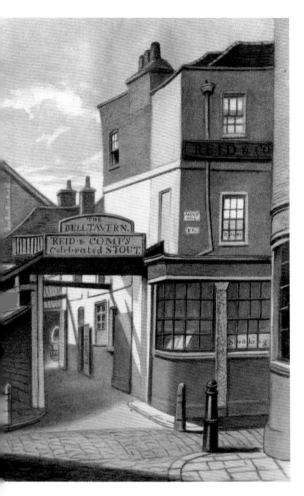

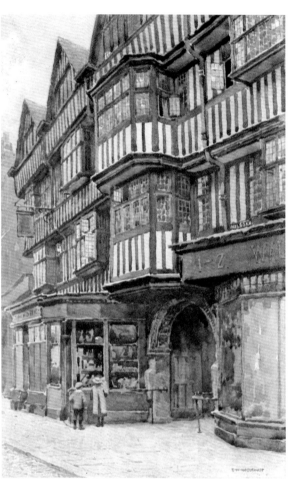

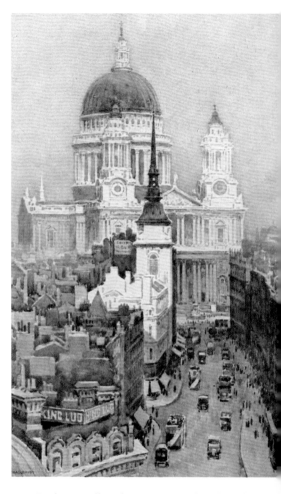

188. The Bell Tavern, Addle Hill, painted by J.T. Wilson in 1868. This was a part of what John Betjeman was to describe as 'Minor London of the narrow lanes, hidden taverns and unsuspected stableyards'. (Stephen Porter)

189. The entrance to Staple Inn, Holborn, the largest Inn of Chancery, which was in existence by 1415. The range facing Holborn is the best surviving half-timbered group in London, erected in 1586; painting by E. W. Haslehust around 1924. (Stephen Porter)

190. Ludgate Hill with St Martin's church and St Paul's Cathedral. St Martin's tower, dome and lantern, topped by a slender lead steeple, were designed by Wren. The painting is by E. W. Haslehust around 1924. (Stephen Porter)

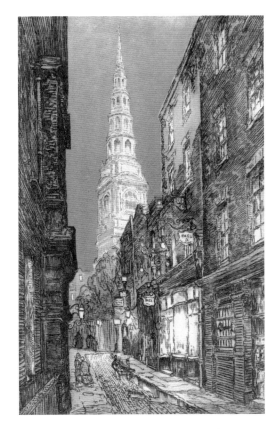

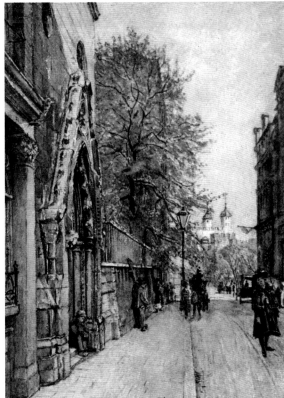

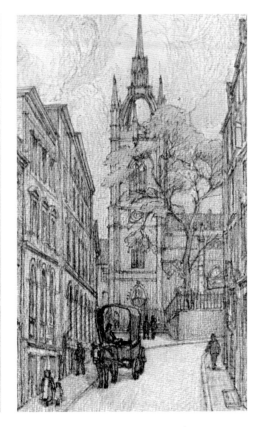

191. St Bride's church, Fleet St, was built in 1671–8 to Sir Christopher Wren's designs. The spire, added in 1701–03, is the best-known and the tallest of his City spires. It is said to have been the source for the form of the traditional wedding cake, introduced by Thomas Rich, a pastry cook on Ludgate Hill, who died in 1811. (Stephen Porter)

192. Great Tower Street looking east towards the Tower, painted by John Fulleylove. Tradition held that Peter the Great of Russia patronised an inn in the street while he was learning about shipbuilding in 1698; it was named 'The Czar of Russia' and had his portrait on its sign. (Stephen Porter)

193. The church of St Dunstan in the East was restored by the parishioners after the Great Fire and the four-stage Gothic tower topped by a slender spire was added by Christopher Wren in 1695–1701. The body of the church was rebuilt in 1817–21 by David Laing. The painting is by Nelson Dawson around 1900; the building was gutted during an air raid in 1941, but the tower and spire were restored and parts of the ruins have been preserved. (Stephen Porter)

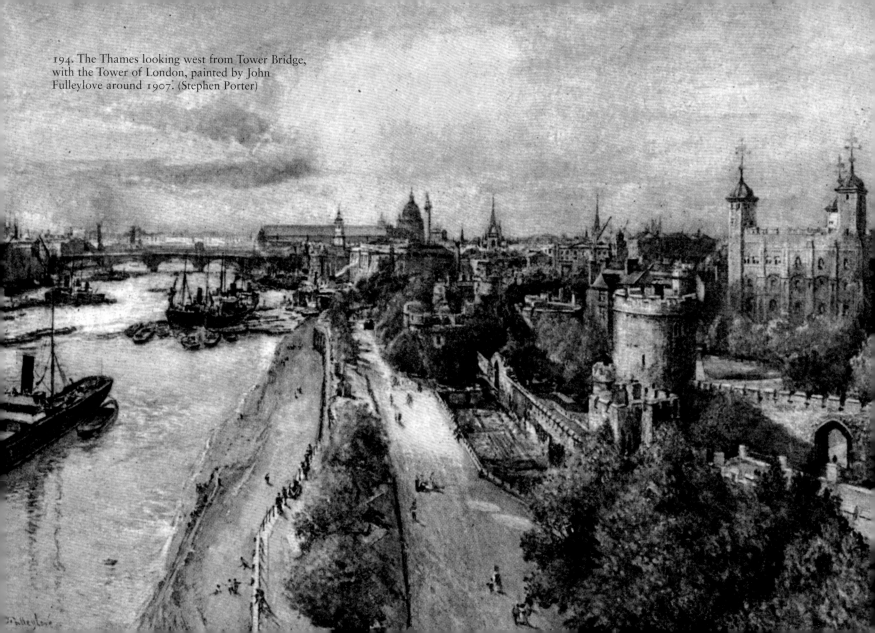

194. The Thames looking west from Tower Bridge, with the Tower of London, painted by John Fulleylove around 1907. (Stephen Porter)

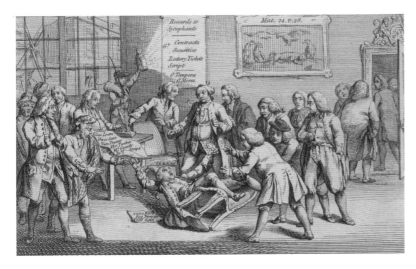

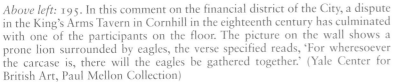

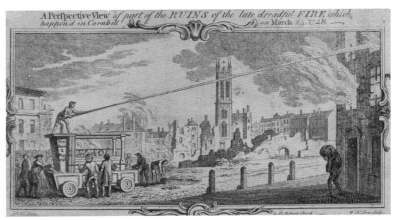

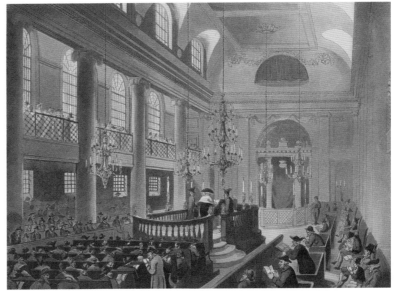

Above left: 195. In this comment on the financial district of the City, a dispute in the King's Arms Tavern in Cornhill in the eighteenth century has culminated with one of the participants on the floor. The picture on the wall shows a prone lion surrounded by eagles, the verse specified reads, 'For wheresoever the carcase is, there will the eagles be gathered together.' (Yale Center for British Art, Paul Mellon Collection)

Above right: 196. The aftermath of the fire in Cornhill and Exchange Alley in March 1748, engraved by William Henry Toms. The fire was one of the worst conflagrations in London in the eighteenth century; the tower is that of St Michael's church. (Yale Center for British Art, Paul Mellon Collection)

Right: 197. Duke's Place was a liberty, outside the authority of the lord mayor, where the great synagogue was erected in 1690, replaced by a new building in 1722 and that in turn was replaced in 1788–90. It is shown in 1808, by Thomas Sunderland, Augustus Pugin and Thomas Rowlandson. (Yale Center for British Art, Gift of Chauncey Brewster Tinker)

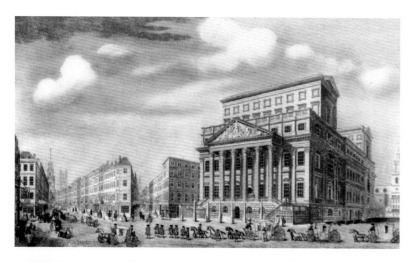

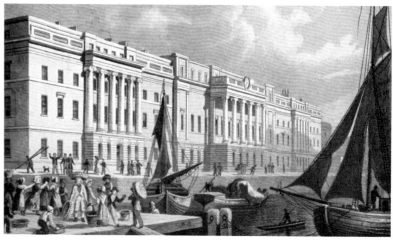

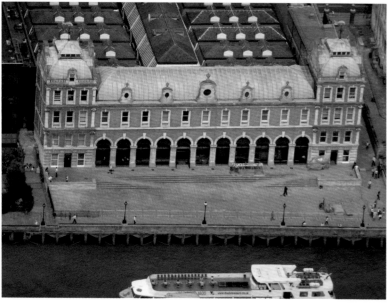

Above right: 198. The Custom House was rebuilt in 1813–17 to the designs of David Laing, Surveyor to the Customs, but Sir Robert Smirke rebuilt the central block and the long front to the river in 1825–28, retaining Laing's wings. The new building was drawn by T. H. Shepherd in 1828. (Stephen Porter)

Above left: 199. The Mansion House, the lord mayor's official residence, first occupied in 1753 by Sir Crisp Gascoigne and depicted here by Samuel Wale. (Stephen Porter)

Left: 200. The riverfront of Billingsgate Market, designed by Sir Horace Jones, the City's architect, in a French Renaissance style and erected in 1874–77. (Stephen Porter)

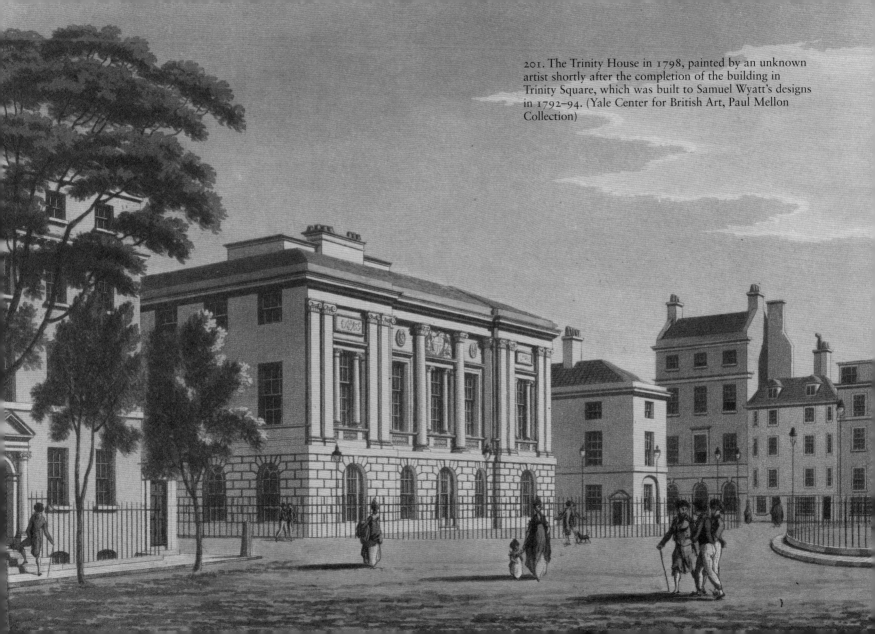

201. The Trinity House in 1798, painted by an unknown artist shortly after the completion of the building in Trinity Square, which was built to Samuel Wyatt's designs in 1792–94. (Yale Center for British Art, Paul Mellon Collection)

10

ST PAUL'S

The first church dedicated to St Paul was founded as a consequence of Pope Gregory's instruction to St Augustine to re-establish the Christian structure in England, centred on London and York. Mellitus was consecrated as bishop of the East Saxons in 604 and, according to the historian Bede, 'King Ethelbert built the church of the holy apostle Paul in the city of London.' This was within the city walls and probably on the crest of the hill where its successors were built. But in 616 Mellitus was expelled and only through the efforts of Erkenwald, abbot of Chertsey, who was consecrated as bishop around 675, was the see securely established. He came to be venerated for his role and in 1148 his remains were placed in a shrine in St Paul's, 'being richly shrined above the choir behind the high altar'.

The cathedral was burnt down in 962 and was said to have been rebuilt within a year, which suggests repair of a stone structure, not the complete reconstruction that would have been required had it been a wooden one. But it is likely that the Anglo-Saxon cathedral had a wooden roof, which made it vulnerable to fire. Indeed, damage inflicted during a general conflagration in the city in 1087 was such that a new building was required. The work was begun under Bishop Maurice (1085–1107) and was continued by his successor Richard de Belmeis (1108–27), but

was hampered by damage during another fire in the city in 1133 that required some rebuilding of the new fabric.

The cathedral was built with Caen stone brought from Normandy and, unsurprisingly given its scale and materials, raising the necessary funds took time. The west end was finished in the late twelfth century and the tower and spire not until the early thirteenth century. The choir was then rebuilt and extended, from 1256, and the chapter house was subsequently reconstructed, as the centre of a cloister in the south-west angle of the nave and south transept; those works were not finished until the mid-fourteenth century. The completed cathedral was a large and impressive building, 596 feet long, with a nave of twelve bays which was 100 feet wide, and with a central tower topped by a tall, slender spire that was 589 feet high. A detached bell tower stood at the north-east corner of the precinct, near Cheapside.

As well as the services within the building, weekly ones were conducted and sermons were preached from Paul's Cross, an outdoor pulpit which stood in the angle between the north transept and the choir. Galleries against the wall of the choir were for the civic dignitaries attending the services. The pulpit was in existence by 1241 and was rebuilt in 1448 and 1595.

Baron Waldstein, from Moravia, described this in 1600 as 'an open space where they hold open air services which the Mayor of the City himself attends. The services last for nearly 3 hours.'

The cathedral was the focus for the diocese and a complex of buildings grew up in the precinct, including the bishop's palace and deanery, colleges housing the chantry priests, which numbered fifty by around 1547, and the residences of the thirty vicars choral and thirty canons. In the fifteenth century the dean's household numbered forty people. By the time of the Reformation the precinct housed roughly 300 people, not including the boys at the school, which had been founded in 1510 by the dean, John Colet. In addition, the undercroft of the choir was used by the parishioners of St Faith's as their church, and St Gregory's parish church stood against the south wall of the nave at its west end.

The cathedral's sheer size and presence within the city's buildings impressed visitors to London, yet all was not well. The cathedral did not attract the bequests of the citizens in the same way that London Bridge did, for example, and the fabric became somewhat neglected. The tower was not entirely stable, despite buttresses at three of its corners, 'for the fourth wants a buttress'. The spire was struck by lightning in 1444 and the fire caused by another strike in 1561 destroyed the steeple, which was not replaced, although the tower and roof were repaired within ten years. The fabric was so neglected that in 1600 a piece of masonry fell from the battlements, killing a horse, and in 1616 Henry Farley, a scrivener, began a campaign for the renovation of the building, which he described as 'cracked, defaced, rent, and almost undone'.

By the early seventeenth century there was concern not only because of the condition of the building but also its profanation. Its position between Cheapside and Ludgate Hill meant that citizens treated it as a thoroughfare, passing from the door into the north transept along the nave to its west end. It was customary to wander through the building, meeting friends to exchange news and gossip, perhaps to do business, hire employees or conclude a transaction. The long central aisle of the nave had become a promenade, known as Paul's Walk. Attempts were made to limit the citizens' activities, at least when services were being held, but the cathedral's many secular functions were not easily suppressed.

One aspect of Farley's campaign was the removal of houses built against the east wall of the north transept. During William Laud's time as Bishop of London (1628–33) a more significant series of improvements was executed, to Inigo Jones's designs. These included the addition of a Corinthian-style portico on the west front, which required the partial demolition of St Gregory's, and the re-casing of the nave, with classical pilasters replacing the buttresses. But following the outbreak of the Civil War and the abolition of bishops and deans and chapters the cathedral was again neglected. Soldiers were quartered in it, using part of the building to stable their horses, and the Dutch visitor Lodewijck Huygens wrote in 1652 that it was 'as dirty as it can be in any stable'. Paul's Cross was demolished during the war, in 1643.

Following the restoration of the monarchy and Church, a commission was set up in 1663 to consider the possibilities for repairing the building. Sir Christopher Wren submitted a plan in May 1666 that proposed the rearrangement of the interior and the construction of a lofty dome over the crossing, to replace the tower. The scheme was approved by the commissioners, but any action was forestalled by the outbreak of the Great Fire on Sunday, 3 September. The fire spread steadily westwards from Pudding Lane and on the Tuesday evening the cathedral roof was ignited by burning debris. The flames then spread to the remainder of the building. The churchyard and Paternoster Row on its north side had become a centre of stationers and booksellers, with St Faith's church in the crypt as their church. They moved their stocks of books and papers there in the hope that it might be fireproof, but the choir's vaulted roof collapsed, breaking through the floor and exposing St Faith's contents to the flames. Ironically, among the losses were 300 copies of Sir William Dugdale's new *History of St Paul's Cathedral*. The building burned and smouldered for several hours and by the time that the fire had burnt out it was left in ruins.

Despite the ravages of the fire, a part of the nave was usable for services and they were continued until 1673. But it was realised that the building could not be reconstructed and that an entirely new one was required. Clearance of the site took until 1676; in all, 47,000 loads of rubbish were carted away for sorting and the retrieval of material that could be reused. Meanwhile, Wren produced a number of designs, including, in 1673–74, a model almost twenty feet long for a building based on a Greek cross that had arms of equal length, with an extension to the westward one. But it lacked a distinct choir and there were other objections, and so that plan was abandoned. He then prepared a new design, which consisted of a Latin cross with a choir of three bays and an additional half-bay and apse at the east end, a nave of five bays with aisles, and transepts of three bays. That received the royal

warrant in May 1675 and the foundation stone was laid in June. But, almost from the outset, Wren set about adapting the design and so both the external appearance and the internal layout were considerably modified in the course of the work. Perhaps most importantly, the planned shallow dome with a tall drum above it that was topped with a lofty steeple was abandoned and he reverted to the central dome that he had conceived for the pre-fire improvement of the cathedral, and had also used for his design based on a Greek cross, although further developing that idea.

By the time that construction work began, skilled labour and materials were becoming more readily available as the other post-fire buildings were completed. And funds from the duty levied on coal brought into the port of London, which had been imposed to pay for the public buildings, including the churches, could increasingly be directed to the work at St Paul's. The east end was completed first and was ready for a service in 1697 celebrating the end of the Nine Years War. Work on the dome began in 1706 and the cathedral was completed in 1710. It had taken thirty-five years to build.

Wren used Portland stone, and 50,322 tons were brought to the site at a cost of £81,357, over a half of which was accounted for by the expense of carriage, together with 25,573 tons of stone from other quarries, which added a further £53,594. The total cost of the building was £738,845. The new cathedral covered a smaller area than did its medieval predecessor, but it was the outstanding architectural achievement of the rebuilding works, dominating London's skyline and providing the centrepiece for the towers, steeples and spires of the post-fire churches. Not only was the grandeur of the building impressive, but so, too, was the fine carved decoration on the external stonework and the decorative internal features, notably the dome over the crossing, with its Whispering Gallery, the choir screen of wrought iron, by Jean Tijou, and the choir stalls by Grinling Gibbons.

The new cathedral stood in an open churchyard, with the chapter house on the north side. Undeterred by their losses in the Great Fire, the booksellers and publishers returned and the precinct continued to be a centre for publishing and bookselling well into the nineteenth century.

St Paul's remained the City's church and services on state occasions continued to be held in Westminster Abbey. But it was the setting for some special services because of its size, including that marking the Peace of Utrecht in 1713 and the funerals of Lord Nelson in 1806 and the Duke of Wellington in 1852. No funerary monuments were placed in the building before 1790, but thereafter the wish to honour those who fought in the wars with France saw the placing of several memorials within the cathedral, including those commemorating Lord Nelson and Sir John Moore. The Victorians followed that practice and their memorials included the imposing Wellington monument, by Alfred Stevens, in the arcade of the nave. They also made a substantial alteration to the appearance of the interior by adding mosaics, firstly to the spandrels of the crossing, from 1864, and then, at the end of the nineteenth century, to the entire vault of the choir. The building faced a serious threat from air raids in 1940–41, during which fires raged nearby, but, apart from a direct hit on the high altar and the destruction of part of the north transept's vault, the cathedral emerged from the Second World War largely unscathed.

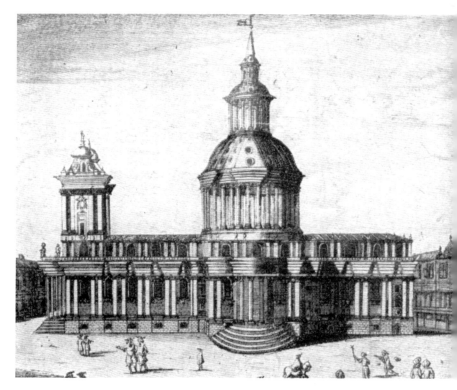

202. Wren's early design for St Paul's cathedral, dated 1673. (Stephen Porter)

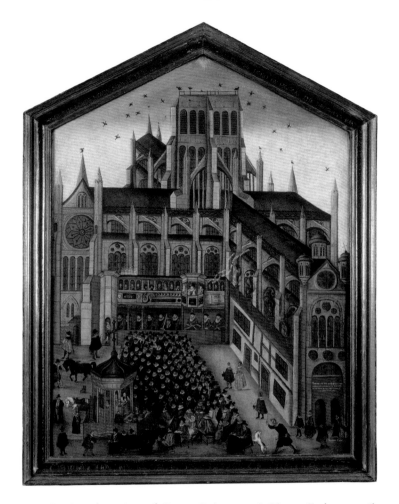

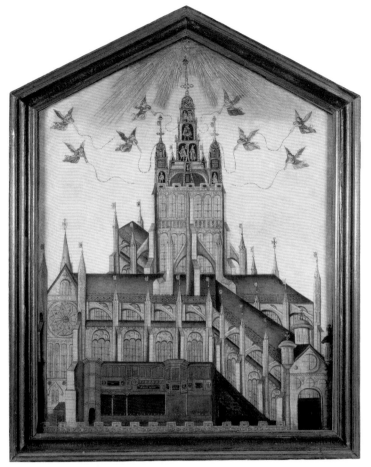

203. During the reign of James I (1603–25) Henry Farley, a tailor, campaigned for funds to restore St Paul's Cathedral. This painting of 1616 shows John King, Bishop of London, preaching from Paul's Cross to the king and his queen, Anne of Denmark, the aldermen of London in galleries, and a numerous outdoor congregation. (Society of Antiquaries of London)

204. The second painting of the St Paul's diptych, from the same perspective, imagines the cathedral repaired, with a new spire, around which angels soar. (Society of Antiquaries of London)

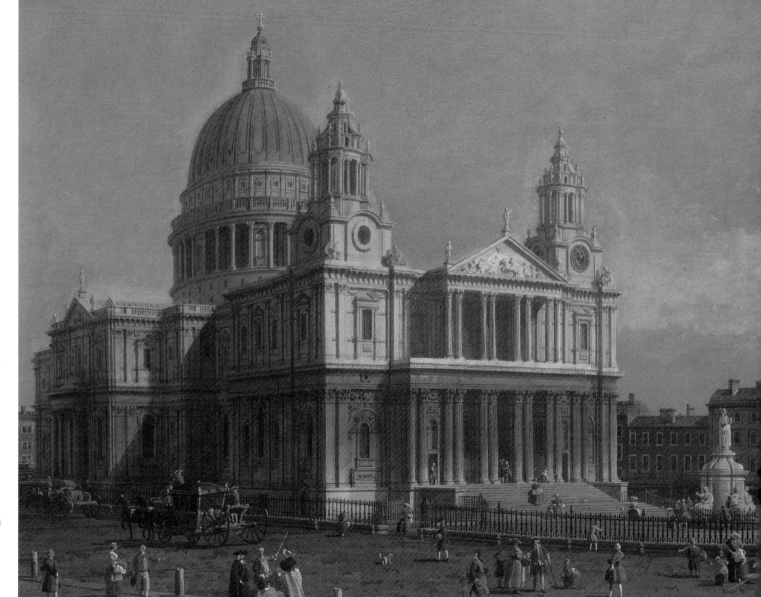

205. Unlike the cathedral destroyed in the Great Fire, the new St Paul's was not enclosed within a precinct, but had busy roadways on both sides, making it a much more integral part of the City's life. This depiction is by Canaletto, painted around 1754. (Yale Center for British Art, Paul Mellon Collection)

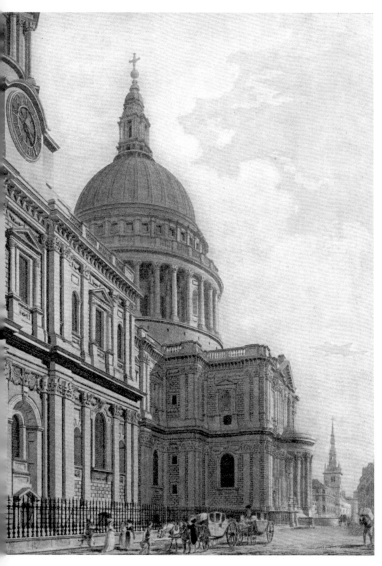

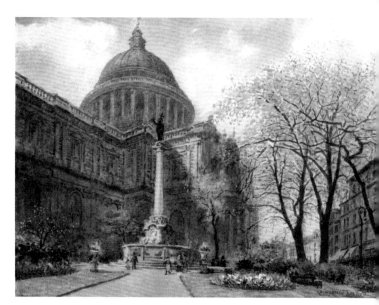

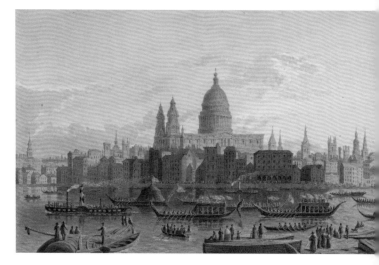

Left: 206. St Paul's Cathedral south side, drawn by Thomas Malton in 1792. The clock in the south-west tower was installed in 1707. (Stephen Porter)

Top right: 207. St Paul's Cathedral from the north-east, by Lawrence Deller, 1914. The tall pillar, of 1910, commemorates Paul's Cross, the open-air pulpit on the site, demolished in 1643. (Stephen Porter)

Bottom right: 208. St Paul's, the City churches and the riverside below the cathedral, which was lined with tall warehouses and other buildings; the many vessels on the Thames include ceremonial barges and a steam launch. Drawn by an unknown artist in the early nineteenth century. (Yale Center for British Art, Paul Mellon Collection)

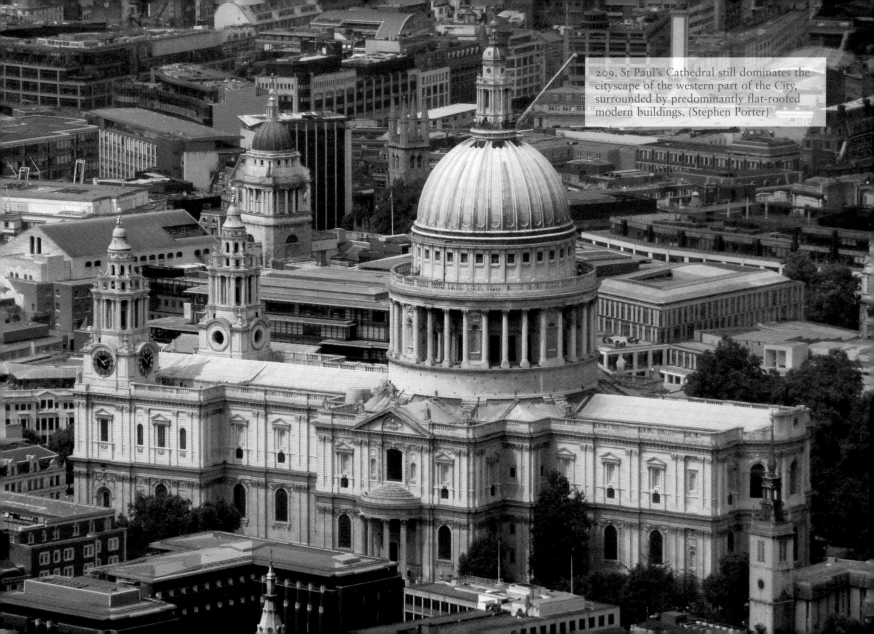

209. St Paul's Cathedral still dominates the cityscape of the western part of the City, surrounded by predominantly flat-roofed modern buildings. (Stephen Porter)

11

CHEAPSIDE

From late Saxon times, this was the principal market in the City, sometimes known as Westcheap, to distinguish it from Eastcheap. The street was set out before 900, but only from the sixteenth century was it known as Cheapside, that is, the street alongside the market. As well as the street markets, by the early thirteenth century Cheapside was lined with small shops. Behind the frontages were yards containing bazaars, known as selds, each of which had twenty to thirty traders' places, where they stored and sold their wares. In 1300 the street had as many as 400 shops and up to ten times that number of traders' places in the selds. But the decline in population after the Black Death in 1348–49 brought a fall in demand for goods, and so a decline in rents. During the later Middle Ages there were fewer, albeit larger, shops, and when demand and rents increased again after around 1500 the smaller shops and selds did not reappear.

As the main street of the City, and because of its width and closeness to both St Paul's and Guildhall, Cheapside was used for jousts, tournaments and processions, royal and civic, including the lord mayor's show. It was also a place where shoddy goods and those that contravened the regulations of the guilds were burned and where miscreants stood in the pillory.

The later Middle Ages saw the erection of buildings which were typically three stories high, and some even had five or six stories. With the rise in rents and increasing prosperity, during the sixteenth century the shops were taken by goldsmiths and silk mercers; indeed it became known as the goldsmiths' street. The Swiss visitor Thomas Platter, in 1599, wrote, 'In one very long street called Cheapside dwell almost only goldsmiths and money changers on either hand, so that inexpressibly great treasures and vast amounts of money may be seen here.' But during the early seventeenth century the goldsmiths began to be replaced by other tradesmen, described as booksellers, stocking men, haberdashers, lacemakers and 'other mean trades'.

Cheapside's buildings were destroyed by the Great Fire and the butchers' stalls were then moved to Honey Lane market. It did recover its former prominence after the rebuilding and continued to be the focus for formal processions, and for demonstrations and bonfires by political agitators. The street maintained its status throughout the eighteenth and nineteenth centuries, despite the attractions of the West End and the fall in the City's resident population. But the luxury trades drifted away westwards and the goldsmiths moved east, to the financial district around the Bank of England and the Royal Exchange. Charles Dickens the younger, in 1888, still regarded Cheapside as 'the greatest thoroughfare in the City of London', though it was blighted by traffic congestion.

Many of its buildings were replaced in the late nineteenth and early twentieth centuries, and again following the air-raids of the Second World War, which destroyed most of the western section of the street.

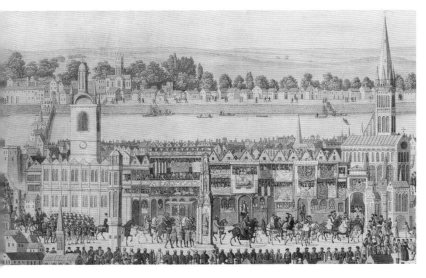

210. It was the practice for monarchs to spend the night before their coronation at the Tower of London, before processing to Westminster. Edward VI's procession in 1547 is shown passing along Cheapside, with the church of St Mary le Bow, St Paul's Cathedral, which still had its spire, and London Bridge prominently shown, and Southwark, St Saviour's church and Bankside across the Thames. This copy was made by Samuel Hieronymus Grimm (1733–94). (Society of Antiquaries of London)

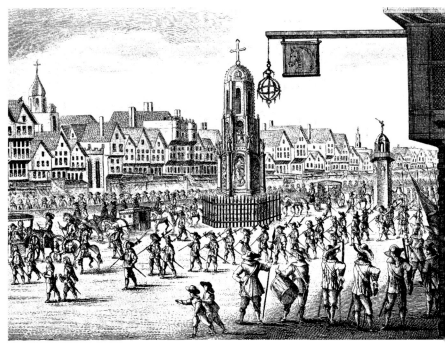

211. The procession of Marie de Medici passing the cross in Cheapside in 1638, accompanied by soldiers of the London Trained Bands. Cheapside's status as one of the wealthiest streets in the city is shown by the large houses. (Jonathan Reeve, JR445b8fp94 16001650)

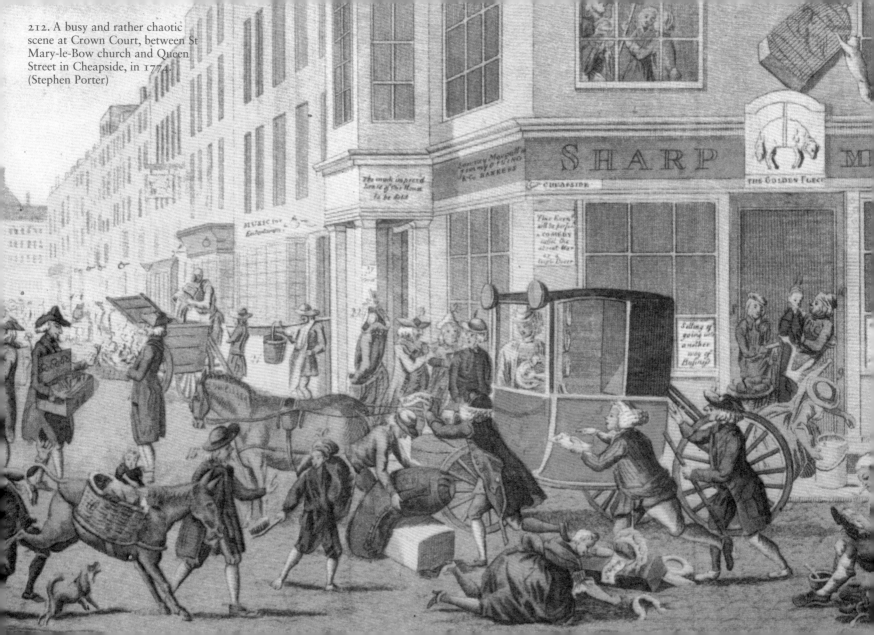

212. A busy and rather chaotic scene at Crown Court, between St Mary-le-Bow church and Queen Street in Cheapside, in 1774. (Stephen Porter)

12

THE TOWER OF LONDON

When William the Conqueror's army reached London late in 1066, it encountered resistance before taking control of the city. After his coronation in Westminster Abbey on Christmas Day, William withdrew to Barking, until fortifications were provided to accommodate a garrison and to overawe the citizens. One of those strongholds was an enclosure within the south-east corner of the Roman city walls, and William later ordered the erection of a great keep of Caen stone within that enclosure. The work began in 1078 and the building, the White Tower, probably was completed within twenty years.

The complex was enlarged over the two centuries following the erection of the White Tower, especially during the reigns of Richard I (1189–99), Henry III (1216–72) and his son Edward I (1272–1307). The inner ward was developed as a royal palace and the defences were extended, with new outer walls, surrounded by a moat. With Edward's extension of the perimeter, by 1300 the Tower had reached its maximum extent of roughly eighteen acres and had the concentric layout which is familiar today.

The palace housed the royal wardrobe and regalia, and became a stronghold for the deposit of bullion, including wealthy Londoners' riches. In the late thirteenth century the minting of coins was centralised and moved into the Tower, which also developed as a centre of royal administration and a repository for the storage of the records of government and the central courts. It also contained a military arsenal where armour, weapons and artillery were made and stored. The Ordnance Office developed from those functions, with workshops and storehouses within the precincts. A garrison was based at the Tower, but it failed to defend the fortress when it was captured by the citizens in 1326 and during the Peasants' Revolt in 1381. After Henry VII's accession in 1485, he appointed a force of about 200 men as part of his household, to be a bodyguard, from which developed the Yeomen Warders, who were responsible for guarding the Tower.

The Tower was the state's prison, with the prisoners held in the various towers. Some were subject to torture, which could be carried out only by warrant. Some eighty-one such warrants were issued between 1540 and 1640, when the Long Parliament put an end to the practice. Many prisoners died within the Tower, some presumed murdered, such as Henry VI, Edward V and his brother (the Princes in the Tower) in 1483, and Sir Thomas Overbury, who was poisoned there in 1613. Others were executed, mostly on Tower Hill, for only members of the royal family were put to death on the green within the Tower. Two of Henry VIII's wives, Anne Boleyn and Katherine Howard, were beheaded there, as was Lady Jane Grey, his great-niece and queen for nine days. In 1399 the Tower was the scene of Richard II's deposition by Henry Bolingbroke, one of his long-standing opponents among the nobility, who took the throne as Henry IV.

The wardrobe, based in the Tower, was responsible for looking after the monarch's collection of exotic animals. By the 1330s the menagerie of lions, leopards and bears was in the barbican at the western entrance, where the Lion Tower housed the king's beasts in the sixteenth century. The office of 'keeper of the lions, lionesses and leopards in the Tower' was created in the fifteenth century.

In 1274 Edward I began the practice of a king preparing for his coronation at the Tower, before processing through London to Westminster to be crowned, which was continued until the coronation of Charles II in 1660. Under the Tudors, the royal quarters gradually fell out of use and were encroached upon by the Ordnance Office, which was increasingly in need of storage space. Overcrowding of buildings and stores became a chronic problem and by the end of the sixteenth century the Tower 'gives visitors the impression of a town'. As the size of the military establishment grew, especially in the late seventeenth century, so did the problem, and in 1663–64 a new Great Store House was constructed against the curtain wall. The congestion was exacerbated by the accumulation of obsolete equipment, for the stocks of body armour, swords, pikes, bows and crossbows, and arrows continued to be held when they were no longer required. The armour included decorative suits, for men and horses, and they, with equipment and trophies captured during military campaigns, came to be arranged as displays. The armouries, royal regalia and the menagerie increasingly became attractions

for visitors to the Tower. The ease of access was exploited by 'Colonel' Thomas Blood, who only narrowly failed in his audacious attempt to steal the Crown jewels.

Another function grew up within the Tower during the eighteenth century. The Corps of Engineers was created within the Board of Ordnance in 1716, with responsibility for surveying, and a map room was established on the east side of the White Tower. In 1791 the Ordnance Survey was formed, as a branch of the board, still based in the Tower, where it remained until a fire in 1841 destroyed the Grand Storehouse. The Ordnance Survey was then moved to Southampton.

The Tower had already ceased to be a prison. The final group of prisoners was the Cato Street conspirators, who hatched a plot, in 1820, to assassinate the cabinet. Their leader, Arthur Thistlewood, and four others were executed. No prisoners were held in the Tower during the remainder of the nineteenth century. Many of the various departments were moved out of the Tower: the Mint in 1811–12, the menagerie in 1831–35 and the records in 1858, to the new Public Record Office in Chancery Lane, while the Bank of England had become the preferred place of deposit for the merchants. On the other hand, the regalia remained, the displays in the armouries became more extensive and increasing numbers of visitors went to the Tower.

Interest was stimulated by the publication of guides to the buildings, their associations and contents, scholarly histories, and historical novels which used the Tower as a setting. They enhanced the impression that the fortress had been close to the centre of political and royal affairs for centuries. The history of the fabric, too, attracted attention, with the Board of Works' architects adopting a policy of presenting what they believed to be the authentic medieval buildings. That involved some rebuilding and the demolition of structures from later periods which were regarded as inappropriate accretions. As the French visitor Francis Wey commented, in the early 1850s, 'the English with their mania for spurious restoring have completely altered its character. The old towers alone now bear witness to its original aspect.' That approach was indeed part of a more widespread treatment of historic buildings deplored by later generations.

The Yeomen Warders pointed out to visitors the rooms where famous prisoners had been incarcerated (although many of the connections were gradually changed as a result of research), showed the graffiti in the plasterwork carved by prisoners and recounted the many traditions. These included the ceremony of the keys, which involved the barring and locking of the gates at curfew, with a set routine and dialogue. They also came to include the notion that ravens had been living at the Tower for centuries and that if they disappeared the monarchy and state would fall, a comment attributed to Charles II. In fact, ravens had begun to visit the Tower in the mid-nineteenth century, as their previous nesting sites in London had been lost. Yet it became the practice to ensure that there were always five ravens there, to maintain the newly created tradition.

Tension arose between those advocating the opening of more of the Tower to visitors and reducing admission prices, and those who wished to retain it solely as a military base, with the displays in the armouries and the regalia shown elsewhere. When prices were reduced and free days were introduced the number of visitors increased considerably, and the presentation of the buildings and the collections within them as a museum of national interest was the course which was followed. Terrorist bombs in 1885 and 1974 demonstrated its significance as a symbol of royal authority and state power. Indeed, it retained a garrison and was again used as a military prison in both world wars. The opening of larger areas to public access as the military presence was reduced was a process which lasted well into the twentieth century. From being a fortress and prison in the eleventh century, over the following 900 years the Tower developed a number of other functions, and then lost them, yet has been maintained and adapted, rather than neglected, and has become a major visitor attraction which is indisputably the best-known castle in the world.

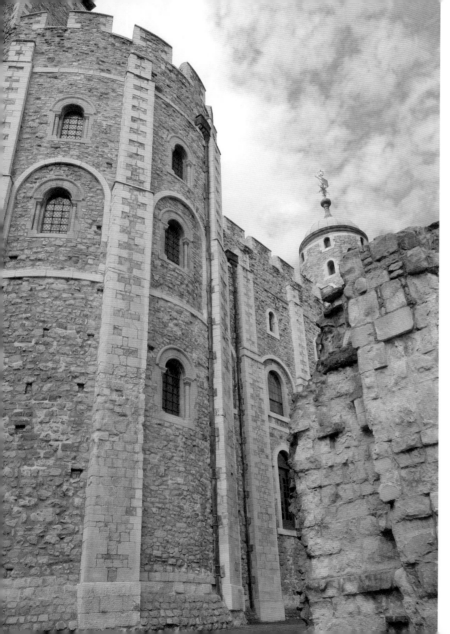

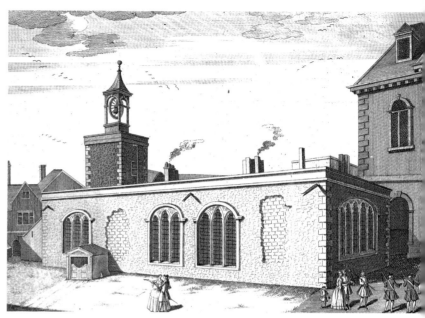

Above: 213. The chapel of St Peter ad Vincula within the Tower of London was built in 1286–87 and rebuilt in 1519–20. Visitors are being shown around the buildings in this print of around 1755. (Stephen Porter)

Left: 214. The dominating keep of the White Tower was built in the late eleventh century as the principal building of the Norman fortress which developed into the Tower of London. (Stephen Porter)

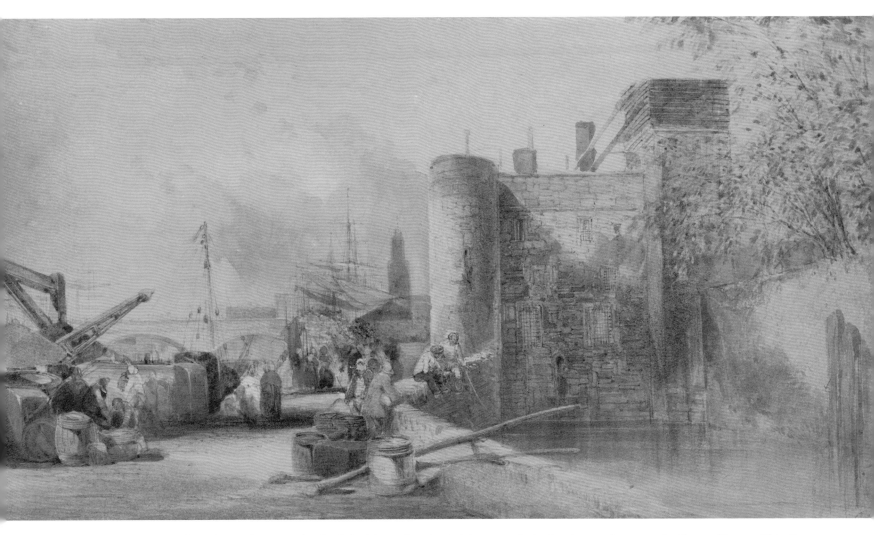

215. The moat of the Tower of London and Tower Wharf, piled with goods unloaded from vessels, in the nineteenth century, by George Howse. (Yale Center for British Art, Paul Mellon Collection)

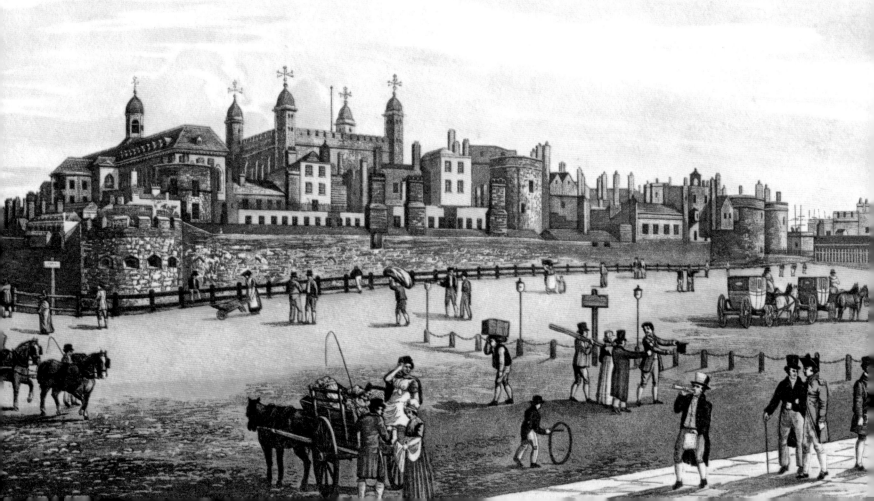

216. Tower Hill in 1821 with coaches and carts full of produce, as well as a mixture of people. The crowded and varied buildings of the Tower were said to resemble a small town. (Stephen Porter)

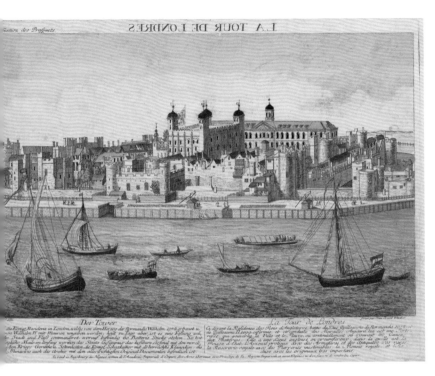

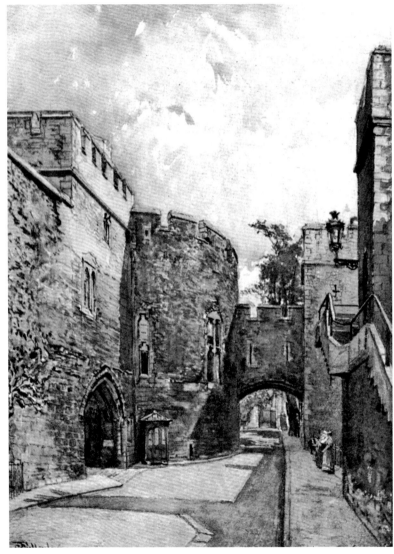

Above: 217. The Tower of London in an engraving by John Winckler, after the Dutch artist Leonard Knyff (1650–1721). The drawing was made after the building of the Grand Storehouse, behind the White Tower, in 1688–89. The accompanying text mentions that the Tower was still a fortress, with sixty cannon mounted on its batteries. (Yale Center for British Art, Paul Mellon Collection)

Right: 218. The Bloody Tower and the Wakefield Tower in the Tower of London painted by John Fulleylove around 1907. (Stephen Porter)

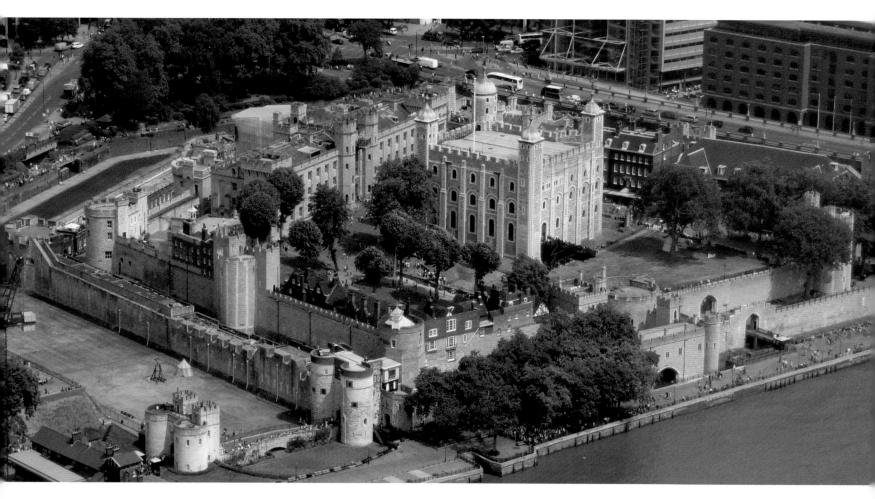

219. The area and configuration of the modern Tower of London was attained by the early fourteenth century, when Edward I completed the works begun by his father. (Stephen Porter)

LONDON BRIDGE

The first bridge across the Thames at London was built by the Romans, perhaps by AD 50, and roughly on the site of the later bridges. The Roman bridge was of wood and must have been over 350 yards long. It survived for some time after the withdrawal of the Roman legions, but, as Londinium was abandoned and Lundenwic developed as the settlement on the north bank, it probably went out of use in the fifth and sixth centuries, later being broken down as a defensive measure.

After London was re-established towards the end of the ninth century, there was again a need for a bridge and one was constructed by the end of the tenth century. Of wooden construction, it was built to improve communications and trade and was described as being wide enough for two wagons to pass. It could also serve as a defensive feature in response to raids by the Norsemen, blocking the movement of ships upstream and giving the defenders positions from which to bombard vessels below, as well as preventing a hostile force from crossing the river, as in 1066.

A rush of water during a severe gale in 1091 destroyed the bridge, its replacement was burnt in 1135 and the new timber bridge, built in 1163, was replaced by a stone one between 1176 and 1212. Peter de Colechurch, a priest, was responsible for overseeing the financing and the early stages of the building work of the stone bridge. Before the end of the twelfth century it was maintained by donations, tolls, and rents of properties bequeathed for the purpose. The fraternity responsible for overseeing the fund was to develop into the Bridge House Trust. A chapel dedicated to St Thomas à Becket, the City's patron saint, was built on the bridge in the early thirteenth century, and rebuilt in 1384–97. It was demolished in 1553.

The bridge was just over 300 yards long, with the deck supported on nineteen piers on broad platforms, known as starlings, with narrow gaps between them. They effectively reduced the width of the river from 900 feet to 200 feet, creating strong pressures on the starlings and increasing the flow of water to such an extent that the passage of boats through the openings was hazardous, except at slack water between the tides.

There were a gatehouse and drawbridge close to the bridge's south end and in 1426 another, larger, gatehouse, known as Drawbridge Gate, was erected further along. In 1437 the Great Stone Gate and two arches 'with alle the housing thereupon' fell into the river. Surprisingly, no one was killed. The gate was rebuilt by the mid-1460s, although a large slab of masonry that had fallen between two of the piers was a hazard to boats passing through.

Drawbridge Gate was demolished in 1577, leaving only the Great Stone Gate. It was used, like the other City gates, to display the heads of executed traitors and others whose offence was so heinous that putting their heads on poles there would serve as an example to others. The last head to be displayed was that of a goldsmith who was executed in 1678 in the furore which surrounded the Popish Plot. The macabre practice then came to an end.

A large and impressive timber-framed building of four storeys known as Nonesuch House replaced Drawbridge Gate in 1577–79. This was the largest and most impressive of the many houses on the bridge, for the roadway was lined on both sides with houses and shops from the early thirteenth century. By 1358 there were 138 shops, occupying prime sites, as most travellers between London and Southwark crossed the bridge rather than take a boat. In 1598 John Stow wrote that 'it seemeth rather a continual street than a bridge'. Although those buildings were much admired by visitors such as Thomas Platter, who noted that the bridge contained 'many tall handsome merchant dwellings and expensive shops, where all manner of wares are for sale', traffic congestion was a growing problem and after a fire in 1633 destroyed more than forty houses an order came before the Privy Council to prohibit rebuilding.

During the 1680s there was a phase of rebuilding on the bridge, but the structures at the southern end were destroyed by fire in 1725, and the Great Stone Gate was demolished in 1727–28. In 1745–47 a block of buildings designated the Piazza, designed by George Dance the elder, was built on the east side of the bridge at the City end. But the Georgians did not have that affection for the bridge which earlier generations had shown and the street along it was described as 'narrow, darksome, and dangerous to passengers from the multitude of carriages'. In 1756 the London Bridge Act empowered the corporation to acquire and demolish the buildings on the bridge, a process that was completed in 1762. Tolls were abolished in 1782 and by 1800 the bridge's demolition itself was being considered, because it was expensive to maintain. It was also an obstruction to navigation, a problem exacerbated by the waterwheels, for raising water and powering mills, between the starlings close to the banks at both ends. An Act of Parliament of 1822 ordered their removal.

Clearance of the buildings and the waterwheels was not enough to save the structure, and in 1821 a competition was held for a design for a replacement. John Rennie's proposal was adopted and the new bridge, of five elliptical arches, was opened by William IV and Queen Adelaide in 1831. It was built about 100 feet upstream from the medieval bridge, with new approaches. But it did not solve the problem of traffic congestion, despite the opening of other bridges along the river in central London. Rennie's structure was removed in 1968, when it was dismantled and re-erected at Lake Havasu City, Arizona. Its replacement was opened in 1973.

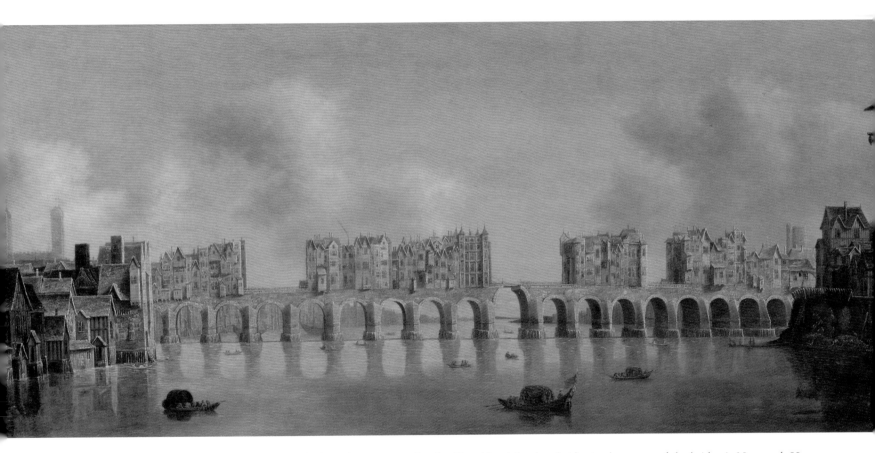

220. View of London Bridge before the fire of 1633, looking downstream. On the City side of the drawbridge in the centre of the bridge is Nonesuch House, built in 1577–79. There are gaps in the buildings along the bridge, but a continuous huddle of buildings on the City side which comes down to the water's edge. By Claude de Jongh, around 1632. (Yale Center for British Art, Paul Mellon Fund)

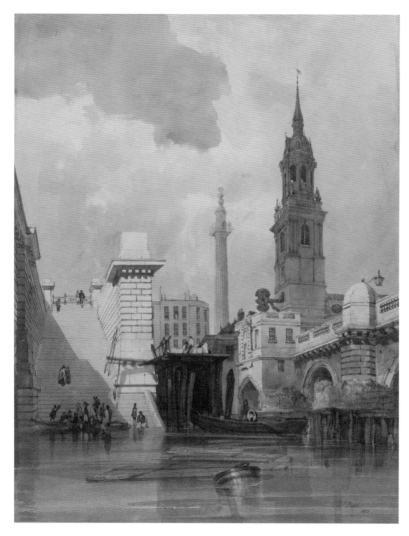

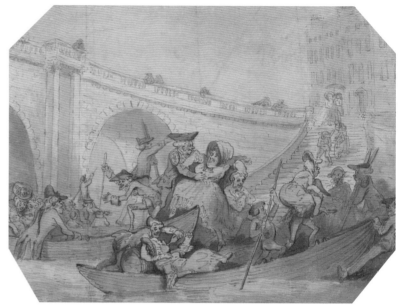

Above: 221. 'The Arrival of Ferries at London Bridge' is a humorous depiction of passengers disembarking, in a rather chaotic manner, from boats to ascend the steps alongside the bridge. By an unknown artist and undated. (Yale Center for British Art, Paul Mellon Collection)

Left: 222. The old London Bridge in 1832, to the right, just before its demolition, and its replacement, to the left, with the church of St Magnus the Martyr and the Monument; by Thomas Shotter Boys. (Yale Center for British Art, Paul Mellon Collection)

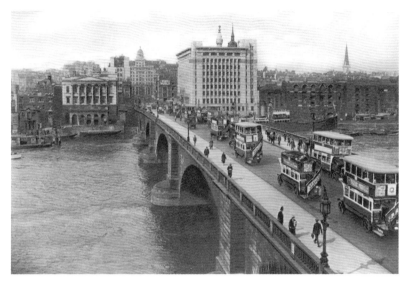

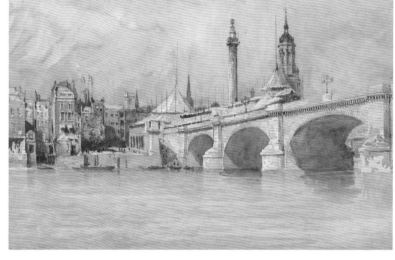

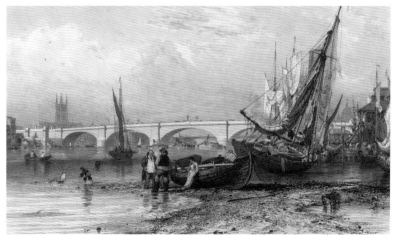

Above left: 223. John Rennie's London Bridge was opened in 1831 and dismantled in 1968; it was re-erected at Lake Havasu City, Arizona. It was flanked by the Fishmongers' Company hall of 1832–35 and Adelaide House of 1921–24, designed by Sir John Burnet & Tait, which was then London's tallest commercial building. (Stephen Porter)

Above right: 224. The ceremony of opening the new London Bridge on 1 August 1831, with pavilions erected on the bridge itself, painted by David Cox. (Yale Center for British Art, Paul Mellon Collection)

Right: 225. The new London Bridge, from Billingsgate, in 1832, by Edward William Cooke. (Yale Center for British Art, Paul Mellon Collection)

14

TOWER BRIDGE

The bridges built across the Thames from the mid-eighteenth century onwards were all upstream of London Bridge. The need for a bridge downstream, to serve the growing East End, was recognised by the mid-1870s, when proposals were invited. The need to provide clearance for ships to enter the Pool of London governed the size and scale of the structure, while its proximity to the Tower of London meant that its appearance had to be sensitive to that setting. The design submitted by Sir Horace Jones, the corporation's architect, was selected in 1885, and was further modified with input from the engineer, Sir John Wolfe Barry. The bridge was built between 1886 and 1894.

The two towers are 213 feet high and between them are two lifting bascules spanning the 200-foot-wide central section, and two upper walkways. The central bridge is approached along smaller suspension bridges which are suspended from lattice girders. The design of the twin Gothic towers was described by Eric de Maré in 1964 as 'some curious sort of Flemish mediaeval style'; their steel structure is clad in granite.

Although its scale and design provoked criticism in the early stages, the bridge's distinctive appearance, and its setting, proved to be appealing once the structure was completed. A French visitor was lavish with his praise, describing the bridge as 'a colossal symbol of the British genius … built on lines of severe simplicity, harmonious, superbly balanced, without exaggeration or emphasis; sober architecture, yet with reasonable audacities'.

Its design had provoked disquiet not only on aesthetic grounds but also because of some qualms among the military establishment, for the scale of the bridge is such that it overlooks the Tower of London. It was feared that if the bridge was seized by a hostile force the Tower would be threatened, and so a clause in the Act of Parliament of 1885 authorising the construction of the bridge permitted soldiers to occupy the bridge and its approaches when necessary. But a proposal to erect a firing platform within the walls of the Tower, from which its defenders could fire on enemy forces on the bridge, was not implemented. Moral rather than defensive reasons led to the closure of the upper walkways in 1910, as they had become the haunt of pickpockets and prostitutes.

Whatever misgivings its position, scale and design aroused, the bridge gradually came to be recognised as making a strong contribution to the identity of London. It is ranked with St Paul's, Westminster Abbey, Trafalgar Square, the Houses of Parliament and the Tower itself as one of the city's distinctive features.

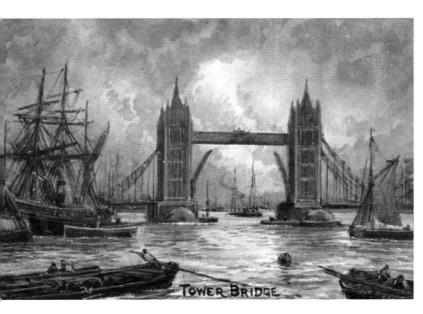

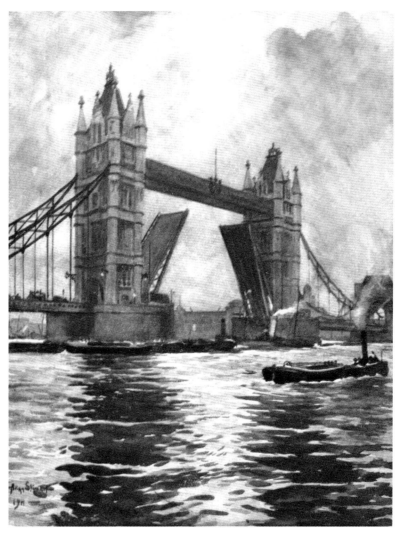

Above: 226. Tower Bridge in 1908, when sailing vessels were still common on the Thames in London. (Stephen Porter)

Right: 227. Tower Bridge was completed in 1894 and quickly became an iconic feature of London's cityscape. It was painted by Allan Stewart in the early twentieth century. (Stephen Porter)

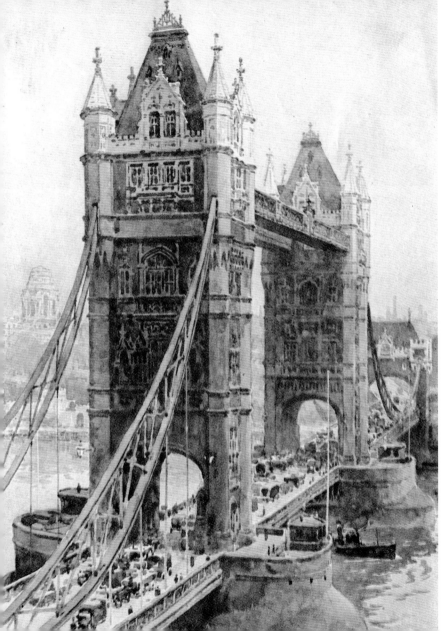

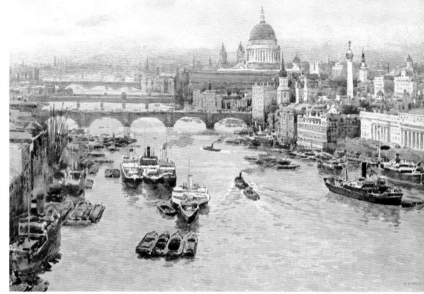

Above: 228. As well as being an eye-catching structure, Tower Bridge provided a new vantage point from which to view the river and the City, as E. W. Haslehust did for his painting in the early 1920s. (Stephen Porter)

Left: 229. By the early twentieth century Tower Bridge was carrying 5,000 vehicles and 20,000 pedestrians daily. (Stephen Porter)

15

THE ROYAL EXCHANGE

The Royal Exchange is the third building on the site, between Cornhill and Threadneedle Street, its predecessors having been destroyed by fire. The first building was erected in 1568 on the initiative of Sir Thomas Gresham, a freeman and member of the Mercers' Company, whose family's business traded through Antwerp. He also acted on the government's behalf there and visited the city intermittently until 1567.

Gresham's model for the London building was the first purpose-built bourse, opened in Antwerp in 1531. In 1565 he proposed to the City that he would pay the costs of a similar building, if it would obtain the site. The City agreed and acquired property, and Sir Thomas appointed the Antwerp mason Hendryck van Paesschen to undertake the work, which was completed in December 1568. In January 1571 Elizabeth I visited the building and, according to John Stow, 'shee caused the same Bursse by an Herauld and a Trumpet, to be proclamed the Royal Exchange, and so to be called from thenceforth, and not otherwise'.

The merchants met in the courtyard, in groups according to the region or city with which they were trading. The Swiss visitor Thomas Platter noted that 'several hundred may be found assembled twice daily'. The courtyard was also a centre for the delivery of letters and messages, and for hearing news from overseas. The gallery and the storey above it, known as the Pawn and the Upper Pawn, contained 120 shops. During the early seventeenth century a quarter of the tenants were haberdashers and just over a tenth were mercers, with painter-stainers, merchant-tailors, clothworkers, grocers, leather-sellers and stationers the other most numerous occupiers. The Royal Exchange was a great success and fulfilled Gresham's objective, providing both a meeting place for the merchant community and a shopping centre in the heart of the City.

The building was completely destroyed by the Great Fire. Its swift rebuilding was a priority and was entrusted to Edward Jerman, one of the City's Surveyors. Charles II laid the first stone on 23 October 1667, but some delays ensued and the merchants were not able to occupy the new building until September 1669; the shopkeepers could not move in until March 1671. Jerman's design was based on the earlier building, with an arcaded courtyard, and an elaborate street front with a lofty tower at its centre.

The costs were shared between the City and the Mercers' Company, and contributed to the company's growing financial problems, exacerbated by the difficulty of finding tenants for the shops in the Exchange. The solution was to take corporate tenants for the Pawns: the Corporation of the Mines Royal and Mineral and Battery Works in 1719 (insuring ships and merchandise), the Royal Exchange Assurance in 1721 and Lloyd's in 1774. The Exchange remained a centre for the dissemination of news and information, and hence a focus for publishers and booksellers who occupied premises in and around Cornhill. The arrangements for the merchants were as before. A list of 'the several Walks for Merchants' of 1712 listed fifteen countries or regions and a later plan showed nineteen, plus seven groups identified by the commodities that they traded.

The second Royal Exchange met the same fate as the first, when a fire began in the Lloyd's rooms on 10 January 1838 and spread throughout the buildings. Again the Joint Committee of the City and Mercers Company moved quickly, obtaining an Act of Parliament for rebuilding in August. But not until May 1840 was a design adopted, by Sir William Tite; the government's attempt to have a say in the choice of the design, because of the building's public significance, was repulsed. Work did not begin until four years after the fire and the new building was opened by Queen Victoria and Prince Albert in October 1844.

The site had been considerably enlarged and the outlay in buying the additional premises exceeded the construction costs. The new Exchange is larger than the two earlier buildings. Clearance of the space to the west of the building allowed Tite to create a grand entrance front, with a Corinthian portico with eight tall columns. The east front has four Corinthian columns supporting a clock tower, which carries a weathervane, in the shape of the grasshopper which is the Gresham symbol and is

from the second Exchange. Within the building, Tite followed the previous layout of an open rectangular courtyard surrounded by a wide ambulatory. In 1883–84 the courtyard was roofed over.

New statues were commissioned, of Queen Victoria and Prince Albert, and Elizabeth I; a copy of Grinling Gibbons's statue of Charles II was also installed. Queen Victoria's statue weathered so badly that it was destroyed in 1891 and replaced by a new one by Sir Hamo Thornycroft. In the niches on the Threadneedle Street front are statues of Sir Richard Whittington and Sir Hugh Myddleton, and the east front niche has one of Sir Thomas Gresham. A special feature of the building is paintings, by a number of artists, which were installed between 1895 and 1922 in the panels around the ambulatory. They illustrate episodes from English history, but lack any clear theme.

The Exchange's pre-eminence for trading in the City was gradually eroded by the specialist exchanges in Mark Lane and Mincing Lane and at the Baltic Exchange. By the 1890s the foreign exchange dealers were the main group still doing business in the courtyard. London Assurance occupied a part of the building from 1845, but moved out in 1922, as did Lloyd's, in 1928, and general trading was ended in 1939.

In 1982 a temporary building was erected in the courtyard for the London International Financial Futures Exchange (LIFFE). It ceased business there in 1991 and the building was then refurbished. The commercial and social life of the courtyard revived, with shops and restaurants. And so the bourse, which epitomised the commercial revolution, has been succeeded by businesses that are manifestations of the retail revolution.

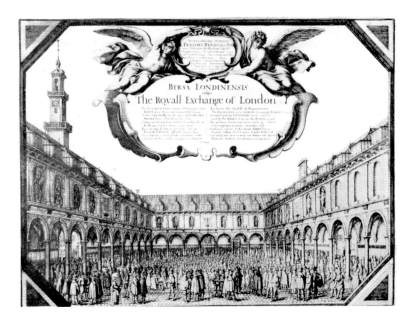

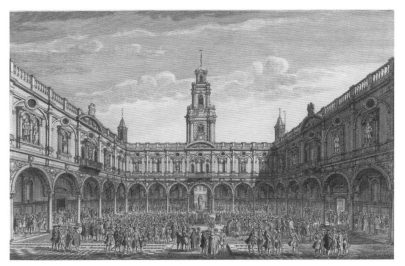

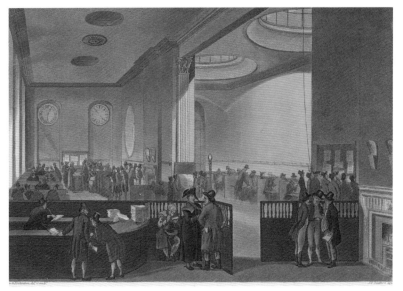

Above left: 230. The first Royal Exchange was erected at Sir Thomas Gresham's expense and opened in 1568 as both a meeting place for the merchant community and a shopping centre. It was destroyed by the Great Fire. (Stephen Porter)

Above right: 231. The Royal Exchange as rebuilt after the Great Fire. Thomas Bowles around 1750 shows the courtyard and ambulatory very crowded with merchants, gathered in groups according to the region of their trade. (Yale Center for British Art, Paul Mellon Collection)

Right: 232. Lloyd's Subscription Room in the Royal Exchange, where the insurance underwriters conducted their business after they had moved into the building in 1774. (Yale Center for British Art, Gift of Chauncey Brewster Tinker)

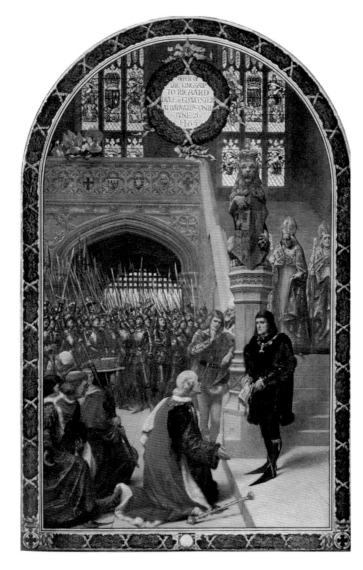

Left: 233. Among the scenes from English history chosen as appropriate for the murals to decorate the ambulatory of the Royal Exchange was the offer of the crown to Richard, Duke of Gloucester, at Baynard's Hall on 26 June 1483. By Sigismund Goetze, it was presented in 1898. (Jonathan Reeve, JR1569b13fp718 14501500)

Right: 234. The second Royal Exchange building was destroyed by fire in 1838 and its successor, designed by Sir William Tite, was erected between 1842 and 1844. Clearance of the space to the west allowed Tite to create a grand entrance front, with a Corinthian portico with eight tall columns, seen here around 1912. (Stephen Porter)

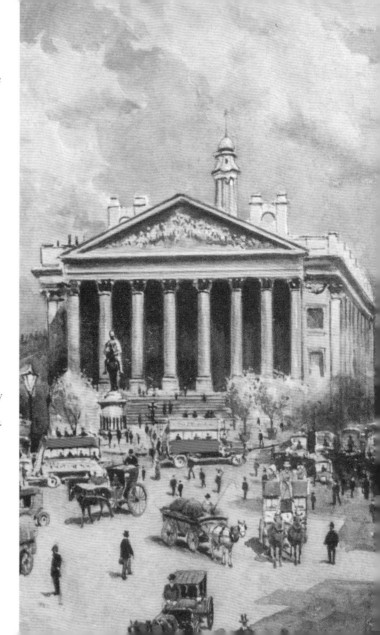

16

THE BANK OF ENGLAND

The Bank of England was established in 1694 as part of the government's efforts to meet the costs of the war against France, which began following the accession of William III and Mary II in 1689. By an Act of Parliament of 1693 creditors who lent to the government were to be repaid from a separate exchequer fund raised on a specific part of the excise, and on the security of Parliament, not on the pledge of the king. This scheme, proposed by Charles Montagu, was the beginning of the national debt and was followed by a project devised by William Paterson and Michael Godfrey, City merchants, for a national bank. Montagu was appointed Chancellor of the Exchequer in April 1694 and piloted the necessary legislation through Parliament. The Tonnage Act of April 1694 provided for a loan of £1.2 million, with interest at 8 per cent payable from duties on shipping and alcohol. Subscribers were to be incorporated as a bank and given power to borrow further sums on the security of parliamentary taxation, and the bank could deal in bullion and bills of exchange, and issue paper money. The full amount was quickly raised and on 27 July 1694 Britain's first joint-stock bank was incorporated as the Governor and Company of the Bank of England.

The first governor was Sir John Houblon, one of seven of the initial twenty-four directors who were of Huguenot descent, as were almost 10 per cent of the subscribers. The Bank was a Whig creation, opposed by some leading Tories, who created a rival land bank. The Bank survived that challenge and the frantic speculation of the South Sea Bubble, which burst in 1720.

The Bank was accommodated initially at the Mercers' Hall in Cheapside and then at the Grocers' Hall off Poultry. When the Bank came to choose a site for a new building, Houblon's mansion on the north side of Threadneedle Street was selected and the Bank's architect, George Sampson, designed a building with an imposing Palladian façade. Erected in 1732–34, this was the first Palladian-style building in the City.

The scale of the Bank's business increased during the eighteenth century, especially during the wars against France. Initially it had fifty-four employees, but a hundred years later the number had risen to 300, and by 1813 it employed 800 clerks. The building was enlarged between 1765 and 1788 by the addition of single-storey wings on both sides of the 1730s block, so that it occupied the whole of the frontage on Threadneedle Street and Prince's Street. Because of the need for security, the outer walls were windowless and within the east wing were four top-lit banking halls arranged on three sides of a rotunda, which served as the stock exchange for consols (Consolidated Government

Annuities) until the governor closed it to stockbrokers in 1838.

By the late eighteenth century the Bank's functions had expanded. It received subscriptions to state loans and managed the national debt, acted as the government's bank and the bankers' bank, made loans to other chartered companies, served as a conventional bank for individuals and institutions, was the holder of bullion, which it supplied to the Royal Mint, and issued its banknotes, which were printed on the premises.

During the wars with France between 1793 and 1815 the Bank's business again increased considerably and so the site was enlarged to the north as far as Lothbury. In 1788 Sir John Soane was appointed architect and surveyor; he held the post until 1833. During that time he rebuilt the Bank in three main phases, replacing most of the existing buildings, including the front to Threadneedle Street. Soane surrounded the whole site with a screen wall. It was necessarily without windows, but added greatly to the architectural grandeur of this part of the City, for Soane based his design upon the Temple of Vesta at Tivoli; the north-west corner was designated Tivoli Corner.

The Bank was sometimes referred to as the Bank of London, but its more common nickname was 'The Old Lady of Threadneedle Street'. That came from a cartoon by James Gillray of 1797, which shows William Pitt, the prime minister, making an amorous advance to the old lady, who is seated on a strongbox marked 'Bank of England'.

The need for security had been emphasised during the Gordon Riots in 1780, when demonstrators were repelled by a detachment of soldiers. In the aftermath of the riots, a detachment of the guards, known as the Bank Picquet, was stationed at the Bank every night. The City objected to the picquet, because it infringed its liberties and, more practically, its arrival each evening at a busy time added to the congestion in the streets around the Bank. The congestion worsened considerably, but the picquet continued to guard the buildings until 1973.

The Victorians came to dislike Soane's cool neoclassical interiors. But it was the Bank's expanding business and growing international role, rather than architectural taste, which prompted another rebuilding. That was carried out between 1925 and 1942, with Sir Herbert Baker as architect, and was achieved by the erection of taller buildings within Soane's curtain walls. The front has a huge portico of coupled columns, incorporating six giant figures and, in the pediment, a relief of the Old Lady, balancing the old building on her knee, with a pile of coins beside her. The curtain wall was retained, but with changes to Tivoli Corner, and many of the elements from the eighteenth- and nineteenth-century buildings were reproduced, although not faithfully, including the rotunda, banking halls, the court room and committee room.

The new buildings did indeed provide the extra space required as the Bank evolved into a modern central bank. Nationalised in 1946, it is responsible for managing the national debt and the government's gold and foreign currency reserves, and its role in implementing monetary policy was augmented when, in 1997, it was given the responsibility to set interest rates.

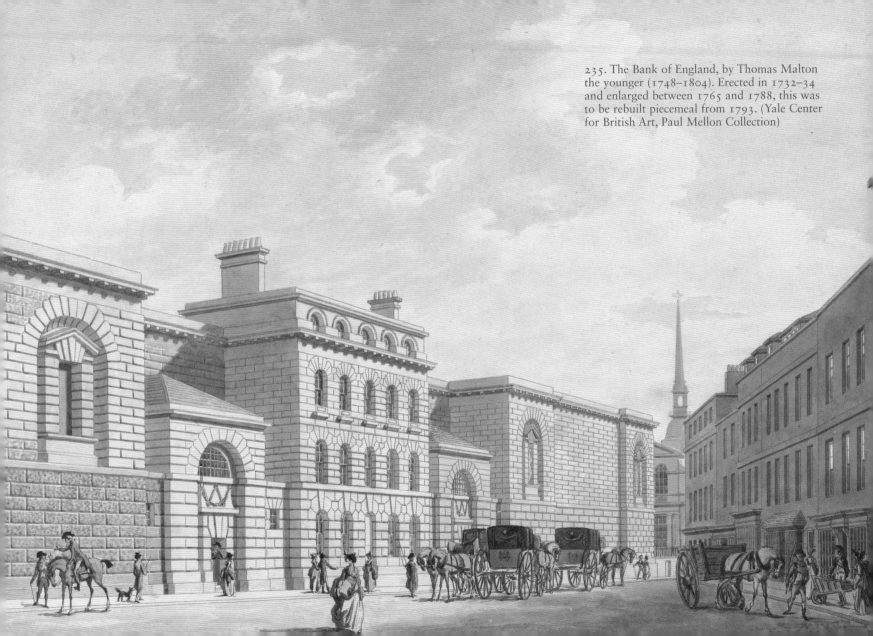

235. The Bank of England, by Thomas Malton the younger (1748–1804). Erected in 1732–34 and enlarged between 1765 and 1788, this was to be rebuilt piecemeal from 1793. (Yale Center for British Art, Paul Mellon Collection)

17

THE STOCK EXCHANGE

Commercial expansion and the development of the London money market in the late seventeenth century saw the emergence of a group of men who specialised in trading in stocks. They attracted criticism, particularly from landowners, for being among those members of the financial sector who were thought to be benefiting from the high taxation levied to finance the war against France. That was the background to the Act of Parliament of 1697 'to restrain the number and ill-practice of brokers and stock-jobbers', which limited their number to 100. They had to be licensed, and unauthorised brokers could be fined up to £100 and made to stand in the pillory.

In 1698 stock dealers were expelled from the Royal Exchange because of their rowdy behaviour and operated instead in the coffee houses in and around Exchange Alley, especially at Jonathan's. From there, in that year John Castaing first issued a list of stock and commodity prices called 'The Course of the Exchange and other things'. A number of stockbrokers and jobbers formed a club at Jonathan's in 1761, for buying and selling shares. A few years later, in 1773, a group of brokers bought a building at the corner of Threadneedle Street and Sweeting's Alley, which they designated the Stock Exchange. When disputes between the members broke out in 1801, a number of them separated and

acquired the site of Mendoza's boxing saloon in Capel Court, off Bartholomew Lane. There they erected the first purpose-built stock exchange, which contained a large room where trading was conducted, with a gallery for the clerks.

In 1812 the first rulebook was introduced. Visitors were not admitted and members were not allowed to advertise. From 550 members in 1801, the number rose to more than 800 by the mid-nineteenth century and 5,500 by 1905. The premises were enlarged accordingly, in 1853–54 and again in 1882–87, but the building's only frontage was that of the general offices facing Old Broad Street.

The London Stock Exchange enforced a division between brokers and jobbers. The former bought and sold for clients, taking a commission, while the latter traded on behalf of the brokers, making their profit on the difference between the buying and selling prices. In the 1960s a replacement building was erected and was opened in 1972, with longer street frontages, and including a twenty-six-storey office block.

A period of considerable change followed. Women were admitted to the trading floor in 1973, and in that year the London Stock Exchange merged with the provincial exchanges and the Dublin Exchange. With the deregulation of 1986, known as Big Bang, the London Stock Exchange became a private limited company, the distinction between brokers and jobbers was removed, member firms could be owned by an outside corporation, and face-to-face trading on the floor was replaced by dealing by computer and telephone. The large trading floor was therefore redundant and was converted to office space. The building was closed in 2004, when the Stock Exchange was moved to Paternoster Square.

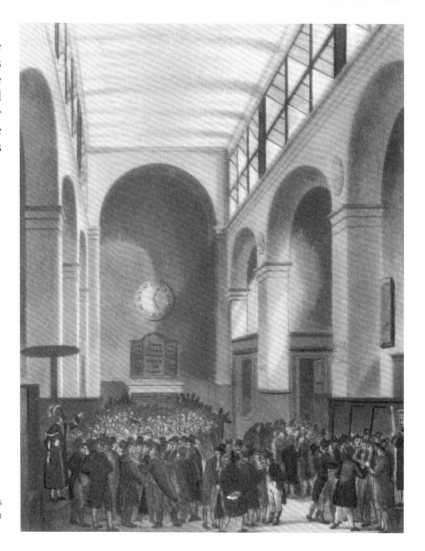

236. The Stock Exchange around 1808, by Thomas Rowlandson and Augustus Pugin, shows the crowded trading room in the Capel Court building erected a few years earlier to the designs of James Peacock. (Stephen Porter)

18

FLEET STREET AND TEMPLE BAR

Fleet Street lies within the City, continuing the line of Ludgate Hill. It was mentioned in 1002. Because of the number of newspapers which had their offices there, its name was long used to describe the British newspaper industry, which was largely based there from around 1825 until the late 1980s. The street was previously noted as a centre of literary London, and for printing, taverns and banks.

Wynkyn de Worde, who had worked with William Caxton, took premises there in 1500–01, beginning its connection with the printing trade. Other printers followed, and so the area became attractive to publishers and literary figures, including Samuel Johnson and Oliver Goldsmith. In 1768 John McMurray acquired a bookseller's premises at No.32, and subsequently changed his name to Murray. He and his son, also John, developed the business into the publishers John Murray, and published, most famously, the works of Lord Byron. In 1812 the business was moved to Albermarle Street, but around 1840 the street still contained several booksellers and map publishers.

The *Daily Courant*, the first regular daily newspaper, began publication in the street in 1702, but Fleet Street's development as the centre of the news industry is usually dated from the establishment of the *Morning Advertiser* in 1825. By 1879, six daily and seventy-three weekly titles were published in Fleet Street and the adjoining side streets and courts. As well as national titles, such as the *Daily Telegraph*, founded in 1866, and the *Daily Express*, established in 1900, a number of provincial newspapers had their London offices there. By the late 1980s technical changes and the outcome of struggles between the newspaper companies and the print unions led to the removal of the newspaper offices and printing works from the street, but they left a fascinating architectural legacy.

In 1791 the printer J. S. Jordan, at No. 166, undertook to publish Thomas Paine's *The Rights of Man*, after another printer had become alarmed at the possible reaction that it may provoke. The book justifies the French Revolution and presents the case for political reform, and over 100,000 copies were sold within two years. Journals published in the district included *Punch*, the *Political Register*, first issued in Bolt Court in 1802, *John Bull*, a scurrilous yet influential publication begun in 1820 that had Queen Caroline as its principal target, and *The Satirist*, launched in 1831. The street had a connection with nineteenth-century radicalism through the headquarters there of two leading political organisations, the Chartists and the Anti-Corn Law League. Among the less contentious organisations were the antiquarian society, which first met in the Mitre Tavern in 1717 and continued as the Society of Antiquaries of London, the Royal Society, which held its meetings at Crane Court from 1710 until 1780, and the Philosophical Society.

Fleet Street also became a centre for banking and insurance. As banking developed in the late seventeenth and early eighteenth centuries, two groups of London banks emerged. One was centred on Lombard Street and served the mercantile community, and the second consisted of the so-called West End banks, in Fleet Street and the Strand, whose customers were chiefly the aristocracy and landed gentry. The prominent banks included Blanchard & Child at Temple Bar, later designated Child's Bank. Francis Child was the dominant partner and is recognised as 'the father of the profession'. Richard Hoare's banking house 'at the sign of the Golden Bottle' was established in Fleet Street in 1690; its business rose fourfold in value between 1725 and 1785. The third of the major Fleet Street banks was Goslings. Francis Gosling was a bookseller and printer, who joined the firm in 1742 and gave it his name. Its business reflected his background, with customers among the local publishers and authors. Both Goslings and Child's had links with the East India Company, as well as among the landed sector. In the nineteenth and early twentieth centuries a number of insurance companies erected new buildings in the street, especially after it was widened when virtually the whole of its south side was rebuilt between 1897 and 1916.

Fleet Street formed part of the ceremonial route through the City from Westminster, and was a favourite place for political processions and demonstrations, focused on Temple Bar, which stood on the boundary between the City and Westminster. The Bar may have consisted originally of a chain slung between wooden posts, but by the mid-fourteenth century this had been replaced by gates and a wooden structure. New battlements were added for the coronation of Edward VI in 1547 and new gates were made in 1554. The Great Fire of London in 1666 did not spread so far west, but Charles II insisted that the corporation replace the old structure, as part of the process of improving the City in the fire's aftermath. The new one, erected in 1672, to Christopher Wren's designs, is a triumphal arch in Portland stone. No other point along the City's boundaries was marked in this way, but Temple Bar was special because it was the point on the ceremonial route where the sovereign was greeted by the lord mayor before entering the City.

Temple Bar was not taken down when the City's gates were demolished in 1761, but came to be regarded as contributing to traffic congestion, and it was no longer seen as an attractive structure. It survived a campaign in 1853 for its removal, but was taken down in 1878 and re-erected at Theobald's Park, Hertfordshire. A memorial designed by Sir Horace Jones replaced it in 1880.

Although the Bar had been preserved, there was a growing feeling that the location was inappropriate, coupled with concerns about its condition. In 1976 the Temple Bar Trust was formed, with the purpose of returning the Bar to the City. Eventually, in 1998 Sir William Whitfield included it in his scheme for the new Paternoster Square and in November 2004 the restored Bar was officially opened at the entrance to the square, facing St Paul's.

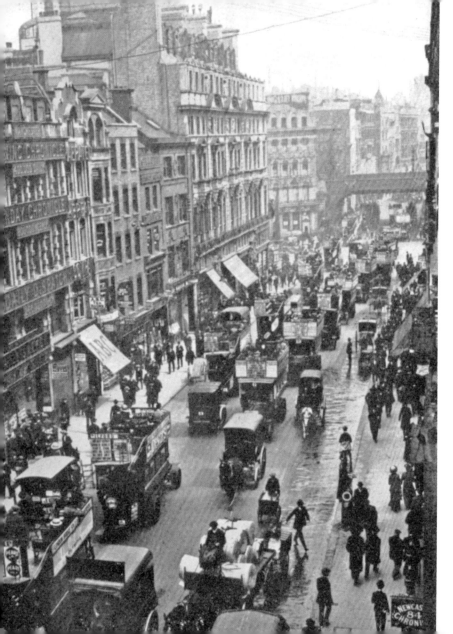

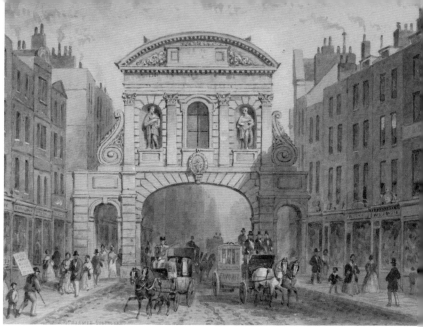

Above: 237. Thomas Hosmer Shepherd's depiction of a busy street scene at Temple Bar in the mid-nineteenth century. (Yale Center for British Art, Paul Mellon Collection)

Left: 238. Fleet Street looking east towards Ludgate Circus in the early twentieth century; its busy traffic contains a mixture of horse-drawn and motorised vehicles. (Stephen Porter)

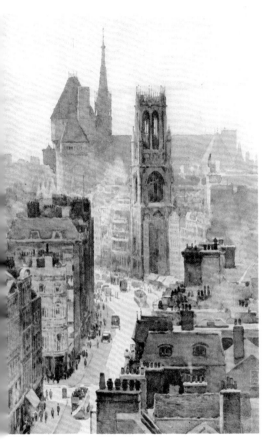

239. Fleet Street looking west to the Royal Courts of Justice building of 1874–82, with the tall lantern of the church of St Dunstan in the West, built in 1831–33 to the designs of John Shaw; it was the last of the City's medieval churches to be rebuilt. The painting is by E. W. Haslehust, around 1924. (Stephen Porter)

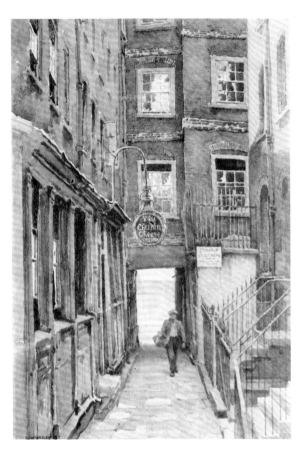

240. Wine Office Court, Fleet Street, at the side of the Old Cheshire Cheese, which was formed from two late seventeenth-century houses, with an eighteenth-century shopfront. Its side entrance and the court are shown in this painting by E. W. Haslehust around 1924. (Stephen Porter)

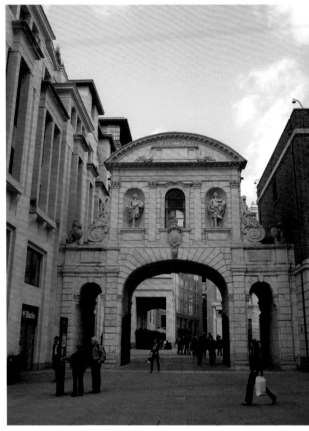

241. Temple Bar was taken down in 1878, re-erected in Theobald's Park and in the early twenty-first century it was moved to the entrance of the new Paternoster Square and opened in 2004. (Stephen Porter)

19

THE TEMPLE

The name is derived from the Knights Templar, formed in the early twelfth century to protect pilgrims visiting the holy sites in Palestine, following its conquest by the Crusaders. A part of the building granted them in Jerusalem stood on the site of Solomon's Temple and they took the name of Poor Fellow-Soldiers of Christ of the Temple of Solomon.

Their first site in London was at the junction of Chancery Lane and Holborn, acquired in the early twelfth century, where they built one of their characteristic round churches, in Caen stone. They moved to a much larger site between Fleet Street and the Thames around 1160, where their round church was consecrated in 1185. In 1240 a rectangular chancel or choir on its east side was consecrated, giving the church its distinctive keyhole shape. A cloister probably was built on its south side, with the clergy's quarters to the east and those of the lay brothers to the west, between the church and Middle Temple Lane.

The Crusader kingdoms of Outremer came under increasing military pressure during the thirteenth century and Jerusalem was captured by the Muslims. The kingdoms were finally extinguished in 1291 and with the loss of the holy places the order was deprived of its principal role. But it had also developed basic banking functions, safeguarding money and valuables and moving them across Europe. The Temple in London held the valuables of Henry III's queen, Eleanor of Provence, among others, and was raided in 1283 by their son, Edward I, who went away with £1,000 from the coffers of those who had deposited money there.

Shorn of their original purpose, the Templars were an obvious target for Philip IV of France when he sought ways to raise money. In 1307 he ordered their arrest throughout France, charging them with sacrilege, idolatry and sodomy. In 1308 Edward II seized the Templars' property in England. The Pope suppressed the order in 1312, at the Council of Vienne. Its assets were assigned to the Knights of St John, known as the Knights Hospitaller. The Temple was attacked during the Peasants' Revolt in 1381, when the rebels 'plucked down the houses and lodgings' and burned documents and books in the street.

William Shakespeare drew upon the earlier Tudor chroniclers when he placed the beginnings of the dispute between the houses of York and Lancaster, which ultimately led to the Wars of the Roses, in the Temple garden: 'Within the Temple Hall we were too loud; The garden here is more convenient.' Here the leaders of the two factions picked red and white roses as their emblems.

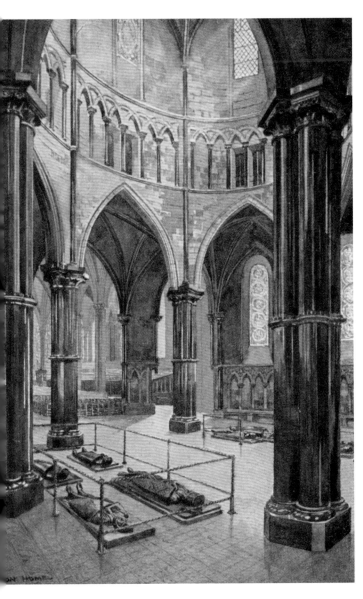

Left: 242. The circular church of the Knights Templar, modelled on the church of the Holy Sepulchre in Jerusalem and consecrated in 1185 by the patriarch of Jerusalem. Depicted by Gordon Home around 1924. (Stephen Porter)

Right: 243. Fountain Court in the Temple around 1912; the court gained its name from what was said to have been the first permanent fountain in London, placed there in 1681. (Stephen Porter)

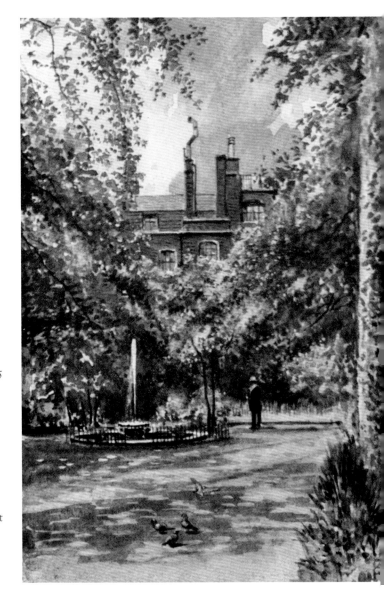

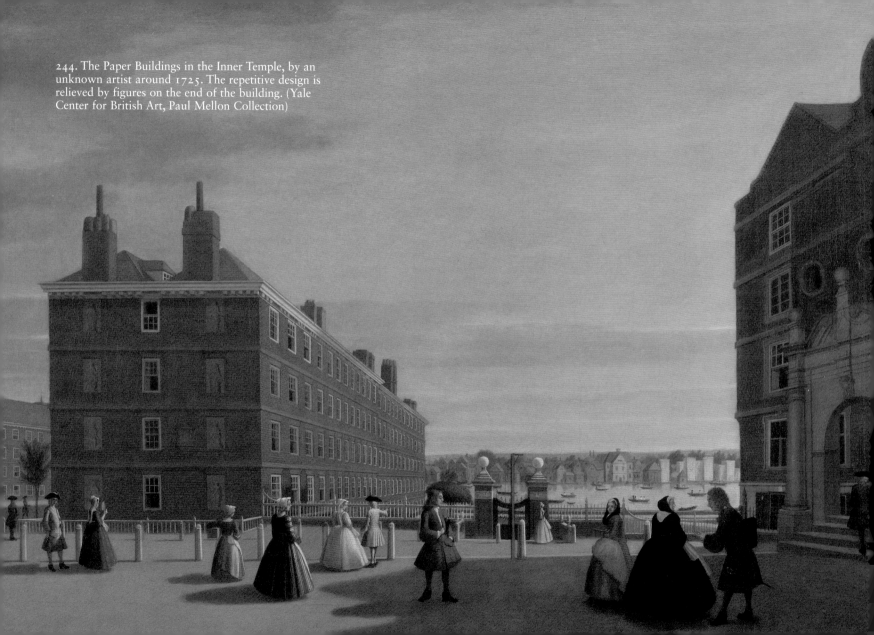

244. The Paper Buildings in the Inner Temple, by an unknown artist around 1725. The repetitive design is relieved by figures on the end of the building. (Yale Center for British Art, Paul Mellon Collection)

20

THE INNS OF COURT

The four Inns of Court evolved in the fourteenth and fifteenth centuries as groups of lawyers in what became London's legal quarter, to the west of the City. In 1326, or earlier, the Knights Hospitaller at the Temple granted property there to a body of lawyers and around 1356 other premises in the precinct were granted to another group. The Middle Temple was mentioned in 1404 and the Inner Temple in 1440, although it may be that the two societies were separate from the first property grants in the previous century. The Inner Temple came to occupy the eastern part of the site and the Middle Temple the western part, up to and beyond Middle Temple Lane. The two societies were allowed to remain after the Knights Hospitaller were suppressed in 1539.

Lincoln's Inn, on the west side of Chancery Lane, may have originated in a group of lawyers that formed at the mansion of Henry de Lacy, 3rd Earl of Lincoln, who died in 1311, on the site of the Dominican priory in Shoe Lane. He was regarded as the founder of the inn, but another society of lawyers was formed at property on the east side of Chancery Lane, acquired by Thomas de Lincoln, the King's Serjeant, between 1331 and 1334. This society was referred to as Lyncolnesynne and may have come into being independently, or perhaps had transferred from the Earl of Lincoln's mansion; it moved across Chancery Lane into the Bishop of Chichester's mansion, between 1415 and 1422, the year in which the inn's records begin.

The fourth Inn is Gray's Inn, to the north of Holborn, where a community of lawyers had formed by 1388 and perhaps earlier, for in 1370 the manor house was described as a hostel. The lawyers were tenants of the de Grey family until the property was sold in the early sixteenth century. In 1513 it was acquired by the priory of Sheen, in Surrey. At the dissolution of the priory in 1539 it passed to the Crown and in 1541 was granted by Henry VIII to the community.

The Inns not only trained men for the law but were also attended by young gentlemen and members of the aristocracy, typically for no more than two years, to study the common law and as part of their general social and intellectual education. This became common after the mid-sixteenth century and by the early seventeenth century roughly 90 per cent of those admitted to the Inner and Middle Temple were ranked as gentlemen or higher, while Grays's Inn was regarded as the most aristocratic of the Inns, with connections to the court and government circles.

The annual average admissions to the Inner and Middle Temple in the 1510s numbered twenty-seven; a century later the figure was 110. At Lincoln's Inn over the same period the annual average rose from twelve to fifty-eight; in Elizabeth I's reign the inn contained 104 chambers and around 200 members during term time and in 1598 John Stow wrote that it was 'lately increased with fair buildings, and replenished with gentlemen studious in the common laws'. Gray's Inn saw the number of annual admissions rise from eighteen during the 1520s to sixty-two during the last forty years of the century, and by the 1620s it was 116. They drew some of their students from the eight Inns of Chancery, which gave initial training to lawyers, and developed an affiliation with particular Inns of Court and so prospered during the period when admissions to them were high.

During the early seventeenth century Lincoln's Inn became a focus for London's puritans, with the chapel frequently full to overflowing, partly due to the influence of John Preston (1587–1628), who succeeded John Donne as preacher in 1622. A new chapel was built in 1619–23, with the chapel above an undercroft at ground level, which was intended to be a meeting place for lawyers and their clients, and for the students. The chapel at Gray's Inn was also rebuilt, in 1619–24; its hall had been built in 1556–58 and the hall at the Middle Temple in 1562–70. All of the Inns erected new buildings during the years of high admissions.

The Inns experienced a decline in numbers after the mid-seventeenth century. By the first decade of the eighteenth century the annual average number of admissions had fallen to fifty at the Middle and Inner Temples and averaged twenty-five at Lincoln's Inn. Attendance by the sons of the aristocracy and gentlemen became less common. Furthermore, attempts to restrict membership to the barristers and exclude members of the junior branches of the legal profession, the attorneys and solicitors, gradually became effective. The number of admissions continued to be low throughout the eighteenth century, but all of the Inns revived in the nineteenth century. During the Second World War bomb damage at Gray's Inn was extensive and almost a half of the Temple was destroyed, requiring extensive restoration and replacement.

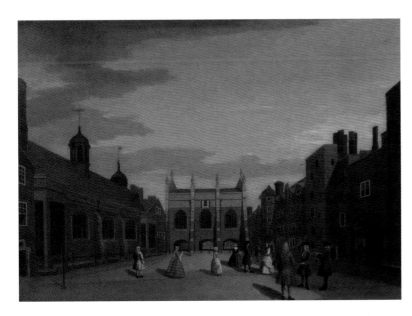

Above: 245. The chapel, gateway and old hall in Lincoln's Inn, by an unknown artist, around 1730. (Yale Center for British Art, Paul Mellon Collection)

Right: 246. The inner side of Lincoln's Inn's gateway to Chancery Lane, built in 1517–21 by Sir Thomas Lovell, Speaker of the House of Commons. Depicted by Gordon Home, around 1924. (Stephen Porter)

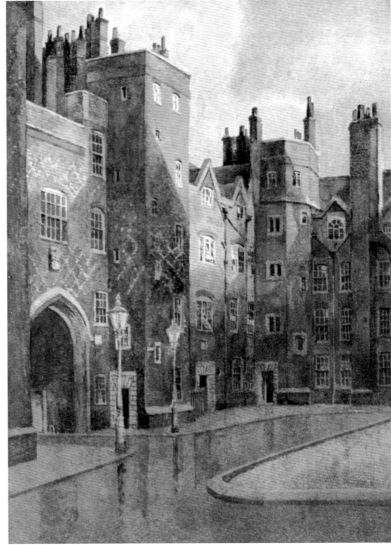

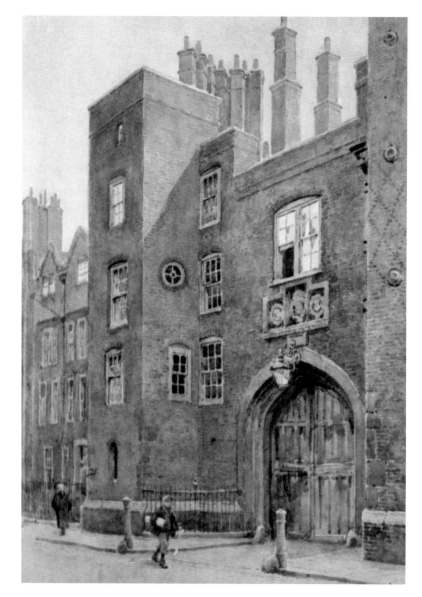

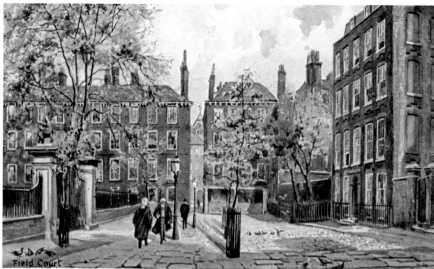

Above: 247. A community of lawyers formed at Gray's Inn during the late fourteenth century. Field Court consisted of mainly eighteenth century buildings; the gateway on the left opens into the Walks. It was depicted by Charles F. Flower around 1910. (Stephen Porter)

Left: 248. The gatehouse of Lincoln's Inn, in Chancery Lane. Henry de Lacy, 3rd Earl of Lincoln, who died in 1311 and whose mansion stood on the site, was regarded as the founder of the inn and his arms were placed on the gatehouse, together with those of Lovell and Henry VIII. Painted by E. W. Haslehust around 1924. (Stephen Porter)

21

SMITHFIELD

The name is a corruption of Smooth Field. The large open space was used for sports, including archery and football, and combats and tournaments. St Bartholomew's fair was established in 1123 by Rahere, founder of St Bartholomew's priory, and was held on the three days centred on St Bartholomew's Day, 24 August, but the period gradually became longer until it lasted for two weeks. In 1708 and again in 1750 the City issued orders to restrict it to three days. The fair was very successful. It became the greatest cloth market in medieval England and leather, pewter, livestock, and butter and cheese were also traded there. The fair was also noted for the entertainments provided by puppeteers, conjurers, players, balladeers, wrestlers, tightrope walkers, fire-eaters and actors. But it was also associated with cheating, petty crime and immorality and became roundly condemned. Its importance to the cloth trade declined after the sixteenth century and many of the other trading functions gradually came to an end. As society became less tolerant and respectability gained ground, denunciations increased and those who went to the fair were disapproved of as idle and dissolute. In 1839 it was limited to just two days and other restrictions were imposed, which led to its steady decline. The last fair was held in 1855.

Smithfield's weekly horse market and its cattle and sheep markets were the largest in the country, with livestock driven long distances to be sold. In 1614–15 the area was drained and paved. But messiness and stench were inevitable in an area used for livestock and hay markets and containing slaughterhouses and stables. The malodorous consequences became offensive to sensitive tastes and, as the suburbs grew, the market, once on the edge of the city, came to be at its centre. The inconveniences of driving animals through the outer areas and the conditions in the markets added to the growing clamour for change and in June 1855 the market at Smithfield was closed. In 1867–68 a meat market was erected there, designed by the city architect, Horace Jones. It was praised, especially for the extensive use of attractive ironwork and the skilfully designed louvred roof, which allows air to circulate but prevents the sun's rays from falling directly into the building. The design produced a cool atmosphere, ideal for the storage of meat.

Smithfield was also known as a place of execution; the Scottish patriot Sir William Wallace was executed there in August 1305. It was the site of executions by burning, for heresy, arson, poisoning, witchcraft, sodomy and bestiality, and for women guilty of high treason or murdering their husbands. Executions for heresy were carried out there from the late fourteenth century, with the Lollards the principal victims in the fifteenth century. But the Protestant burnings during Mary I's reign made the deepest impression. The last person burned in England for religious beliefs was executed in 1612, but burning of those condemned for other crimes continued well into the seventeenth century.

249. *Bartholomew Fair* by Thomas Rowlandson, around 1808, shows the annual fair at Smithfield, which provided a range of entertainments and drew large numbers. The Baroque gateway of St Bartholomew's Hospital of 1702, designed by Edward Strong, is on the left and the tower of St Sepulchre's church is in the distance. (National Gallery of Art, Rosenwald Collection, acc. 1945.5.1227)

Opposite: 250. Smithfield held the country's most important horse market; it was depicted in 1824 by the Swiss artist Jacques-Laurent Agasse, who specialised in animal paintings. In the foreground a grey horse's qualities are being subject to a thorough examination. (Yale Center for British Art, Paul Mellon Collection)

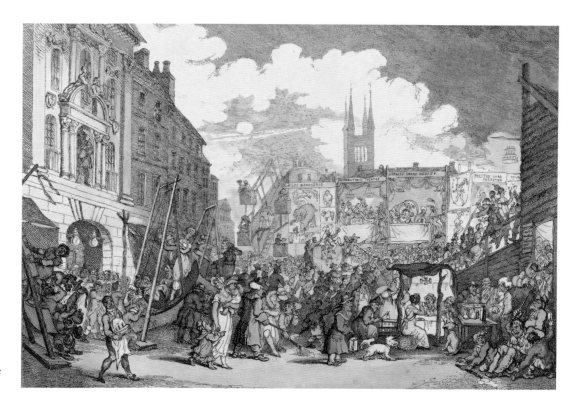

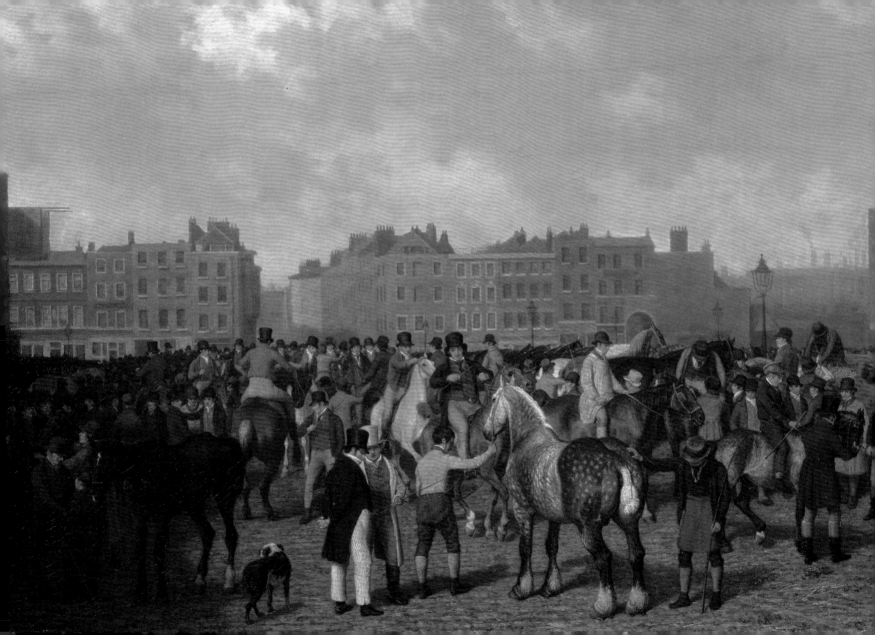

22

THE CHARTERHOUSE

The Charterhouse has been a monastery, aristocratic house and an almshouse and school. The site was acquired by Sir Walter de Mauny in 1349 as a burial ground for victims of the Black Death. The chapel which he built there became the church of a Carthusian priory which he founded in 1371. That was the largest of the nine Carthusian priories in medieval England. Initially a 'double house' of twenty-four monks and a prior, by 1534 it housed the prior, procurator, twenty-five monks, twenty-one priests, three professed religious (who had taken their vows but were not ordained), and thirteen lay brothers. But their opposition to Henry VIII's plans to make himself head of the English Church saw sixteen of them lose their lives, through execution or imprisonment. The priory was suppressed in 1538.

After its dissolution parts of the buildings were incorporated in an impressive mansion built for Sir Edward North in 1545–46. In 1565 it was bought by Thomas, 4th Duke of Norfolk, who embellished and extended the buildings while he was there under house arrest, suspected of involvement in a plot to place Mary, Queen of Scots, on the throne. When the plot was unravelled by the government in 1571, Norfolk's role as leader of an insurrectionary force that was to cooperate with an invading Spanish army was revealed. Convicted of high treason, he was executed in June 1572.

In 1611 the buildings were bought from Norfolk's son Thomas Howard, Earl of Suffolk, by Thomas Sutton, reputedly the wealthiest commoner in England. He died later that year, but he had already overseen the establishment of an almshouse for eighty male pensioners, known as Brothers, and a school for forty foundation scholars. After his death the buildings were converted under the direction of Francis Carter. Sutton's legacy created the most lavishly endowed charity established between the Reformation and the foundation of Guy's Hospital in the 1720s. Its governors have included leading figures in Church and State, and a royal connection established under James I has continued to the present day.

The school was moved to Godalming in 1872 and its part of the site was occupied by the Merchant Taylors' School until 1933, when it was acquired for St Bartholomew's Medical College. In 1873 the Charterhouse school building, which incorporated Norfolk's tennis court, was demolished for the site of the Merchant Taylors' new school.

The almshouse remains, within the Tudor buildings, although they have been altered and augmented, and restored by the architects Seely & Paget after a blaze begun by a firebomb in May 1941 gutted much of the historic core. Their work was intended to recapture the appearance of the Tudor house by removing accretions of the eighteenth and nineteenth centuries. It emphasised the buildings' resemblance to the quad of an Oxford College; James Pope-Hennessy aptly described the Charterhouse as 'that piece of Oxford in London'. The most recent addition, in Preacher's Court, is the Admiral Ashmore Building, by Michael Hopkins & Partners, completed in 2000.

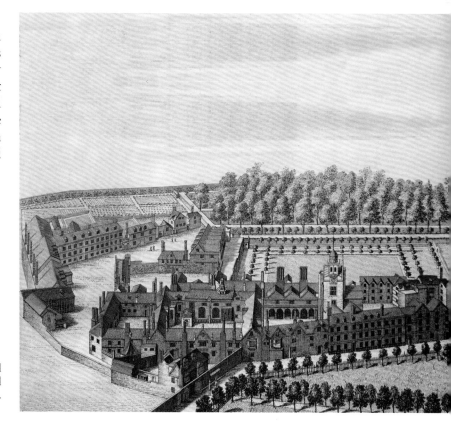

251. The buildings of the Carthusian priory in Clerkenwell were converted into a courtyard mansion in the 1540s and adapted as an almshouse and school in 1614. Johannes Kip's perspective view was drawn around 1688–94. (The Governors of Sutton's Hospital)

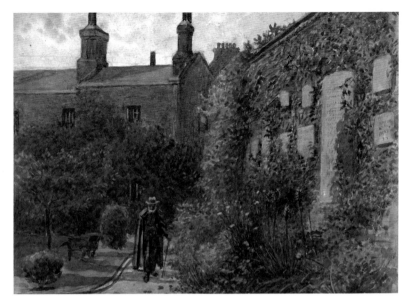

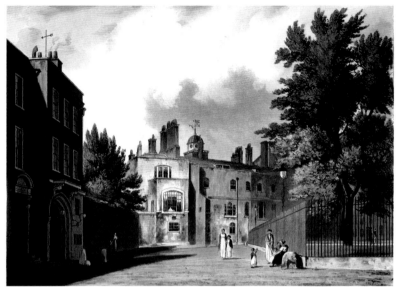

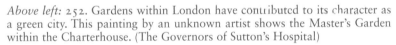

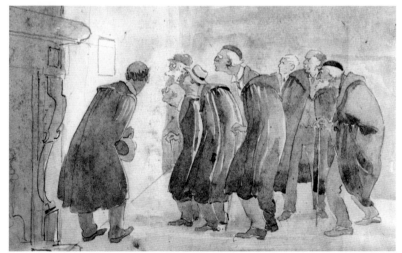

Above left: 252. Gardens within London have contributed to its character as a green city. This painting by an unknown artist shows the Master's Garden within the Charterhouse. (The Governors of Sutton's Hospital)

Above right: 253. The Charterhouse's gateway on the left of William Westall's painting is the early fifteenth-century gateway to the Carthusian priory, with an early eighteenth-century house both to the side and over it. Peeping above the other buildings is the distinctive Jacobean bell-turret. (The Governors of Sutton's Hospital)

Right: 254. 'What's for dinner?' The Brothers at the Charterhouse, established in 1611 by Thomas Sutton, peruse the menu with great interest, 1939, as shown by one of their number, Ronald Gray. (The Governors of Sutton's Hospital)

23

FROST FAIRS

The stone bridge erected over the Thames between 1176 and 1212 had only narrow gaps between the piers, which restricted the flow of water. From the late sixteenth century the current was further restricted by waterwheels in some of those gaps. The first one at the north end was constructed in 1580 by Pieter Morice, a Dutchman, whose 'artificial forcier' could deliver river water from the northern end of London Bridge as high as Leadenhall; eventually five were constructed at the north end and at the south end a wheel for grinding corn was put in place in 1591 and others were added later. The water above the bridge froze in severe winters, when the tidal stretch below the bridge remained open. A Londoner noted the difference in 1646: 'Noe water to be seene on westminster side of the bridge, only at the bridge, but on the tower side almost noe ice.'

Between 1408 and 1814 the Thames was recorded to have been frozen over in twenty-four winters, as the bridge prevented ice floes from passing downstream and so they blocked the passages between the starlings. When the ice was thick enough a frost fair was held. During the winter of 1683/84, the worst in the historical record, the Thames could be crossed by pedestrians for seven weeks and 'whole streets of Booths' were erected, visited by thousands of people. Oxen were roasted, 'Ale and Brandy and Gingerbread and Cakes' were sold, a printer set up his shop on the ice and coaches ran upstream to Lambeth and Vauxhall. The harsh winter of 1708/09 did not produce ice thick enough to support a frost fair, but one was held in 1715/16 and another in 1739/40, when the frost lasted for nine weeks. The last frost fair was held over four days in February 1814, when thirty booths were erected on the ice. As the climate warmed after the Little Ice Age of the sixteenth to eighteenth centuries, severe winters became fewer, and the flow of water was increased when the waterwheels were removed by an order of 1822, the medieval bridge was demolished in 1832 and the Victoria Embankment was constructed in the 1860s, so that the Thames no longer froze over.

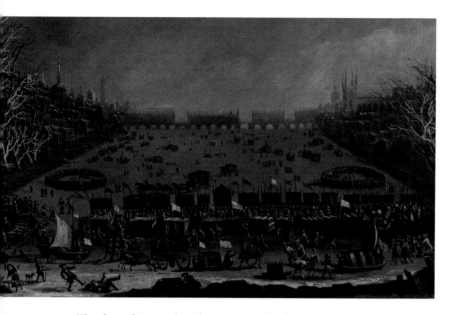

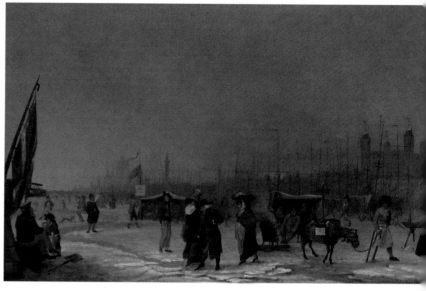

255. The frost fair on the Thames in 1684, looking downstream towards London Bridge. The painting shows the street of booths, carriages being driven and boats being hauled across the ice, and events which have attracted crowds of onlookers. The view was painted by an unknown artist. (Yale Center for British Art, Paul Mellon Collection)

256. The winter of 1788 was harsh enough to freeze the Thames and a frost fair was held on the ice. Unusually, the ice covered the Thames below London Bridge, as depicted by Samuel Collings. (Yale Center for British Art, Paul Mellon Collection)

24

COFFEE HOUSES AND GENTLEMEN'S CLUBS

Coffee houses were rapidly established as places for men to socialise, do business and exchange news and gossip, following the opening of the first such establishment by Pasqua Rosee in St Michael's Alley, off Cornhill, in 1652. According to Thomas Rugg, a barber in Covent Garden, by the end of the decade there was 'a Turkish drink to bee sould, almost in evry street, called coffee, and another kind of drink called tee, and also a drink called chacolate, which was a very harty drink'. Within ten years of the opening of Rosee's, the capital contained more than eighty coffee houses, and the number continued to increase until there were hundreds across the city. They came to form a part of the daily round for many Londoners and attracted a wide clientele, which varied in background and occupation, from district to district, and also at different times of the day.

Clubs were formed which met in the coffee and chocolate houses and taverns for dining and conviviality, with the members sharing common interests or enthusiasms, perhaps professional ones, or a political outlook. Some clubs had a distinguished membership and became well established. The Kit-Kat Club was begun at the very end of the seventeenth century and attracted the Whigs, the October Club was Tory, while those who attended the meetings at the Cocoa Tree Coffee House had Jacobite leanings. Clubs were exclusive, in contrast to coffee houses, which Isaac D'Israeli described as 'the common assemblies of all classes of society'. The Society of Dilettanti was formed in 1733 for young men who had been to Italy on the grand tour, which in itself restricted the potential membership, and they were to be 'noblemen or men of wealth and position', although Horace Walpole commented that the real qualification was that of having been drunk. Many clubs were small; the Literary Club founded by Samuel Johnson and Sir Joshua Reynolds in 1764 originally had twelve members and in 1780 its membership was limited to forty. Throughout the eighteenth century the clubs did not own the premises, which were in the hands of the proprietors, who profited from the food and drink consumed by their affluent clientele. As gambling became a feature of some clubs, especially from the 1770s, the proprietors advanced loans to the members, which provided further income. Francis White opened a chocolate house in St James's Street in 1693 where a club was formed; he died in 1711 but his widow continued the business and was succeeded in 1730 by John Arthur. A fire in 1733 caused a move to new premises and in 1736 the chocolate house became a private club, moving to its present site in St James's Street in 1755. White's was the club favoured by Tory, and later Conservative, politicians. St James's became the district where the more socially elevated clubs were based, convenient for the West End and Parliament, although there were only seven clubs in the district in the early nineteenth century. They included Almack's, established in 1764 in Pall Mall and moved in 1778 to St James's Street as Brooks's, and Boodle's, founded in the same street in 1762.

In the later eighteenth century the St James's clubs in particular came to be noted for the scale of the gambling in which their members indulged. Captain Rees Gronow wrote that the losses were such that they 'made ravages in large fortunes' and explained that at Brooks's 'for nearly half a century, the play was of a more gambling character than at White's. Faro and Macao were indulged in to an extent which enabled a man to win or lose a considerable fortune in one night.' Horace Walpole commented that at Brooks's 'a thousand meadows and cornfields are staked at every throw, and as many villages lost as in the earthquakes that overwhelmed Herculaneum and Pompeii'. The most notorious gambler in Brooks's, and at Newmarket, was the Whig politician Charles James Fox, whose father paid off no less than £120,000 of his gambling debts between 1772 and 1774.

By the early nineteenth century the coffee and chocolate houses were in decline. In 1817 d'Israeli noted that 'frequenting of coffee houses is a custom which has declined within our recollection, since institutions of a higher character, and society itself, has so much improved within late years'. But some of the clubs had become so exclusive that many felt left out, including John

Wilson Croker, who in 1823 wrote to the scientist Sir Humphry Davy bemoaning that 'the fashionable and Military Clubs not only absorb a great portion of society, but have spoiled all the coffee houses and taverns so that the artist, or mere literary man, neither of whom are members of the established clubs, are in a much worse position than they were'. His suggestion for a new club for such literary, scientific and artistic figures produced the Athenaeum, founded in the following year. Its membership was initially restricted to 500, but was soon raised to 1,000, and in 1881 the waiting list for membership contained 1,673 names.

The coffee houses virtually disappeared and not until the late twentieth century did establishments existing chiefly to serve coffee reappear in London's streets. Some clubs were short-lived, but new ones continued to be formed, including the Travellers' in 1814, at the end of the Napoleonic War; Crockford's in St James's Street, primarily a gambling house, in 1828; the Garrick in 1831; and the Arts Club, in 1863. By the mid-century the character of the membership was changing, implied by Gronow's recollection that the members of the West End clubs around 1814 were 'persons, almost without exception, belonging exclusively to the aristocratic world. Bankers and merchants, had not then invaded [them].' The members' wealth is reflected in the scale and style of the buildings: White's was designed by James Wyatt, Brooks's by Henry Holland, Boodle's by John Crunden, Crockford's by Benjamin and Philip Wyatt, the Travellers' by Charles Barry and the Athenaeum by Decimus Burton. They form a distinctive element in the townscape of St James's.

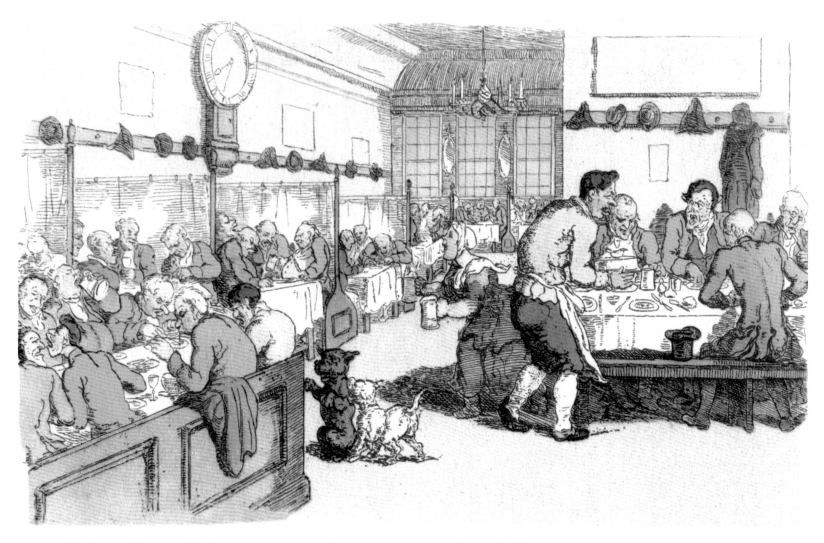

257. A coffee house with a colourful, if somewhat grotesque, clientele around 1800, as depicted by Thomas Rowlandson. (Stephen Porter)

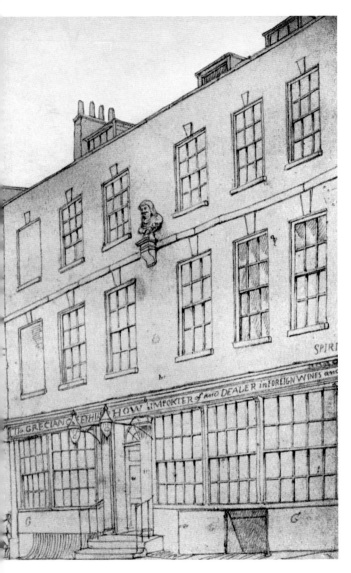

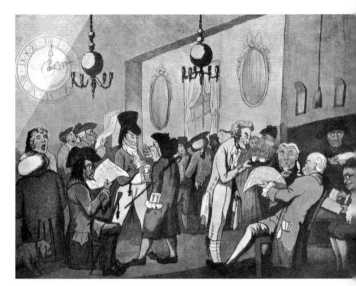

Left: 258. Like other coffee houses, the Grecian in Devereux Court, off the Strand, was favoured at various times by particular groups of patrons. The Grecian attracted Whig politicians in the late seventeenth century and leading scientists in the early eighteenth. (Stephen Porter)

Top right: 259. Lloyd's coffee house, illustrated by William Holland in 1798, was where the business of ship and cargo insurance developed. (Stephen Porter)

Bottom right: 260. The Great Subscription Room at Brooks's, one of the clubs for the aristocracy and gentry in St James's; the opulence of the interior and the table setting indicate the social milieu from which its members were drawn. Depicted by Augustus Pugin and Thomas Rowlandson, 1808. (Stephen Porter)

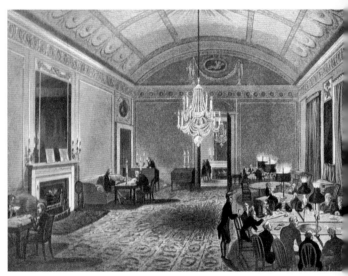

25

THE STRAND

One of London's main thoroughfares, this street runs from the City boundary at the site of Temple Bar to Charing Cross, following the line of the Thames. It connected the royal and ecclesiastical community at Westminster with London and formed part of the ceremonial route for royalty processing between them.

During the Middle Ages the south side of the street came to be occupied by the London houses of bishops and abbots. In the 1530s Whitehall Palace became the centre of the court and the government, and the Strand was conveniently close by, for courtiers and administrators. The senior churchmen were then displaced from their large houses, usually by a process of exchange, the houses being granted to senior figures at court, who rebuilt them. They were occupied by members of the aristocracy and their entourages, and used to lodge royal visitors from abroad, or their ambassadors. From 1552 Somerset House was a royal palace, assigned to the queen consort or royal favourites.

The great houses mostly had no more than a gatehouse on the street front, so that shops and inns fronting the street could provide a rental income. In 1610 the Earl of Salisbury built the New Exchange, which contained 150 shops. The considerable variety in the types of shop did much to give the street a distinctive character; Pastor Philip Moritz in 1782 wrote that 'one shop jostles another and people of very different trades often live in the same house'.

Prostitution was another activity for which the street came to have a reputation and remained a feature through the eighteenth and nineteenth centuries. Prosecution of the prostitutes made scarcely any impact on the scale of the activity and a House of Lords Committee reported in 1881 that 'from three or four o'clock in the afternoon, Villiers Street and Charing Cross Station and the Strand are crowded with prostitutes who openly solicit in broad daylight. At half-past twelve at night, a calculation was made a short time ago that there were 500 prostitutes between Piccadilly Circus and the bottom of Waterloo Place.'

The printing trade had a major presence. In the mid-nineteenth century more than thirty newspaper and magazine companies had their offices in the Strand and its tributary streets. With the printing trade were bookshops, together with those in Holywell Street, off its north side, which made it one of the centres of London's book trade. Because of the newspaper and magazine offices and the Inns of Court nearby, the Strand's various social establishments were where young writers and lawyers socialised, forming a Bohemian set that included the novelist William Makepeace Thackeray and his friend Douglas Jerrold. Some of them held radical political and social views and during the period of reform agitation in the late eighteenth and early nineteenth centuries, the Strand was one of those London streets where groups of activists congregated. In the early twentieth century, according to E. V. Lucas, it still had a reputation for being the most Bohemian of London's streets and 'the best-dressed men and women are not seen on its pavements'.

Its character gradually changed. Somerset House was demolished and replaced by an office building for government departments from 1776, and in 1817 Waterloo Bridge was opened, with its approach road requiring the demolition of buildings in the Strand. Charles Dickens the younger described the street in 1888 as having 'somehow an air of greater lightness and gaiety than is apparent in the City. There are more women among the foot passengers, more looking into shop windows, and an absence of that hurried walk and preoccupied look which prevail in the City proper.' Another appeal was that the Strand was 'essentially the home of the theatres'. Dickens named seven in the street itself and five just off it, plus Exeter Hall on the north side, built in 1830–31 as a popular meeting place for religious and scientific groups, and for concerts. By the end of the century the Strand contained 'the largest number of theatres of any street in London' and it remained a popular place to go to in the evenings in Victorian and Edwardian London.

The amount of traffic became a growing problem, exacerbated by the churches of St Mary le Strand, built in 1714–17, and St Clement Danes, which created a traffic bottleneck. In 1868 the *Building News* described the street as 'an indirect, a tortuous, an obstructed, and a narrow lane, which it is a mockery to call a thoroughfare'. Yet in the later nineteenth century it attracted new, large and grand hotels, and they and Charing Cross station, opened in 1864, with a hotel facing the Strand, helped give it a cosmopolitan air. According to Lucas, 'probably at no hour of the day or might are more than half the Strand's population true Londoners'.

The erection of the Royal Courts of Justice, opened in 1882, and the Aldwych improvements in the early years of the twentieth century transformed the east end of the street. Shopping came to be concentrated west of the Savoy, where the theatre was opened by the impresario Richard D'Oyly Carte in 1881 and the hotel in 1889. The theatre gave its name to Gilbert and Sullivan's hugely popular operettas, eight of which opened there between 1881 and 1889. The Strand's importance for entertainment was enhanced by the building of other new theatres, although, as Walter Besant observed, by the early twentieth century, its former 'architectural glories have almost all vanished'. A fire in 1990 gutted the interior of the Savoy theatre, which was restored by 1993, and a refurbishment of the hotel was completed in 2010, but the number of theatres in the Strand declined. Street widening and property rebuilding during the second half of the twentieth century contributed to the changes in its character and also its decline as London's 'popular' shopping street, as Oxford Street gradually developed that role.

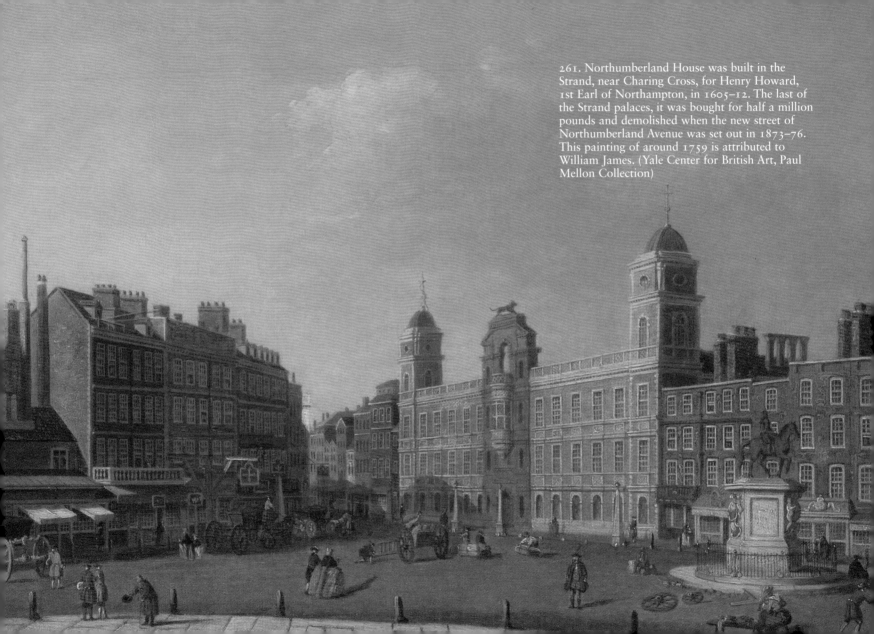

261. Northumberland House was built in the Strand, near Charing Cross, for Henry Howard, 1st Earl of Northampton, in 1605–12. The last of the Strand palaces, it was bought for half a million pounds and demolished when the new street of Northumberland Avenue was set out in 1873–76. This painting of around 1759 is attributed to William James. (Yale Center for British Art, Paul Mellon Collection)

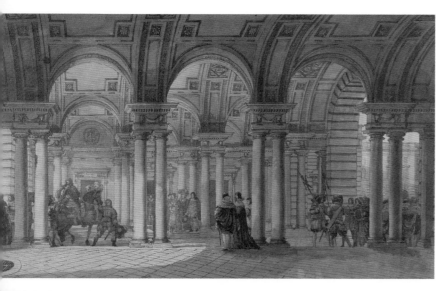

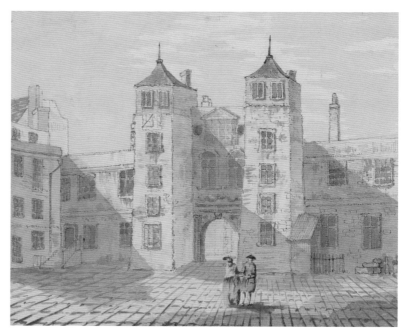

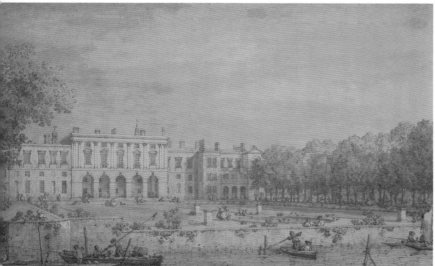

Above right: 262. The courtyard of Somerset House and the gateway to the Strand, by Thomas Theodosius Forrest (1728–84). (Yale Center for British Art, Paul Mellon Collection)

Above left: 263. The Strand entrance to Somerset House, designed by Sir William Chambers and begun in 1776. Louis Jean Desprez anachronistically showed the figures in seventeenth-century dress. (Yale Center for British Art, Paul Mellon Collection)

Left: 264. View of Old Somerset House and its grounds, seen from the Thames, by Canaletto (1697–1768). (Yale Center for British Art, Paul Mellon Collection)

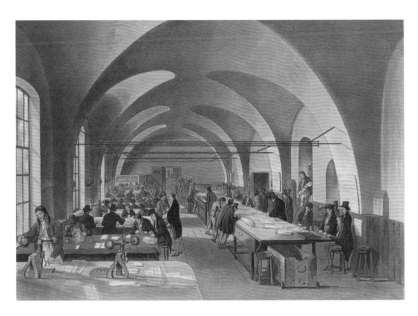

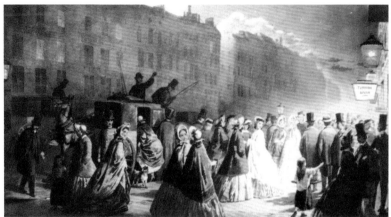

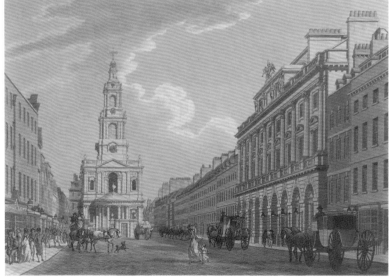

Above left: 265. The Stamp Office in Somerset House, around 1808, by Joseph Constantine Stadler, Augustus Pugin and Thomas Rowlandson. (Yale Center for British Art, Gift of Chauncey Brewster Tinker)

Above right: 266. The Strand was one of London's busiest shopping streets and also a street of theatres and other entertainments, attracting many visitors at night, as shown by the Dutch artist Willem Testas, around 1860. (Stephen Porter)

Right: 267. The church of St Mary le Strand and the front of Somerset House in 1796, by an unknown artist. The earlier church was demolished by Edward, Duke of Somerset, Lord Protector, in 1547–48 as part of his preparations for building Somerset House. The new one was built in 1714–17. Designed by James Gibbs, it was the first church built under the direction of the Commissioners for Building Fifty New Churches. (Yale Center for British Art, Paul Mellon Collection)

26

COVENT GARDEN

This began as a development in the 1630s on part of the former lands of Westminster Abbey. After the abbey's dissolution in 1540, the area was acquired by Edward Seymour, created Duke of Somerset and made Lord Protector on the accession of Edward VI, in 1547. Somerset lost power in 1549 and was executed in January 1552; the former convent garden was granted a few months later to John Russell, Earl of Bedford. A substantial mansion, Bedford House, fronting the Strand, was built around 1586 for the 3rd earl and along the northern edge of the site a new street, Long Acre, was set out in 1615, but was not built up until the 1630s.

The area was within the large parish of St Martin-in-the-Fields and proposals were made in the late 1620s for a new church. The 4th Earl of Bedford gained consent from the Crown to set out a new development in association with the Church, paying £2,000 for a building licence. The work was carried out under the direction of Inigo Jones, who formed an Italianate piazza, the first square in London, between the gardens of Bedford House and Long Acre, with colonnaded buildings on the north and east sides, and the church, flanked by houses, on the west. Because William Laud, Bishop of London and subsequently Archbishop of Canterbury, insisted that the altar should be at the east end, that wall on to the piazza is blank

and the principal doorway is at the west end. The development was built between 1633 and 1638; the Dutch artist William Schellinks described it in 1662 as 'a large piazza or market place with excellent residences resting on pillars, which form a large arcade to walk through'. The new parish of St Paul's, Covent Garden, was created in 1645. A column surmounted by a sundial was erected in the centre in 1668.

The gentility of the new district was not maintained for very long, partly because the aristocracy and gentry moved further west, to the developments set out after the mid-seventeenth century, and partly because of the markets held in the square. These were formalised in a patent granted in 1670, which permitted a market on every day except Sunday, for 'all manner of fruits and flowers, roots and herbes'.

The area became a popular haunt of the literati of late seventeenth-century and eighteenth-century London, drawn there by its coffee houses, and it developed a raffish atmosphere. The theatrical and artistic professions also gravitated there, especially after the Covent Garden Theatre was built by John Rich, in 1732. The considerable fortune which he had made from *The Beggar's Opera* was invested in the new theatre, on the west side of Bow Street and adjoining the north-east corner of the square. It was replaced in 1809 by a new theatre, designed by Robert Smirke; the present building, designed by E. M. Barry, was opened in 1858 and in 1892 it became the Royal Opera House. St Paul's came to be the 'actors' church' and contains memorials to well-known actors and actresses.

Covent Garden also became noted for its brothels. César De Saussure, in 1726, commented that some coffee houses were 'temples of Venus', identifiable by signs showing a woman's arm or a hand holding a coffee pot: 'There are a great number of these houses in the neighbourhood of Covent Garden; they pass for being chocolate houses and you are waited on by beautiful, neat, well-dressed, and amiable, but very dangerous, nymphs.' A satirical verse of 1756 described the district as the 'grand Seraglio to the nation' and John Harris's 'List of Covent-Garden Ladies', a directory of prostitutes, was issued from 1757 for almost forty years.

Bedford House was replaced by houses in 1705–06 and Jones's terraces were rebuilt by 1890. Long Acre was from the mid-seventeenth century a centre for coachbuilders and associated trades, but later its premises were occupied by fruit and vegetable traders, as the market came to dominate the district. A market hall was built for the 6th Duke of Bedford in 1828–30, the Floral Hall was erected in 1860 and in 1904 a new flower market was opened in the Jubilee Hall. The market became one of the sights of London. Charles Dickens the younger wrote, in 1888, that 'no visitor to London should miss paying at least two visits to Covent-garden: one, say at 6 a.m., to see the vegetable market; the other, later on, to see the fruits and flowers'. He commented

on the wagons which arrived early, loaded with vegetables stacked up to twelve feet high.

The congestion caused by the traffic drawn to the central markets led to proposals to move them. A suggestion in 1927 that Covent Garden market could transfer to Bloomsbury was abandoned 'owing to widespread opposition'. But it was realised that, should the market be closed, street improvements could follow. The closure of the market eventually was carried through in the late twentieth century and Covent Garden was moved to a new site in Battersea in 1974.

A redevelopment plan had been produced earlier by the Greater London Council, Westminster Council and Camden Council, and a revised one was prepared in anticipation of the removal of the market. That would have involved a substantial amount of demolition, replaced housing with offices and given space to a new road that was part of a proposed inner London motorway system. A bruising controversy ensued between a growing and forceful conservationist lobby and the GLC. A public enquiry found in favour of the plan, but it was subsequently scuppered by the Secretary of State for the Environment, who ordered a revision that would provide more residential accommodation and who also gave no fewer than 250 additional buildings within the area listed buildings protection. The council then changed its strategy and opted to regenerate the area, with the central market building converted to small shops. The scheme, completed in 1980, proved to be a model of urban regeneration, enhanced by the reconstruction of the Royal Opera House in 1997–99.

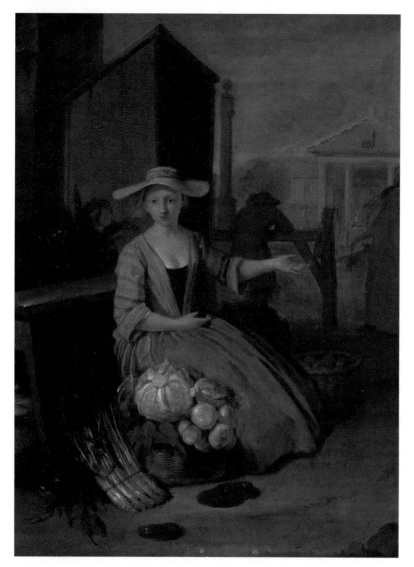

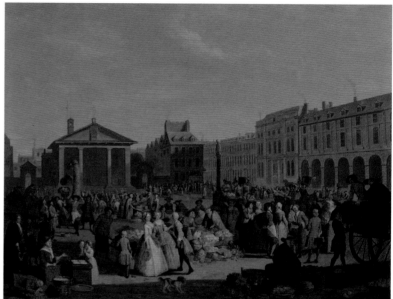

Above: 268. A market day in Covent Garden around 1726, looking towards St Paul's church, by Pieter Angelis, or Angillis, who was in England around 1719–28 and worked from a shop in Covent Garden, depicting local scenes. (Yale Center for British Art, Paul Mellon Collection)

Left: 269. From being a select development when it was built in the mid-seventeenth century, Covent Garden became one of London's most important markets. A vegetable seller in the market is depicted by Pieter Angelis, or Angillis, around 1726. (Yale Center for British Art, Paul Mellon Collection)

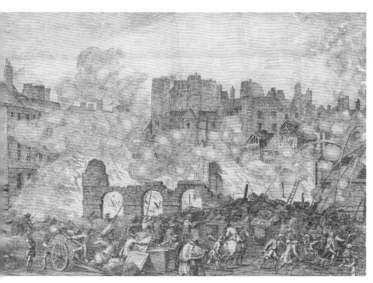

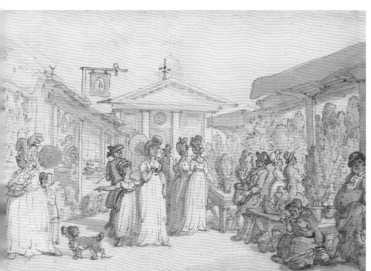

Top left: 270. *A View of the Fire in Covent Garden* by the Swiss artist Samuel Hieronymus Grimm, depicting the fire which took place on 20 March 1769, may well be a record by an eyewitness, for Grimm had lodgings in the neighbourhood after his arrival in England in the previous year. (Yale Center for British Art, Paul Mellon Fund)

Bottom left: 271. Thomas Rowlandson's depiction of Covent Garden Market, between 1795 and 1810, which shows a mixture of people, including some rather genteel figures, browsing through the market, with St Paul's church in the background. (Yale Center for British Art, Paul Mellon Collection)

Right: 272. The profusion of blooms on the flower stalls in Covent Garden Market, around 1912. (Stephen Porter)

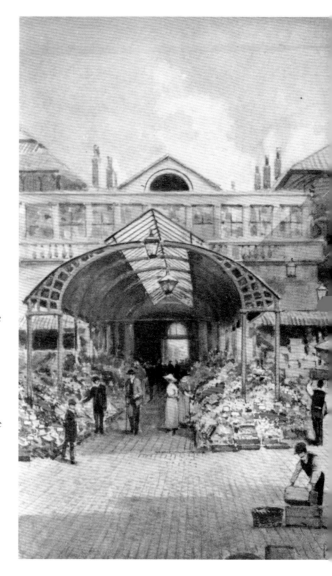

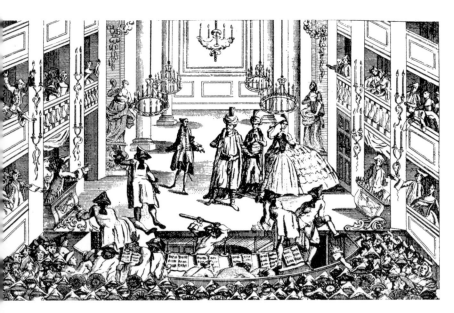

274. The riot at the Covent Garden theatre in 1763 was caused by the management refusing to allow half-price admissions for the current production of Thomas Arne's opera *Artaxerxes*. The rioters are belabouring the musicians in the orchestra pit and are just beginning their invasion of the stage. (Stephen Porter)

273. The capacious auditorium of the New Covent Garden Theatre, 1810, designed by Robert Smirke and opened in the previous year, depicted by John Bluck. (Yale Center for British Art, Paul Mellon Collection)

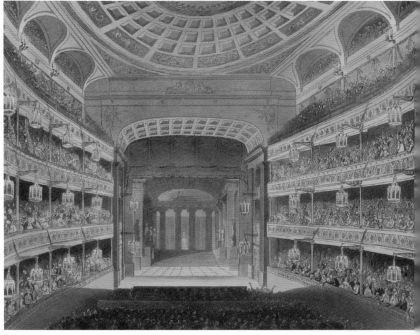

27

TRAFALGAR SQUARE

On 21 October 1805 a British fleet under the command of Admiral Lord Nelson defeated the combined fleets of France and Spain off Cape Trafalgar, on the south-west coast of Spain. That overwhelming victory established British naval supremacy, which was to last throughout the nineteenth century. But Nelson, already a national hero, was killed during the battle.

The square was not, however, a swift response to commemorate the victory and Nelson's achievement; the name was not applied until the mid-1830s, when the newly created space was being formed, and the column carrying Nelson's statue was not completed until 1843. The new square was a development northwards from the junction of Whitehall and the Strand at Charing Cross, where the Royal Mews stood. On the east side of the mews was the St Martin's parish workhouse and St Martin's Lane, with the parish church of St Martin-in-the-Fields on its east side. But only after the decision in 1820 to move the mews to Buckingham Palace could plans for the site be developed and the square was set out during the 1830s, by clearance of the mews, workhouse and, according to Bradshaw's *Hand Book to London*, 'a nest of wretched courts'.

The church faced the new square, which has the National Gallery, built in 1833–38, on its north side. As the land slopes from north to south, a terrace was built in front of the gallery in 1840–45, and the two fountains were completed in 1845. The column, designed by William Railton, is 170 feet high and the statue of Nelson, by E. H. Baily, adds a further seventeen feet. The reliefs against the base were made in 1849–54 and the four lions, designed by Sir Edwin Landseer, were added in 1867. More than sixty years elapsed between the battle and the completion of the scheme commemorating the victory and the admiral. The square also contains equestrian statues of Charles I, made in 1633 by Hubert Le Sueur and placed at the north end of Whitehall in 1675, and George IV, made in 1843 by Sir Francis Legatt Chantrey.

From the outset the square was a paved, not grassed, public space, the setting for the column and statue and a place of public recreation. Some critics described the square as the most wasted space in Europe, while the artist Paul Cohen-Portheim wrote, around 1930, that 'the central asphalt desert of the square is really very depressing', relieved only by the many pigeons and the orators who, on Sundays, chose it as a place where they could pronounce on issues of current concern.

It attracted more attention through the demonstrations and political meetings held there, because of its size and its proximity to Whitehall and Westminster. The best-known meetings during the nineteenth century were held during the Chartist agitation in 1848, at a republican rally in 1871 and protests against the level of unemployment in 1886 and 1887. The square remained a place for both demonstrations and celebrations through the twentieth century.

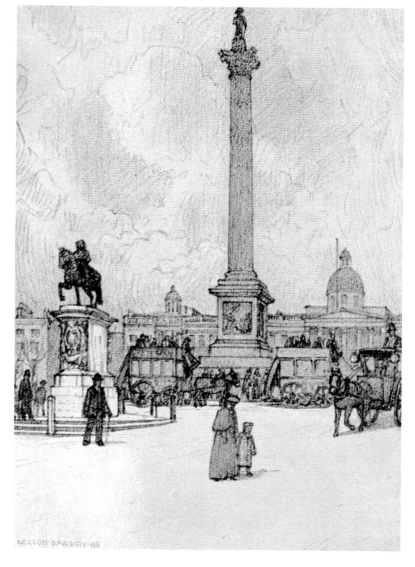

275. The statue of Charles I and Nelson's column, made in 1840–43, in Trafalgar Square, painted by Nelson Dawson around 1900. (Stephen Porter)

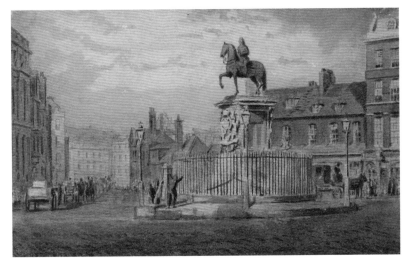

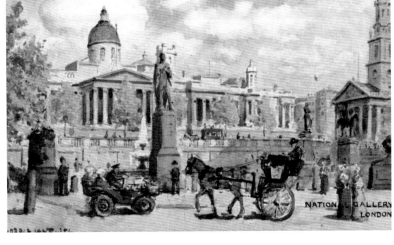

Above left: 276. After the abolition of the monarchy in 1649 the statue of Charles I, made in 1633 by Hubert Le Sueur, was bought by a brazier, who sold mementoes allegedly made from it, yet he produced the statue intact at the Restoration. In 1675 it was placed at Charing Cross, which became part of Trafalgar Square when it was created in the 1830s. Painting by an unknown artist, around 1815. (Yale Center for British Art, Paul Mellon Collection)

Above right: 277. The National Gallery on the north side of Trafalgar Square was designed by William Wilkins and opened in 1838. This painting shows it in the early twentieth century. (Stephen Porter)

Right: 278. Trafalgar Square in the 1920s. (Stephen Porter)

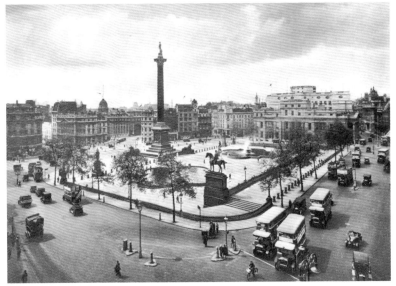

28

WHITEHALL

As Westminster developed into the focus of English government and a major ecclesiastical centre, so the area to the north alongside King Street, leading to Charing Cross, was chosen by those who needed to live close to the court. One of the properties there was acquired in the 1240s by the Archbishop of York and he adapted it as his London town house, known as York Place. Edward I occupied it twice, while Westminster Palace was being extended and repaired, and he enlarged it, partly to provide accommodation for the queen. York Place was enlarged again in the fifteenth century by George Neville, archbishop from 1465 until 1476, who doubled its size. But Neville's rebuilding was modest compared to that carried out by Thomas Wolsey, archbishop from 1514, appointed chancellor in 1515, created a cardinal in 1516 and from 1518 successively bishop of Bath and Wells, Durham and Winchester. To provide space for his extra buildings, he enlarged the site by acquiring neighbouring properties. The palace included state rooms and reception chambers, residential apartments, a new chapel, erected in 1528, and a long gallery. Wolsey's pre-eminent role in government as well as the Church gave the palace a special significance as a centre for those wishing to transact official or legal business.

Wolsey fell from power in 1529 and died in 1530. Without a London palace since 1512, when fire had destroyed the royal apartments in Westminster Palace, Henry VIII then took possession of York Place. He further enlarged the site by acquisitions and reclaiming land along the riverfront, and by new building and improvements he made Whitehall the principal palace of the English Crown. Land on the west side of King Street was acquired and used for recreation, with a tiltyard, tennis courts and a cockpit. It was connected to the main part of the palace by two gatehouses which spanned the street. The later Tudor monarchs did little to improve the palace, although a banqueting house, of timber and canvas, was hastily erected on Elizabeth's orders in 1581. The palace certainly impressed visitors, not for any overall form or architectural distinction, which indeed it lacked, but for its interiors. In 1600 Baron Waldstein wrote that it 'fills one with wonder, not so much because of its great size as because of the magnificence of its bed chambers and living rooms which are furnished with the most gorgeous splendour'. James I replaced the Elizabethan banqueting house with a more substantial structure in 1606. That banqueting house was destroyed by fire in 1619 and its replacement was designed by Inigo Jones in an innovative and striking classical design. The building had a greater significance than its predecessor in that it was also used as a presence chamber. Charles I completed the building, commissioning from Peter Paul Rubens the painted ceiling, depicting his father's apotheosis. On 30 January 1649 Charles was executed on a scaffold specially erected outside the banqueting house.

A blaze in 1691 damaged the southern part of the palace buildings and its core was destroyed in a more devastating fire in January 1698. The blaze began when a maid left a bag of charcoal too near a fire and when it caught fire the servants hoped to quench the flames without further assistance, 'but it increas'd soe violently it occasion'd ye ruine of ye whole pallace'. The banqueting house and the gatehouses escaped, but much of the remainder was gutted. Although plans were produced for rebuilding, they were not proceeded with and the site remained derelict, dotted with ruins, well into the eighteenth century. The King Street gate was demolished in 1723 and the Holbein Gate in 1759.

Whitehall ceased to be a focus for the monarchy, but the street's role as a centre of government continued to develop. The process had begun before the fire, with the erection of the Horse Guards on the former tilt yard in the 1660s and the Admiralty Office, outside the palace precincts, in 1693–94. South of the Horse Guards, Downing Street was set out in 1682 and included 'four or five very large and well built houses fit for persons of honour and quality'. One of these, No. 10, was offered by George II to the prime minister, Sir Robert Walpole, who accepted it on condition that it would be used by his successors. In 1735 Walpole moved in and the building has been the prime minister's official residence since then. The Admiralty building was erected in 1726, the Treasury was built in the 1730s and the new Horse Guards was completed in 1760, with an office for the Secretary at War as well as a barracks. The process continued in the nineteenth and twentieth centuries, with ever larger and imposing government offices built along the street; a large part of the frontage on the west side was taken by a complex erected in the 1860s and 1870s to accommodate the Foreign Office, the India Office, the Colonial Office and the Home Office. On the east side the War Office was built between 1899 and 1906, the Ministry of Defence building, although designed in 1936, was erected in the 1960s and Richmond House was constructed in the 1980s, for the Ministry of Health. A part of Scotland Yard, to the north, became the Metropolitan Police's headquarters soon after its creation in 1829.

The former King Street had been widened to create a spacious thoroughfare, designated Whitehall, which was the appropriate setting for a national monument to commemorate the dead of the First World War. The Cenotaph, designed by Sir Edwin Lutyens, was first hastily erected in plaster for the victory parade on 19 July 1919, in the presence of the French and American commanders, and was then replaced in Portland stone and unveiled on Armistice Day, 11 November, in 1920. William Teignmouth Shore was among those who admired it for its 'dignified simplicity too often lacking in British memorials'.

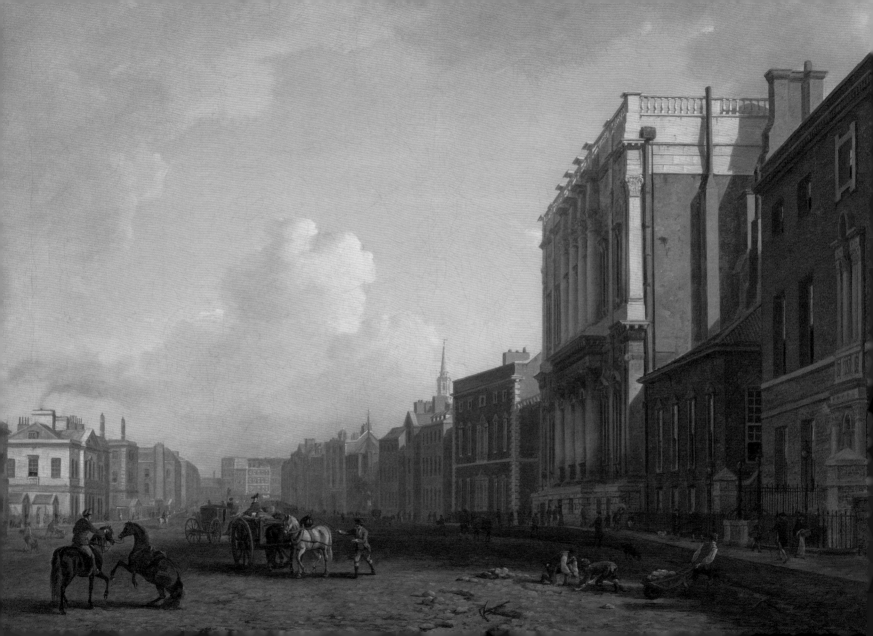

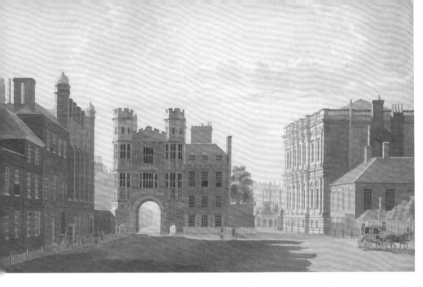

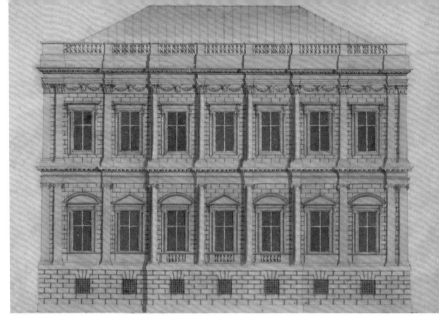

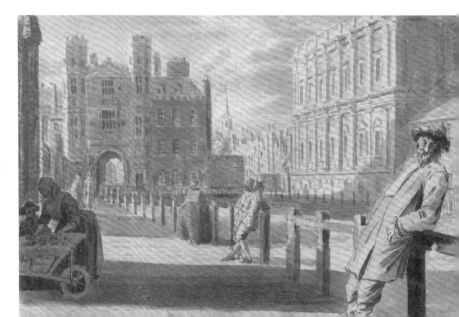

Opposite: 279. William Marlow's painting of around 1775 shows Whitehall looking north, with the Banqueting House on the right. He illustrates the street's variety of buildings, before large government offices had begun to dominate the district. (Yale Center for British Art, Paul Mellon Collection)

Above left: 280. Surviving elements of Whitehall Palace, destroyed by fire in 1698: Holbein's Gate, which was to be demolished in 1759, and the Jacobean Banqueting Hall, painted by Thomas Sandby around 1758. (Yale Center for British Art, Paul Mellon Collection)

Above right: 281. The Banqueting House of Whitehall Palace, designed by Inigo Jones for James I and built in 1619–22, drawn by Thomas Forster around 1700. (Yale Center for British Art, Paul Mellon Collection)

Right: 282. Louis Philippe Boitard's depiction of figures in Whitehall, including a woman selling fruit from a barrow, before 1759. (Yale Center for British Art, Paul Mellon Collection)

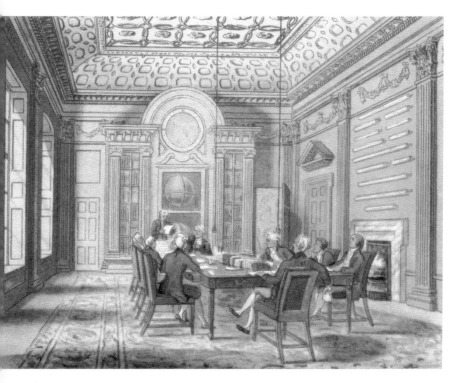

283. The board room of the Admiralty building, Whitehall, designed by Thomas Ripley of the Office of Works and built in 1723–26; illustrated around 1808 by Thomas Rowlandson and Augustus Pugin. (Stephen Porter)

284. The Horse Guards building in Whitehall, erected in the 1750s, containing a barracks and the offices of the Secretary at War, a post created in the reign of Charles II. (Yale Center for British Art, Paul Mellon Collection)

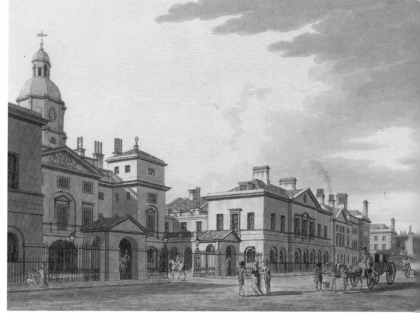

29

WESTMINSTER

The name was recorded as Westmynster around 975, although there may have been a minster, or monastery, on Thorney Island, west of London, after the mid-seventh century and certainly by the early eighth century during the reign of Offa, king of the West Saxons (not to be confused with Offa, king of Mercia). The decline of Lundenwic and reoccupation of London after 886 saw the adoption of St Paul's as the principal civic church. The house on Thorney Island was refounded as a Benedictine monastery by Dunstan, who was appointed Bishop of London shortly after returning in 957 from a period of exile in Ghent. The abbey was a small one, with twelve monks, and had St Peter as its patron saint, and that was said to have been a factor in it being favoured by Edward the Confessor, who came to the throne in 1042. It had already attracted royal patronage during Cnut's reign, receiving gifts of relics from him, and Harold I was buried there in 1040, but under Edward, with the encouragement of Robert, Bishop of London, the church was rebuilt and a royal palace was erected adjoining the abbey from around 1050. The church at the abbey of Jumièges in Normandy had been built during Robert's time as abbot and his influence probably produced a Norman style for the church at Westminster, which was consecrated in 1065. It was unusually large for the period, with an east end of two bays and a nave of twelve bays, and an overall length of 322 feet.

Edward effectively created a royal enclave at Westminster, which was then adopted by the Norman kings. Edward had been crowned at Winchester and his successor, Harold II, was the first English king to be crowned in Westminster Abbey, in 1066, as was William I, on Christmas Day in the same year; the practice of royal coronations in the abbey has continued since. The cloister and other monastic buildings probably were erected in the late eleventh century and William II added Westminster Hall to the palace buildings in 1097–99. Edward the Confessor was buried in the abbey and his cult developed from the early twelfth century, after an inspection of his corpse in 1102 produced a favourable assessment of his piety. He was canonised in 1161 and his body was moved to a new shrine in the abbey two years later. A community grew up around the abbey and palace which was served, probably from the late eleventh century, by a parish church dedicated to St Margaret.

In 1220 work began on a Lady chapel at the east end of the abbey church, but that was followed by the complete rebuilding of the rest of the abbey, with the building as far west as the nave demolished in 1245. The rebuilding, which included a new chapter house, was carried out under the patronage of Henry III, who bore the costs, which had reached around £45,000 by the time of his death in 1272. The king probably was influenced not only by a devotion to the cult of St Edward, whose body was moved to a new chapel in 1269, but also a need to match the great church buildings being erected in France, such as Reims and Sainte-Chapelle, which greatly influenced the style of his new church. Henry's death brought the work to a halt; no future king was prepared to take on the whole expense of the works and the Crown contributed rather less than 30 per cent of the subsequent costs down to 1534. Much of the outlay fell on the monastery itself at a time when its funds were also needed to restore buildings damaged by a fire in 1298. The monks attracted the anger of Edward I in 1303 when they were discovered to have colluded in the theft of some of the royal jewels, stored in the abbey for safe keeping. Among the suspects were forty-eight monks and thirty-two lay members of the community, who were imprisoned in the Tower, but the monks claimed benefit of clergy and so were released.

Not until 1375 was the programme for building the nave revived. A burst of activity during Richard II's reign saw much of it erected, under the direction of the architect Henry Yevele, but progress was slow during the fifteenth century. The west window and the clerestory windows were finished in 1496 and a further spurt of work followed in 1528–34. The monastery was dissolved in January 1540 and in the December of that year the abbey was created the cathedral of the newly formed diocese of Westminster, which was suppressed ten years later. The west towers, designed by Nicholas Hawksmoor, were added in 1734–45. Following the dissolution of the abbey, the school attached to it was refounded by Henry VIII, with forty scholars.

A Lady chapel was erected at the east end of the abbey church between 1503 and 1510, replacing the early thirteenth-century one. The chapel was begun by Henry VII and completed as his chantry chapel after his death in 1509. It is in a bold Perpendicular style, with a splendid fan vault, and contains the tomb and effigies of Henry VII and his queen, Elizabeth of York, made in 1512–17 by the Italian sculptor Pietro Torrigiano. As a student, Torrigiano had trained in the workshop of Domenico Ghirlandaio in Florence alongside Michelangelo and on one occasion, irritated beyond endurance by his teasing, he had broken Michelangelo's nose with a firm punch. Torrigiano arrived in England in 1511 and created a masterpiece.

The palace at Westminster gained in size and significance as the monarchs became less peripatetic; the White Hall was built in the eleventh century; the chapel of St Stephen's College, which was independent of both monarch and abbot, was begun in 1292; the Painted Chamber was both Henry III's bedchamber and an audience chamber; a jewel tower for the safe keeping of the royal treasure was built by Edward III in 1365–66; and in 1394 Richard II began the remodelling of the hall, under Yevele's direction, which was completed in 1401. Medieval Westminster also became the centre of the administration of justice, with the establishment there of the central courts as the common law evolved following the organisation of the English judicial system by Henry II (1154–89). To serve the growing number of parishioners, St Margaret's church was rebuilt during Edward I's reign and again between 1482 and 1523.

In 1512 a fire destroyed the royal accommodation of the palace and the buildings were not repaired; Henry VIII used other palaces and then, from 1530, enlarged Cardinal Wolsey's former palace in Whitehall as his principal London residence. Westminster Palace's remaining buildings included the hall, St Stephen's chapel, the Painted Chamber and the White Hall. These came to be used for the law courts and for Parliament, which met with increasing frequency, especially after 1640. The House of Lords assembled in the Queen's Chamber and the Commons, which had used the abbey's chapter house, met in St Stephen's chapel, after the college was dissolved in 1547. The Commons continued to use the abbey as its church until 1614, when it adopted St Margaret's for its services.

The palace was the location for the courts of common law and equity from the late twelfth century and for King's Bench from the early fifteenth century. By the late Middle Ages three courts met in Westminster Hall: Chancery and King's Bench on either side of the south end, and Common Pleas along the west wall. The Court of Requests, established in 1540, met in the White Hall. By the early eighteenth century two other courts met outside the hall, with the Exchequer in a Tudor building abutting its north-west tower and the Bail Court to the east of the hall. Changes were proposed by William Kent in 1739 and, although most were not adopted, he did create a courtroom for Common Pleas against the west wall of the hall, between a pair of buttresses, with a portal opened in that wall for access. Within the hall, he erected Gothick partitions to enclose the courts of Chancery and King's Bench, and a new Common Pleas courtroom.

By the early nineteenth century the pressure for new courtrooms was increasing. Not only was more space required and the existing arrangements inconvenient for the legal profession, but they were thought inimical to the dignity necessary for courts of law. A more pressing reason for creating new accommodation for the courts was the need to clear the hall for the coronation banquet of George IV, which took place in July 1821. Lord Liverpool, the prime minister, was so impressed by the grandeur of the uncluttered hall that he decided that the courts should be accommodated elsewhere. Sir John Soane of the Board of Works was appointed to erect new courts on the west side of Westminster Hall and to restore its north front. Soane created further openings in the wall of the hall, leading to a public corridor serving the five new courtrooms, which were arranged between the hall's buttresses. They were completed in 1825 and their decorated white ceilings, hanging arches, delicately carved canopies and the red of the curtains and carpets combined to give them what one observer described as 'more the air of fairy halls than of seats of justice'. In 1831 the Master of the Rolls moved to Westminster and three years later a new Bankruptcy Court was established; both were accommodated in the existing buildings. The Westminster courtrooms remained in use until their replacement, the Royal Courts of Justice in the Strand, was opened in 1883, when they were demolished. The west side of Westminster Hall was then restored.

As the centre of power and patronage, Westminster drew the nobility and gentry, and those seeking influence and wealth. In the mid-seventeenth century it was said to have 'most of the Nobility and Gentry residing in, or about her Precincts'. To the south of the abbey and palace, Smith Square was set out in the 1720s, with St John's church, designed by Thomas Archer, as its striking centrepiece. But Westminster's fine houses stood cheek by jowl with some poor dwellings and miserable streets. Buildings cleared away from the front of Westminster Hall in 1807 were described as 'sheds, hovels, taverns, and alehouses'.

A fire in October 1834 destroyed most of the palace's buildings, although the hall and adjoining courtrooms were saved. After a competition, Sir Charles Barry's design was selected and he, with the assistance of Augustus Pugin, directed the construction of the new Palace of Westminster. The Lords' chamber was ready in 1847 and the Commons' chamber was occupied in 1852, with the whole palace virtually finished by 1860. Pugin died in 1852 and Barry in 1860. The royal gallery, Lords' chamber, central lobby and Commons' chamber form a central spine, parallel to the river. The striking features of the exterior are the distinctive front to the Thames and two imposing towers of similar height, the Victoria Tower and the Clock Tower, the latter containing the bell of 13½ tons affectionately known as 'Big Ben', cast at the Whitechapel Bell Foundry in 1858. The completed building was hailed as 'the finest specimen of Gothic civil architecture in Europe'. The Commons' chamber and lobby were rebuilt after bomb damage in May 1941.

Royalty had withdrawn from Westminster and Whitehall by the eighteenth century and the area developed as the centre of national government, the growing Civil Service and also local administration, with the Middlesex Guildhall erected in 1912 on the west side of Parliament Square, which had been created in 1868. Government buildings came to dominate the

district. But the abbey continued to serve as the nation's church, for coronations, celebrations and state funerals, and as the place of burial of figures of national importance, in politics, military service and the arts, many of them commemorated by monuments. Westminster's evolution as a royal, ecclesiastical and government enclave gave it a character which was quite distinct from that of the City.

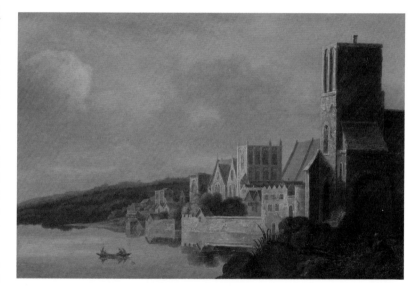

285. Claude de Jongh's painting of the Thames at Westminster in the 1620s shows that it marked the limit of building on the left bank of the river. (Yale Center for British Art, Paul Mellon Collection)

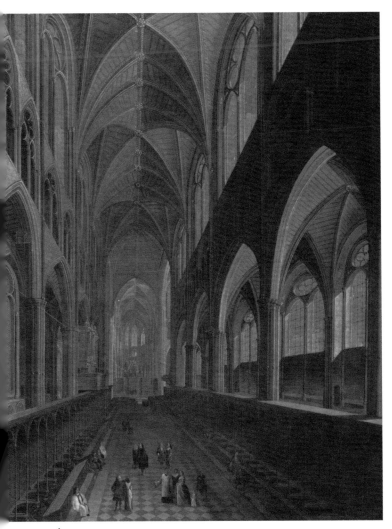

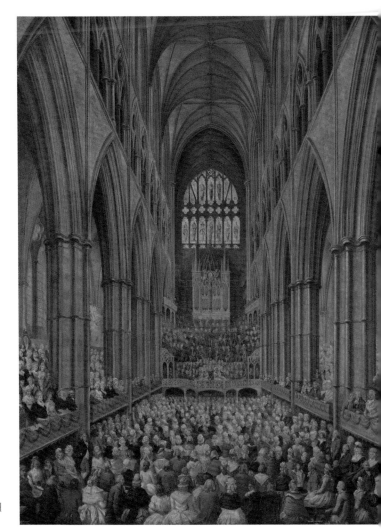

Left: 286. The interior of Westminster Abbey being admired by visitors, by an unknown artist around 1714. (Yale Center for British Art, Paul Mellon Collection)

Right: 287. Commemorations of the composer Georg Frederic Handel were held in Westminster Abbey from 1784 to 1791, with up to 4,500 people crammed into the nave and the specially built galleries in the aisles. The painting, by Edward Edwards, may represent an amalgam of more than one of the events. The viewpoint is a structure erected in front of the choir screen, looking west. (Yale Center for British Art, Paul Mellon Collection)

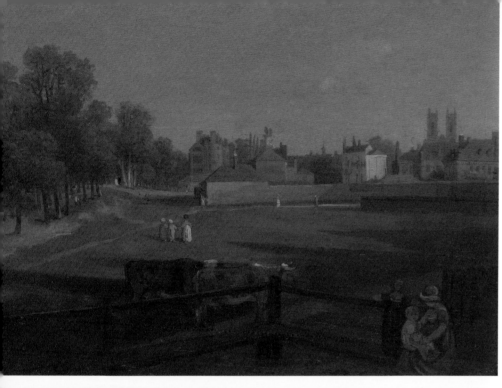

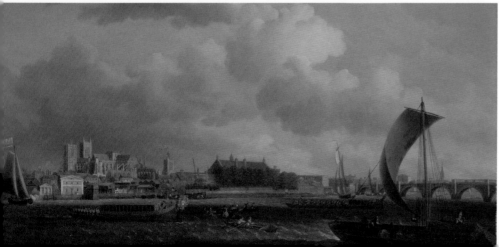

Top left: 288. A view of Westminster and Bird Cage Walk from the west in 1808, by George Arnald, which illustrates how little development there had been in that area by the early nineteenth century. (Yale Center for British Art, Paul Mellon Collection)

Bottom left: 289. The London livery companies kept a barge for ceremonial occasions. The more prominent of the two depicted by Samuel Scott at Westminster around 1750 is that of the Ironmongers' Company. (Yale Center for British Art, Paul Mellon Collection)

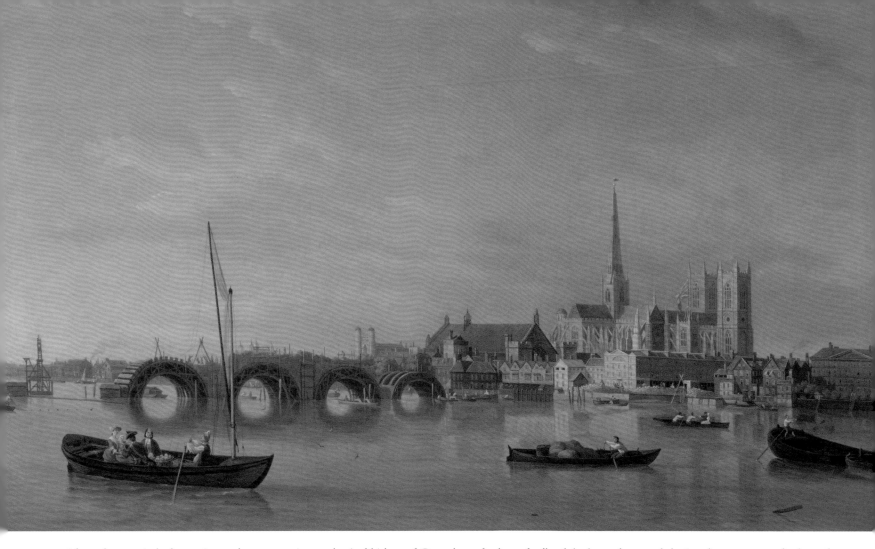

290. After a long period of gestation and compensation to the Archbishop of Canterbury, for loss of tolls of the horse ferry, and the London watermen, for loss of business, Westminster Bridge was built between 1738 and 1750. Samuel Scott depicted the process around 1742. (Yale Center for British Art, Paul Mellon Collection)

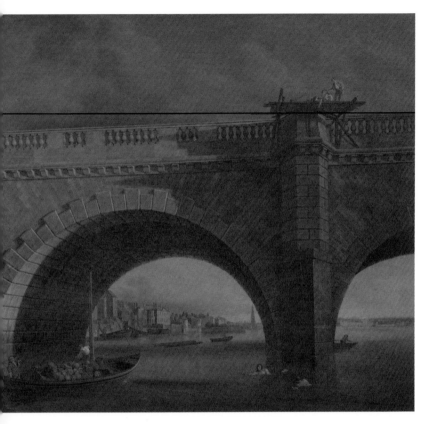

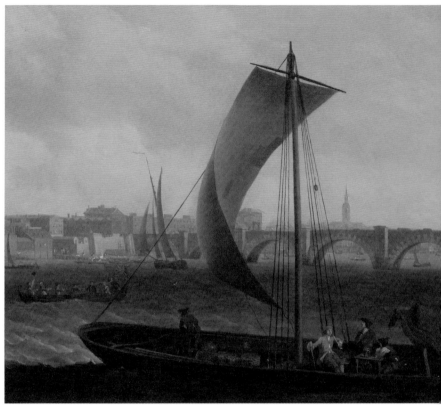

291. Westminster Bridge was the second stone bridge over the Thames in London, after London Bridge. Completed in 1750, it attracted the attention of artists, including Samuel Scott, who shows a boat passing beneath the bridge, while work is being carried out on one of its piers. (Yale Center for British Art, Paul Mellon Collection)

292. Boats on the Thames near Westminster Bridge, with Westminster beyond, by Samuel Scott. (Yale Center for British Art, Paul Mellon Collection)

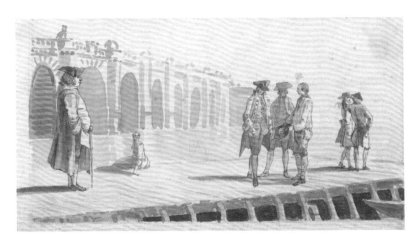

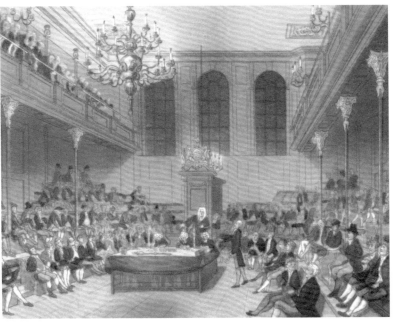

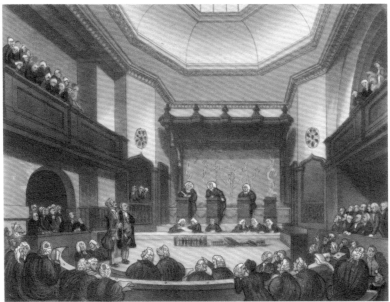

Above right: 293. William Kent's building adjoining Westminster Hall for the Court of Common Pleas was designed in 1739. Thomas Rowlandson and Augustus Pugin's illustration of around 1808 gives the impression of greater scale than was in fact the case, for the room was just thirty-six feet by fifteen and a half feet. (Stephen Porter)

Above left: 294. Paul Sandby's atmospheric watercolour of around 1752 shows a group of men on Westminster Pier, watched by a woman seated on the edge of the pier. (Yale Center for British Art, Paul Mellon Collection)

Left: 295. The House of Commons was enlarged to accommodate the influx of members representing Irish seats following the Act of Union in 1800; the chamber was illustrated by Thomas Rowlandson and Augustus Pugin during that period. (Stephen Porter)

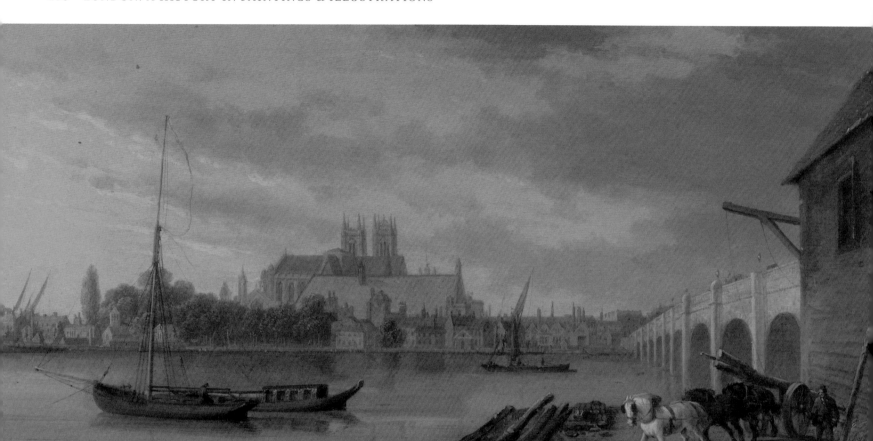

296. A view across the Thames at Westminster in 1818, close to Westminster Bridge, shows modest buildings on the riverfront, with the long roof of Westminster Hall and the abbey behind; by William Anderson. (Yale Center for British Art, Paul Mellon Collection)

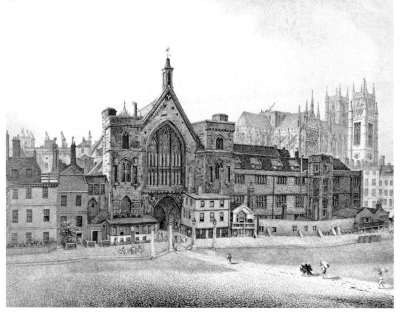

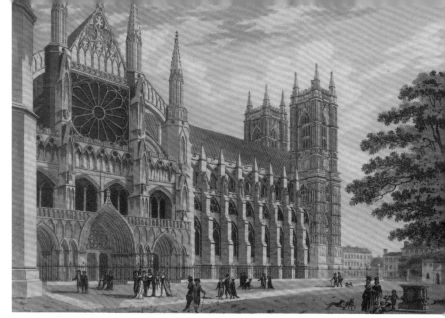

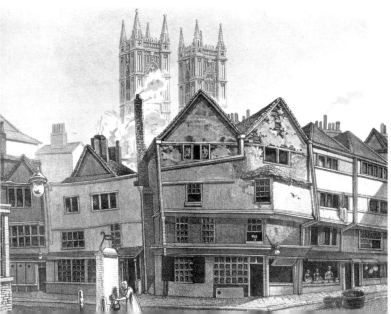

Above right: 297. The north side of Westminster Abbey, with the elaborate doorway and rose window of the north transept, by an unknown artist, after Thomas Malton (1726–1801). (Yale Center for British Art)

Above left: 298. The south side of New Palace Yard with Westminster Hall and the buildings erected right up against it, drawn by Joshua Bryant in the early nineteenth century. (Stephen Porter)

Left: 299. The rather neglected-looking buildings of Thieving Lane and the street pump, close to Westminster Abbey, drawn by J. T. Smith in 1808. (Stephen Porter)

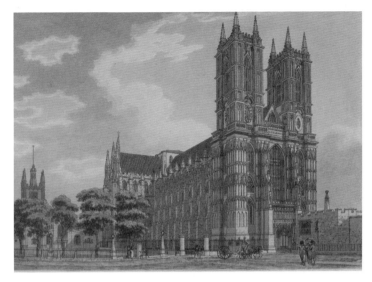

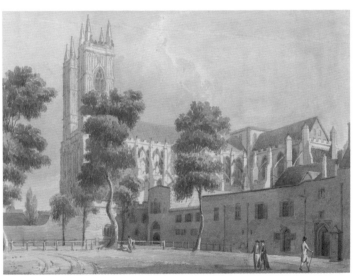

Top left: 300. Westminster Abbey from the north-west in 1793, by an unknown artist, after Thomas Malton. (Yale Center for British Art)

Bottom left: 301. Dean's Yard, Westminster, in 1793, by an unknown artist, after Thomas Malton (1726–1801). The former abbey buildings here were used by Westminster School, but were mostly demolished in the mid-eighteenth and early nineteenth centuries. (Yale Center for British Art)

Right: 302. The Victoria Tower, one of the Houses of Parliament's two tall towers, seen from the south along Millbank, around 1912. It is the repository for Parliament's records. (Stephen Porter)

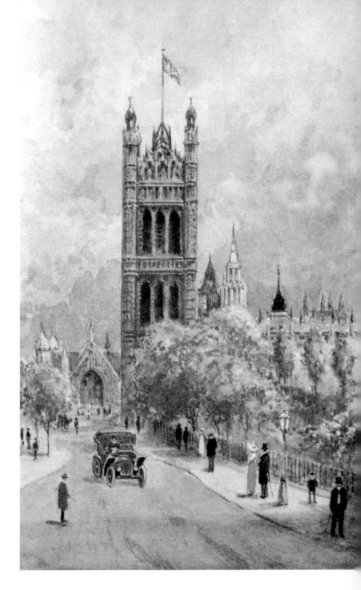

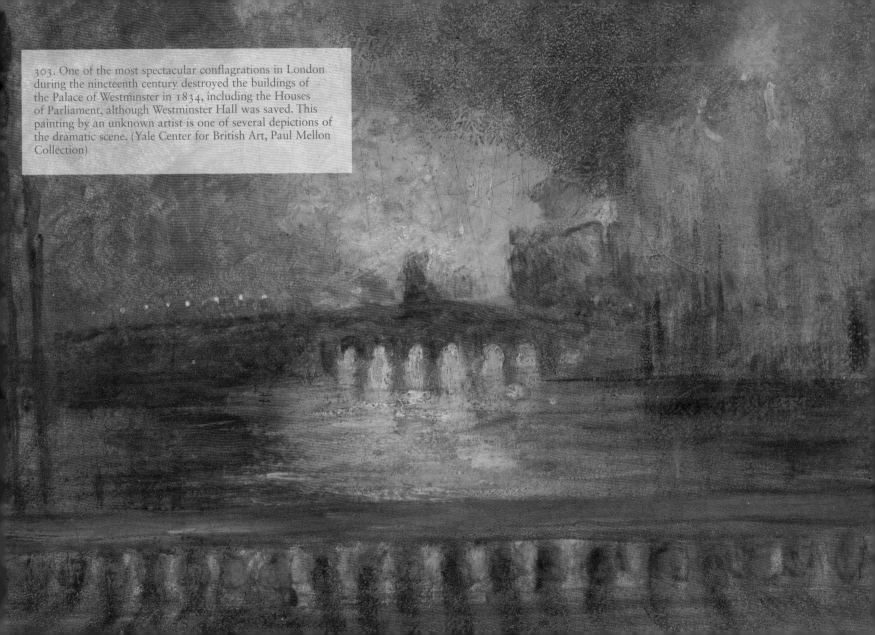

303. One of the most spectacular conflagrations in London during the nineteenth century destroyed the buildings of the Palace of Westminster in 1834, including the Houses of Parliament, although Westminster Hall was saved. This painting by an unknown artist is one of several depictions of the dramatic scene. (Yale Center for British Art, Paul Mellon Collection)

30

THE WEST END

The designation West End was adopted in the early nineteenth century for the wide sweep of developments that were set out just beyond the western edge of the metropolis, from Westminster to Bloomsbury. The housing was designed for the wealthy and was built around squares, with grand houses fronting them and the subsidiary streets, and perhaps a market and a chapel. These were developed from the late seventeenth century, typically by an aristocratic landowner who built a mansion along one side of the square, with a speculative builder engaged to develop the other frontages. Pastor Moritz, in 1782, noted that the squares 'contain the most splendid houses in London'. At the rear were the mews, with stabling and room for carriages, while the minor streets had accommodation for those who provided services for the grand households. The central parts of the squares were railed off from the roadways, lined with trees and perhaps set out as a garden, or laid to grass to provide pasture for a few animals, offering a glimpse of the countryside in town.

The more or less standard form of the square and its secondary streets gave coherence to the area, but there was no overall planning. And, while squares were the typical form, the West End also included fashionable shopping streets, notably Regent Street, Oxford Street and Bond Street. In 1708 Bond Street was described as 'a fine new street, mostly inhabited by nobility and gentry', and in 1717 the *Weekly Journal* commented that the new buildings between Bond Street and Marylebone 'go on with all possible diligence and the houses even let and sell before they are built'. Bond Street retained its role as a fashionable shopping street, but Oxford Street fell away and in 1931 Virginia Woolf wrote that it was 'not London's most distinguished thoroughfare. Moralists have been known to point the finger of scorn at those who buy there, and they have the support of the dandies.'

The West End was unrivalled as the most fashionable part of London, attracting members of the aristocracy and gentry, and, increasingly during the nineteenth century, successful City men as well. It acted as the focus of society during the London season, with its round of balls, *soirées* and visits, and was the place to be seen, to admire and to envy. Thomas Pennant in 1790 noted that those who 'lounged' in Bond Street did so to 'get a nearer glimpse of the fashionable and generally titled ladies that pass and repass from two to five o'clock'. The well-to-do did not need, or wish, to go even so far as the Strand, let alone to Temple Bar, and might venture into the City only occasionally to check on their financial affairs. Moreover, the West End remained the fashionable part of town, unlike districts such as Covent Garden, which were fashionable for a time but later fell into disfavour with the wealthy, who abandoned them.

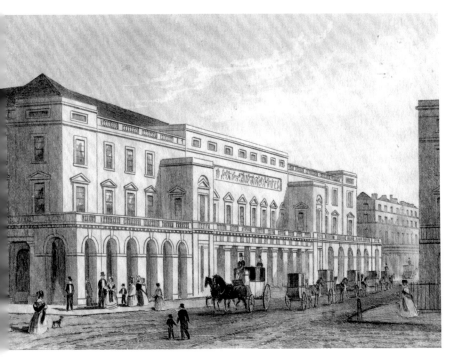

304. Her Majesty's Theatre in the Haymarket around 1840. The first theatre on the site was established by Sir John Vanbrugh in 1705 and it became the King's Theatre in 1714; the change of name to Her Majesty's Theatre followed the accession of Queen Victoria in 1837. (Stephen Porter)

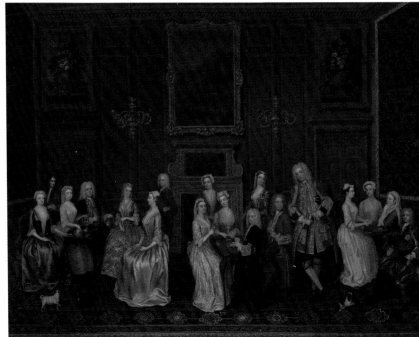

305. A tea party in a room furnished in a typically aristocratic early eighteenth-century style at Lord Harrington's House, St James's, 1730, painted by Charles Philips. (Yale Center for British Art, Paul Mellon Collection)

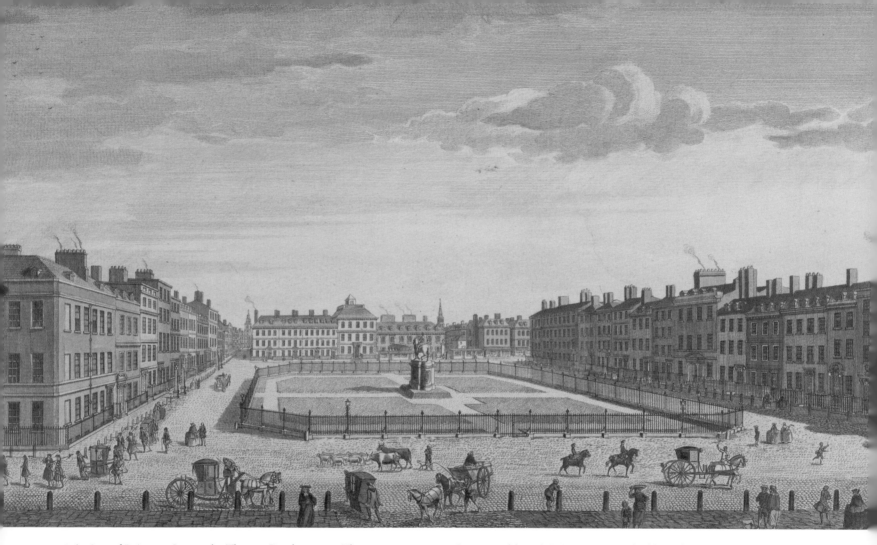

306. A view of Leicester Square, by Thomas Bowles, 1753. The square was set out in 1670, although Leicester House had been built in the early 1630s and did not have a dominant position in the square. (Yale Center for British Art, Paul Mellon Collection)

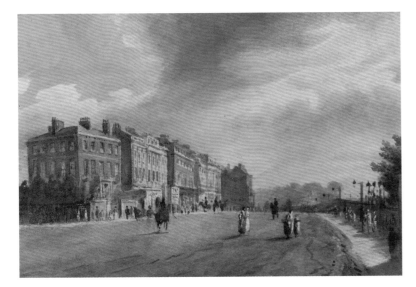

Left: 307. The Duke of Wellington's Apsley House and Piccadilly seen from Hyde Park Corner, by Frederick Nash (1782–1856). (Yale Center for British Art, Paul Mellon Collection)

Below left: 308. The regular façades of Regent Street are shown in this view looking towards Piccadilly from Waterloo Place, by Thomas Shotter Boys, undated. (Yale Center for British Art, Paul Mellon Collection)

Below right: 309. The Quadrant, Regent Street, in 1827, by Thomas Shepherd. (Stephen Porter)

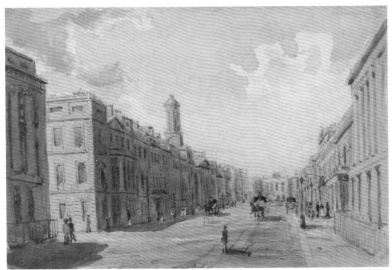

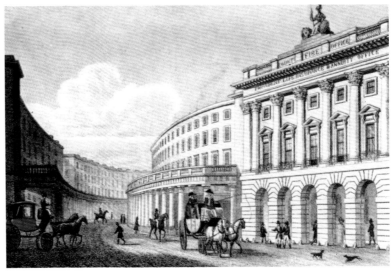

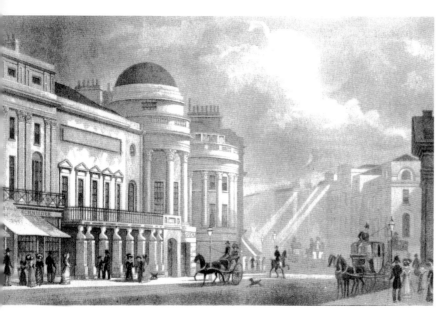

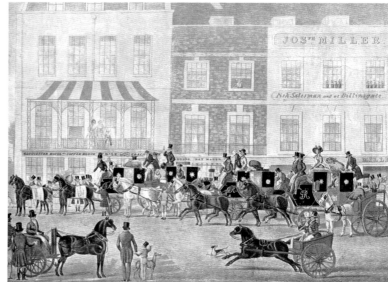

Above left: 310. The Argyll Rooms in Regent Street, built for the Harmonic Institution by John Nash. A group of eighteen musicians established the Institution in 1818, to publish their music and that of other composers; it ceased to exist after the building was burned down in 1830. The site was then cleared for houses. (Stephen Porter)

Above right: 311. The West Country mail coach outside the Gloucester Coffee House in Piccadilly in 1828. The premises of the fishmonger Joseph Miller shows that although this was one of London's smartest streets, it also contained shops selling everyday supplies. (Stephen Porter)

Right: 312. St James's Street, looking towards the gatehouse of St James's palace. The Conservative Club, established in 1840, occupied the prominent building on the right from 1845. (Stephen Porter)

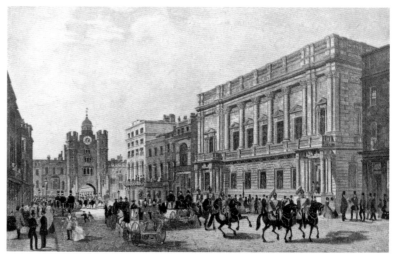

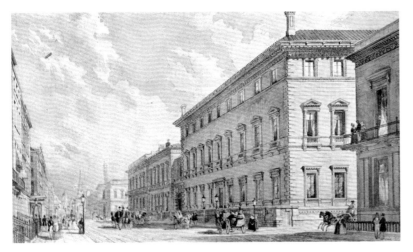

Left: 313. Pall Mall, with the Reform Club, painted by George Moore in 1837. (Stephen Porter)

Below left: 314. Carlton House in Pall Mall was built in 1709 and was acquired in 1732 for Frederick, Prince of Wales. It remained a royal residence and the Prince Regent created an opulent interior in a mixture of styles. But after he had become king, as George IV, in 1820 he did not need the house, which was demolished in 1827. The interior was illustrated around 1808 by Thomas Rowlandson and Augustus Pugin. (Stephen Porter)

Below right: 315. A popular viewing at the Royal Academy in Somerset House, where the works of art crowd the walls, around 1808, by Thomas Rowlandson and Augustus Pugin. (Stephen Porter)

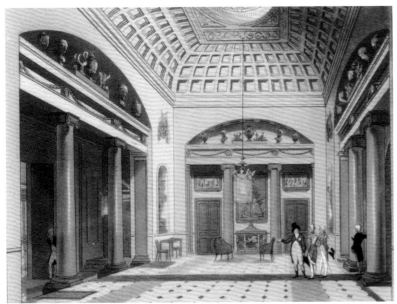

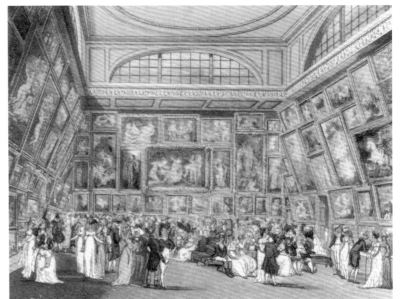

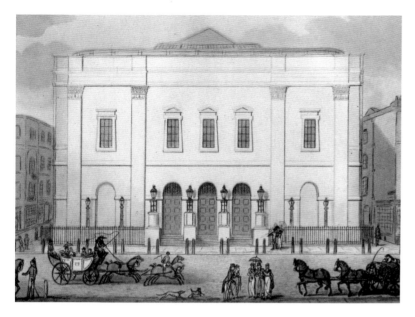

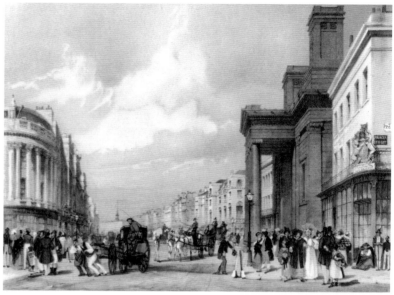

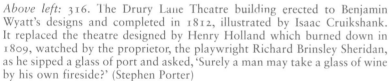

Above left: 316. The Drury Lane Theatre building erected to Benjamin Wyatt's designs and completed in 1812, illustrated by Isaac Cruikshank. It replaced the theatre designed by Henry Holland which burned down in 1809, watched by the proprietor, the playwright Richard Brinsley Sheridan, as he sipped a glass of port and asked, 'Surely a man may take a glass of wine by his own fireside?' (Stephen Porter)

Above right: 317. Regent Street was set out in the early nineteenth century and completed in 1825; it is shown in 1842, by Thomas Shotter Boys. (Stephen Porter)

Right: 318. Founded by James Christie in 1766 north of Oxford Street, Christie's quickly became a leading auction house; Thomas Rowlandson and Augustus Pugin show a well-attended sale in progress, around 1808. The firm moved to premises in King Street, St James's, in 1823. (Stephen Porter)

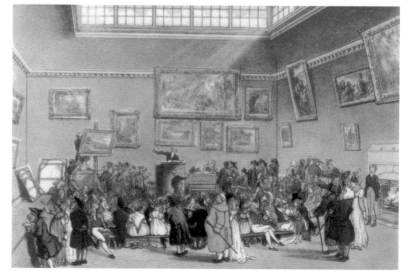

31

PARKS AND PLEASURE GARDENS

The royal parks of Hyde Park and St James's Park were formed by Henry VIII, who acquired the site of Hyde Park from Westminster Abbey. It was opened to the public in the 1620s and became a fashionable spot, especially with the aristocracy and gentry, who ostentatiously paraded in their coaches. Charles II set out a part of the land acquired by the Crown in 1668 from the Poultney family as Upper St James's Park, which by the 1740s was known as Green Park. St James's Park was increasingly used by the public for promenading. On a visit to London in 1782 Pastor Moritz was not impressed either with St James's Palace or the park, yet was pleased to see 'the astonishing medley of people who take their evening walk there in fine weather ... with dense crowds of people strolling up and down'.

Moritz's reaction to the pleasure garden at Ranelagh, adjoining Chelsea Hospital, was similar, being delighted to watch 'the play and gathering of this happy carefree world', as well as enjoying the fare and entertainment. He noted, too, that at Ranelagh the company 'looked superior to that at Vauxhall', a distinction that was fostered by the admission charge of 2s 6d, whereas at Vauxhall it was only 1s 0d. The gardens at Vauxhall had been opened in 1661, replacing those at Spring Garden near Charing Cross, while Ranelagh was not opened until 1742. The pleasure gardens were popular places for all social groups and provided activities ranging from firework displays, ballooning and romantic assignations to the more deadly serious practice of duelling. Music formed an important part of the entertainment, especially in the large rotunda at Ranelagh. In the 1730s the music at Vauxhall was performed by 'a Band consisting of above thirty of the ablest Performers'; a statue of the composer George Frederic Handel was set up there and a rehearsal in 1749 of his suite of music celebrating the peace treaty of Aix-la-Chapelle drew a crowd of 'above 12,000' and caused severe traffic congestion as far away as London Bridge.

The pleasure grounds declined in the nineteenth century; Ranelagh was closed in 1803, although Vauxhall limped on until 1859. But other parks and open areas were expanded: Regent's Park was planned during the Napoleonic War and opened after the peace, while spaces under threat from development were preserved for public recreation, such as Blackheath and Hampstead Heath. From the mid-nineteenth century municipal parks were created, the first of which was Victoria Park, in the East End, opened in 1845, and others followed, such as Battersea Park (1853), Finsbury Park (1869) and Dulwich Park (1890), and they became a feature of the city in the late nineteenth and early twentieth centuries.

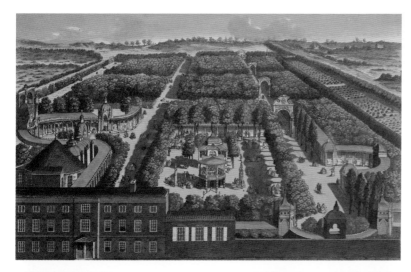

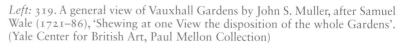

Left: 319. A general view of Vauxhall Gardens by John S. Muller, after Samuel Wale (1721–86), 'Shewing at one View the disposition of the whole Gardens'. (Yale Center for British Art, Paul Mellon Collection)

Below left: 320. The Temple of Comus in Vauxhall Gardens, by John S. Muller around 1794. (Yale Center for British Art, Paul Mellon Collection)

Below right: 321. A view of the Centre Cross Walk in Vauxhall Gardens, with groups of fashionable visitors, by Edward Rooker. (Yale Center for British Art, Paul Mellon Collection)

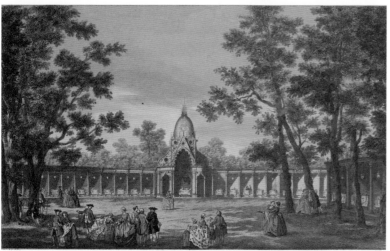

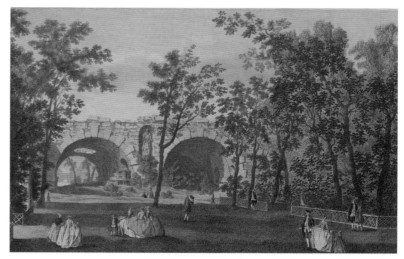

Right: 322. A band of musicians and a soloist entertain the visitors from a gallery in Vauxhall Gardens, although they scarcely seem to be paying attention to the performance, as shown by Thomas Rowlandson, around 1784. (Yale Center for British Art, Paul Mellon Collection)

Below left: 323. Milkmaids serving gentlemen and a soldier in St James's Park, while another maid is milking a cow, depicted by Thomas Rowlandson. (Yale Center for British Art, Paul Mellon Collection)

Below right: 324. Soldiers exercising in St James's Park, while the genteel characters taking their leisure are shown by Thomas Rowlandson continuing with their promenade. (Yale Center for British Art, Paul Mellon Collection)

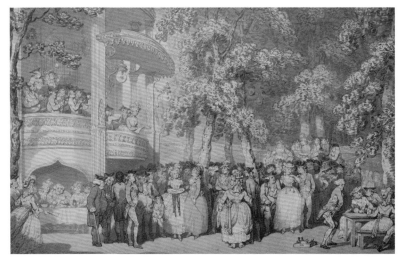

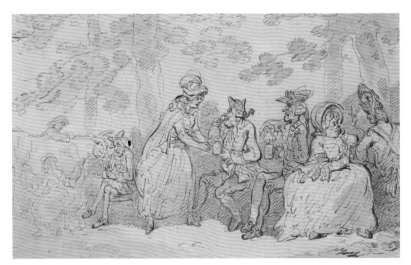

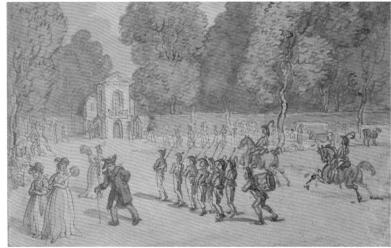

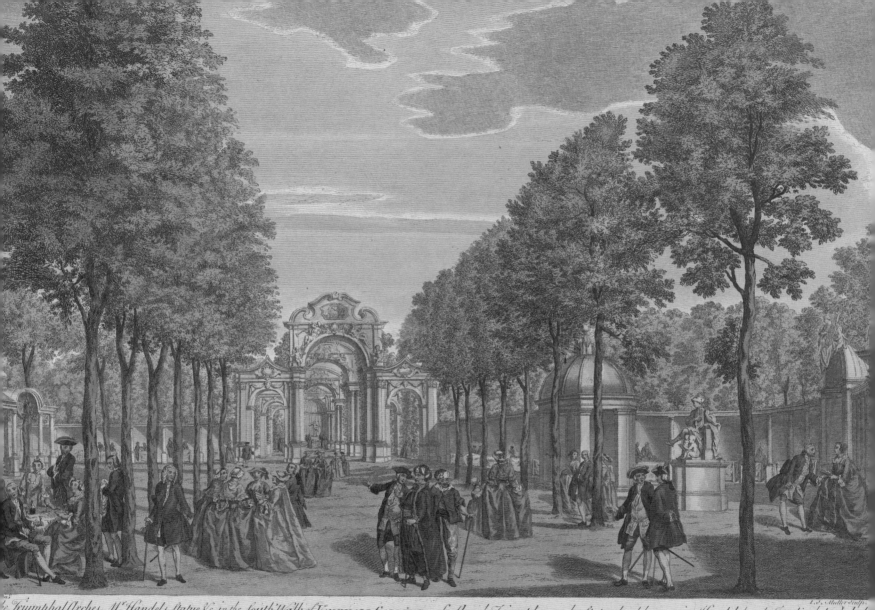

I. S. Muller Sculp.

e Triumphal Arches, Mr Handels Statue &c. in the South Walk of VAUXHALL GARDENS. Les Ares de Triomphe avec la Statue du celebre musicien Handel dans les Jardin de Vauxhale

Published by F. West, 83, Fleet Street, London.

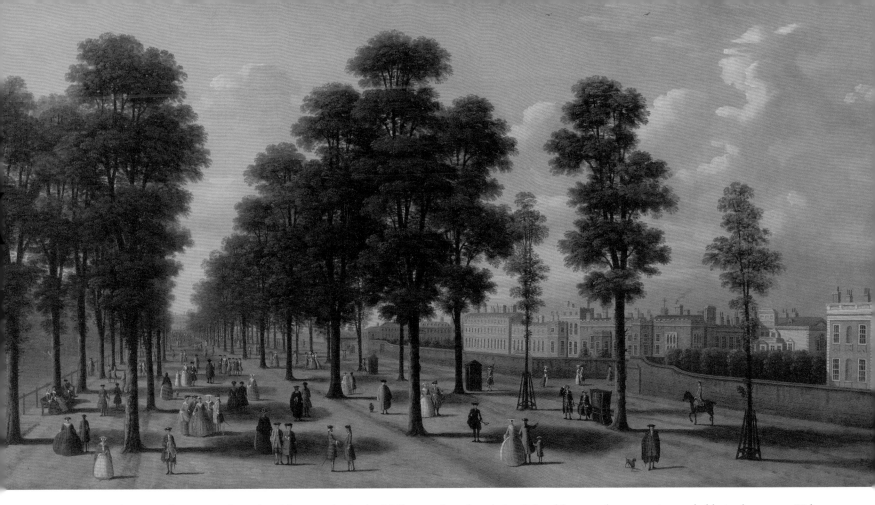

Above: 326. A rather genteel mixture of people taking exercise in the Mall, some in sedan chairs. Painted by an unknown artist, probably in the 1740s. (Yale Center for British Art, Paul Mellon Collection)

Opposite: 325. Genteel visitors promenading in the south walk of Vauxhall Gardens in the mid-eighteenth century, with the statue of Handel by Louis-François Roubiliac, which was placed there in 1738; painting by John S. Muller. (Yale Center for British Art, Paul Mellon Collection)

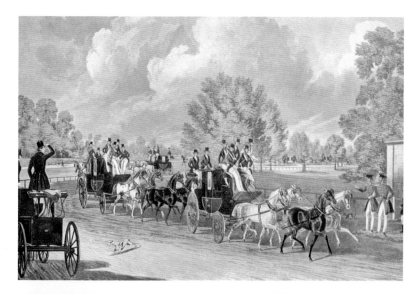

Left: 327. Members of the Four-in-Hand Club take their vehicles around Hyde Park, painted by James Pollard. The club was formed in 1808 and continued until 1820, with a brief revival in 1822–4; it was an exclusive club with only thirty to forty members. (Stephen Porter)

Below left: 328. The Serpentine in Hyde Park in the mid-nineteenth century, attributed to George Sidney Shepherd. (Yale Center for British Art, Paul Mellon Collection)

Below right: 329. Hyde Park was not only a place for leisure but also where the military could camp and train. This painting of a review of the London Volunteer Cavalry and Flying Artillery, by an unknown artist, was made in 1804, during the war with France, and shows that a military exercise of that kind attracted curious onlookers. (Yale Center for British Art, Paul Mellon Collection)

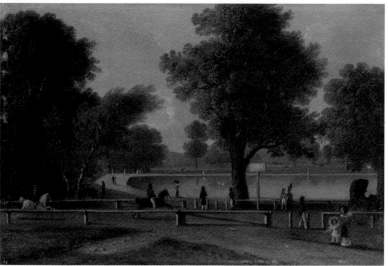

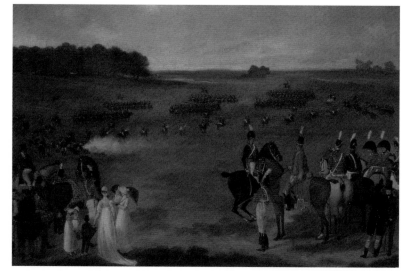

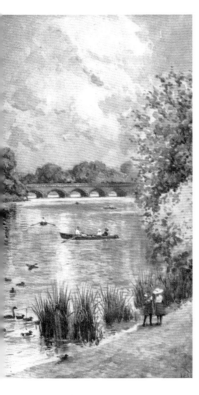

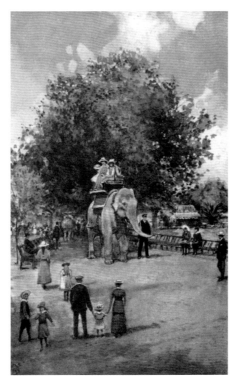

332. Promenaders and soldiers in St James's Park in 1808, painted by H. Schulz, when the canal was still rectangular; in 1826–27 it was given a more curved and 'natural' form. (Stephen Porter)

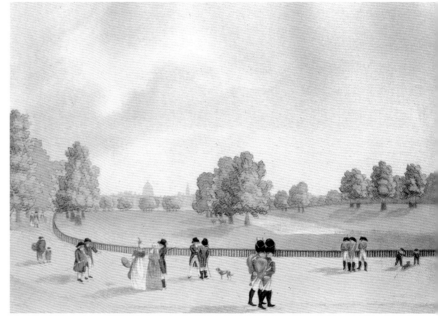

Above left: 330. The Serpentine was created in Hyde Park in 1731, probably by William Kent for Queen Caroline, by enlarging and connecting a series of pools formed by the Westbourne Brook. This illustration dates from around 1912, when boating cost between 1s and 1s 6d per hour. (Stephen Porter)

Above right: 331. London Zoo was established in Regent's Park by the Zoological Society of London in 1828 and the royal collections of animals were added to it during the 1830s. By the early twentieth century young visitors could take rides on the elephants. (Stephen Porter)

32

SPITALFIELDS

The district takes its name from the medieval priory of St Mary Spital, alongside Bishopsgate, which had a large burial ground on its south side. After its dissolution, in 1539, the area was developed. According to John Stow, from 'pleasant fields' by around 1600 it had become 'a continual building throughout, of garden-houses and small cottages'. The fields had been made into gardens, tenter-yards for stretching newly made cloth, bowling alleys 'and such like', from Houndsditch to Whitechapel.

Spitalfields was a separate hamlet of Stepney parish from 1662 and in 1729 the new parish of Christ Church, Spitalfields was created. The imposing parish church, designed by Nicholas Hawksmoor, was erected in 1714–29. The streets set out in the late seventeenth and eighteenth centuries were more regular than those developed in the sixteenth century and contained some fine houses.

Part of the priory site was used as the target range of England's Master Gunner, known as the Artillery Garden. This was the training ground of the Guild of St George, granted a charter by Henry VIII in 1537, which became known as the Society of the Artillery Garden. It remained until the mid-seventeenth century. A market was then established there, which came to be a major feature of the district, specialising in vegetables and fruit. It was acquired by the Corporation of London in 1920 and new buildings were erected in 1928. The market was closed in 1991.

The area attracted Huguenot immigrants from France, especially following Louis XIV's revocation of the Edict of Nantes in 1685. By 1700 it had nine French churches and a *Maison de Charité* had been established, distributing food to the poor. The Huguenots developed a silk industry, which became by far the largest employer in Spitalfields in the eighteenth century, with 500 master weavers and about 15,000 looms by 1750. But it was subject to fluctuations in the supply of the raw material and changing fashions, and the downturns saw periods of great hardship. In 1773 Parliament responded to pressure from the silk weavers and popular unrest and passed the Spitalfields Act, to control entry into the trade and regulate wage levels. Competition from provincial silk manufacturers and the policy of free trade led to the decline of the industry in the area during the nineteenth century, although by 1914 there were still forty-six silk workshops in Spitalfields and Bethnal Green.

By that time there had been another wave of immigration, of Jews from eastern Europe, who settled in the inner East

End, including Spitalfields. Their main employment was in sweatshops, producing readymade clothes. In the mid-twentieth century the Jewish community gradually moved away and the Spitalfields Great Synagogue, the principal synagogue in the East End, was closed in 1968. They were replaced by immigrants from India and Bangladesh and in 1977 the building, erected in 1742 as the Neuve Eglisé by the Huguenot community, was adapted again, as the Jamme Masjid mosque.

333. Huguenot immigrants settled in Spitalfields in the late seventeenth century and the French Hospital, known as La Providence, was built on the site of a pesthouse and was opened in 1718. (Stephen Porter)

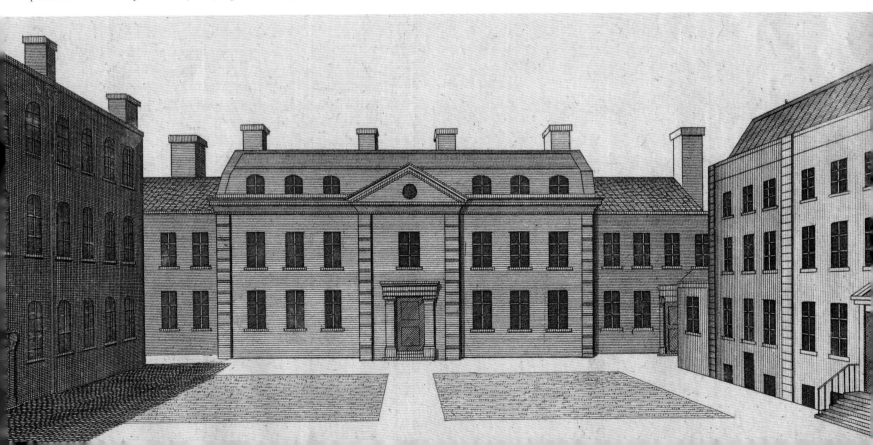

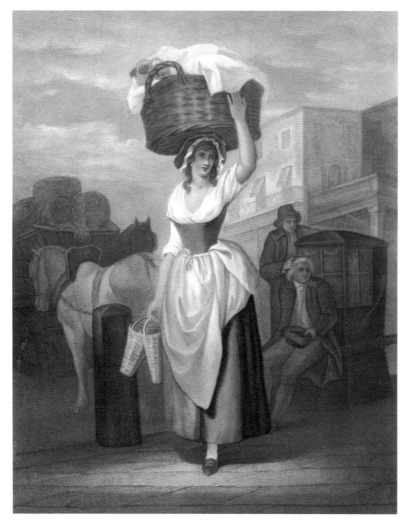

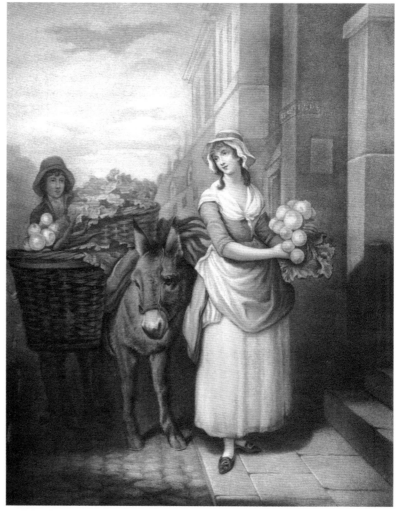

334. The strawberry seller, one of Francis Wheatley's series *Cries of London*, 1795. (Stephen Porter)

335. Turnips and carrots for sale, one of Francis Wheatley's series *Cries of London*, 1797. (Stephen Porter)

33

THE EAST END

The name Stepney was in use by around 1000 and was applied to the area east of the City which came to form the unusually extensive parish of St Dunstan's between the City boundary and the River Lea, which divided Middlesex from Essex. The parish was subdivided for administrative purposes into separate hamlets and in 1329 Whitechapel was taken from it to become a separate parish. Most development before the seventeenth century was along Whitechapel High Street and the riverside, in Wapping, Shadwell, Limehouse, Poplar and Blackwall.

Whitechapel attracted those unpleasant and polluting trades typical of a suburban area, and inns for travellers stood along the street. The Boar's Head was one of the establishments first recorded as used for playhouses, and another was the Red Lion, where a theatre was built in 1567. Some of the sixteenth-century development consisted of small houses occupied by poor people. In 1598 John Stow complained about the 'filthy cottages' and rubbish dumps that stretched for half a mile beyond St Mary's church. More than 700 new houses were erected between 1620 and 1677, and by 1710–11 the population of the parish was estimated at 18,000. The area had a high level of poverty, with 70 per cent of householders exempt from paying the hearth tax in 1664, compared to 45 per cent in nearby Spitalfields and 47

per cent in the Tower Liberty and Shadwell. The conditions made it an unhealthy district: at the time of the Civil War there were three burials for every two baptisms and during the Great Plague in 1665 deaths were seven times the normal level, one of the highest mortality rates in London. Yet the population within the whole Stepney division increased from 143,436 in 1710–11 to 188,609 in 1801. The separate parishes created from St Dunstan's give some idea of the progress of development: Shadwell (1669), Wapping (1694), St George's-in-the-East (1729), Spitalfields (1729), Limehouse (1730), Bethnal Green (1743) and Poplar (1817).

The riverside grew swiftly following the construction of enclosed docks: the West India Docks across the Isle of Dogs in 1802, the London Docks in 1805, the East India Docks in 1806 and St Katherine's Dock, just east of the Tower, in 1828. Two canals improved communications for waterborne traffic: the Limehouse Cut, connecting the River Lea and the Thames, was built in 1767–70 and the Regent's Canal was completed in 1820, with a basin at Limehouse. Road connections with the city were greatly improved with the construction of the Commercial, West India Dock and East India Dock roads in the first decade of the nineteenth century. A major boom in the middle of the century, especially in shipbuilding, saw the construction of the Millwall Docks in 1864–67, and although a recession in the late 1860s led to a decline in shipbuilding and related industries, new docks were built downstream from the Lea.

The East End, as it became known in the late nineteenth century, had a reputation for being rough and tough, with its inhabitants, typified by truculent dockers, hostile to outsiders. Yet it drew waves of immigrants, especially Jews from central and eastern Europe and Chinese. The Chinese community in Limehouse became a source of fascination for polite metropolitan society, who associated it with opium dens and the generally seedy and shabby conditions which, they presumed, pervaded the East End. It seemed to consist of 'crowded and insanitary courts and alleys … the streets littered and ill-kept, the beer-shops full, the schools shut up'. Flower and Dean Street, off Whitechapel, gained a bad reputation and was described as 'the foulest and most dangerous street in the whole metropolis'. But that was typical of the smaller streets rather than the High Street, a wide thoroughfare lined with booths on market day and where a hay market was held until 1928.

Whitechapel High Street was the focus of the East End's lively social life, described in 1891 by the young Anglo-German writer John Henry Mackay as 'the greatest public pleasure-ground of the East End, accessible to all. Large music halls with broad lobbies and high stories and galleries are located there, and small hidden penny gaffs, in which there is little to see on account of the tobacco smoke, and little to hear on account of the noise.' (A gaff was a low-grade theatre, where the admission charge was usually a penny.) The Passmore Edwards library and museum were opened in 1892–93 and an art gallery was built next to the library in 1897–99 in an art nouveau style. Further along the street was the Pavilion Theatre, opened in 1828 and twice rebuilt, which catered for the local Jewish population until it was closed in 1933. Yiddish plays were also presented at the Wonderland, opened in 1880 and converted to a boxing saloon in 1894; it was burned down in 1911. On the south side, the London Hospital was built in 1753–57 and, with rebuilding and additions in the late nineteenth and early twentieth centuries, it became the largest hospital in the country.

The high street continues as Whitechapel Road, leading to the districts beyond the Lea that were developed from the mid-nineteenth century, stimulated by the coming of the suburban railways, where West Ham, East Ham, Plaistow, Canning Town and Stratford expanded enormously. The population of the inner East End, on the other hand, peaked around 1900 and fell thereafter, as its river-based economy changed. In 1931 Virginia Woolf arrived along the Thames to be confronted with 'surely the most dismal prospect in the world. The banks of the river are lined with dingy, decrepit-looking warehouses.' Bomb damage during the Second World War was extensive; the ruined property and substandard houses were mostly replaced by public housing, and the regeneration of docklands followed in the late twentieth century.

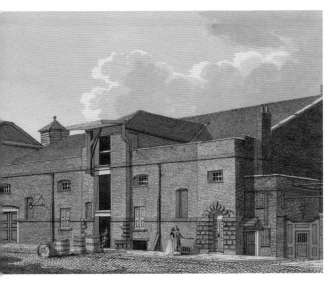

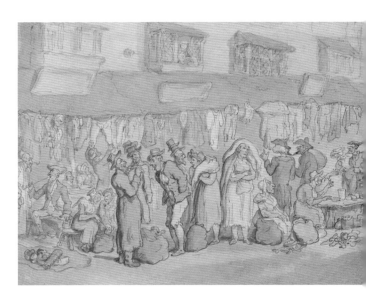

Top left: 336. The former Goodman's Field Theatre in Whitechapel in 1801, painted by Charles Tomkins; it had been converted to a warehouse and the building was burned down in 1809. (Yale Center for British Art, Paul Mellon Collection)

Top right: 337. Rosemary Lane, renamed Royal Mint Street in 1850, ran east from Little Tower Hill. From the late seventeenth century a street market was held there, chiefly for second-hand clothing. Ned Ward, around 1700, described the characters which frequented it as 'a Tatter'd Multitude … all the Ragg-pickers in Town'. A century later the market was depicted by Thomas Rowlandson. (Yale Center for British Art, Paul Mellon Collection)

Bottom left: 338. A view looking downstream taken near Limehouse Bridge in the eighteenth century, by an unknown artist. (Yale Center for British Art, Paul Mellon Collection)

Bottom right: 339. The church of St John, Wapping, in the mid-eighteenth century, set in a churchyard crowded with tombs. (Stephen Porter)

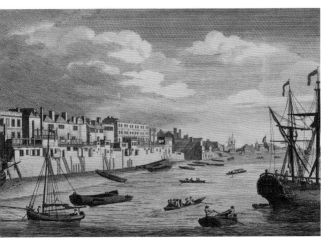

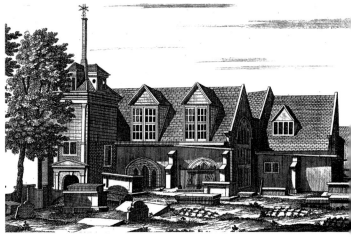

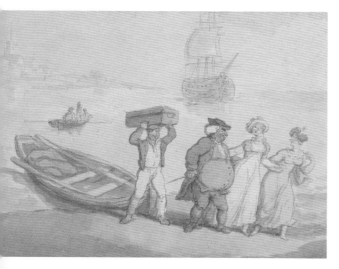

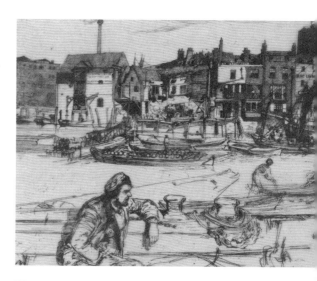

Top left: 340. Many passengers arriving at London disembarked at Blackwall, to avoid the river journey around the Isle of Dogs. The process was depicted by Thomas Rowlandson. (Yale Center for British Art, Paul Mellon Collection)

Top right: 341. The somewhat dilapidated nature of the Thames riverside in the mid-nineteenth century is evoked in James McNeill Whistler's etching of 1859 showing Black Lion Wharf and a number of adjacent wharves, on the north side of the river, east of St Katherine's Dock. (Yale Center for British Art, Gift of Janet and James Sale, Yale College 1960)

Bottom left: 342. Passengers alighting from a boat at Wapping Old Stairs, which are shown by Thomas Rowlandson to be in a rather shabby riverfront. (Yale Center for British Art, Paul Mellon Collection)

Bottom right: 343. A fireproof sugar refinery in Leman Street, Stepney in 1851, illustrated by Vincent Brooks. (Stephen Porter)

Opposite: 344. With the continued increase in shipping using the river and the persistent problem of pilfering from cargoes, plans were made for enclosed docks downstream from the City. The bold proposal to cut across the Isle of Dogs, with separate docks for incoming and outgoing vessels, is shown in Ralph Walker's plan for the West India Docks, 1802. (Yale Center for British Art, Paul Mellon Collection)

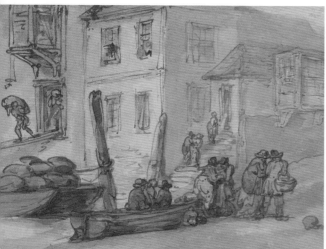

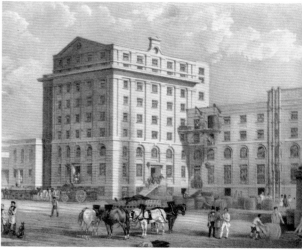

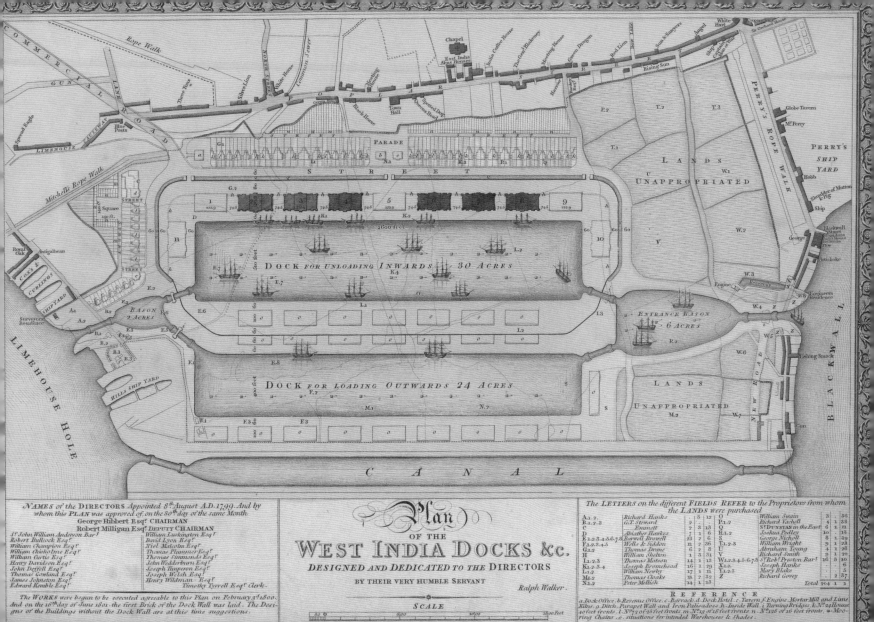

Plan
OF THE
WEST INDIA DOCKS &c.
DESIGNED AND DEDICATED TO THE DIRECTORS
BY THEIR VERY HUMBLE SERVANT
Ralph Walker.

SCALE

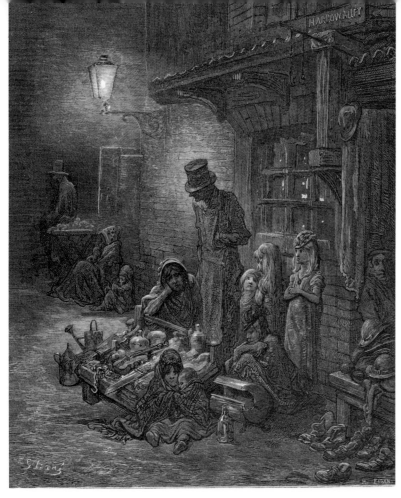

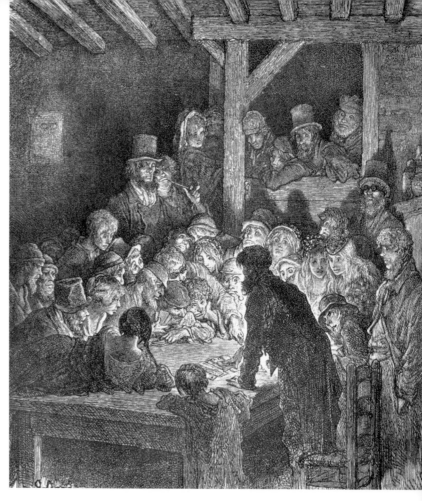

345. Harrow Alley, off Petticoat Lane, is shown by Gustave Doré in *London: A Pilgrimage* (1872), where a woman and children are trying to sell a miscellany of small items, including a violin, outside a doorway; outside the next house hats and boots are for sale. An air of melancholy pervades the scene. (National Gallery of Art, William B. O'Neal Fund, acc. 2007.98.1)

346. Gambling in a low lodging house on Ratcliff Highway, 1850; this is in one of the areas of the East End which both fascinated and appalled middle-class Londoners. (Stephen Porter)

SOUTHWARK

Southwark grew up on a tongue of dry ground, or perhaps an island, projecting northwards into the Thames, which the Romans chose as the southern point for their bridge, erected by around AD 50. Settlement on the south side of the Thames during the Roman period was confined to the approach to the bridge and for roughly 600 yards along the river. The area was abandoned soon after around 400 and was not reoccupied until the late ninth century. Thereafter, as Saxon London grew, so the settlement on the south side of the rebuilt bridge developed.

Southwark was to become known as the Borough, using the term in the sense of an extramural suburb, and its principal street of Long Southwark running southwards from the bridge was later to be designated Borough High Street. The area's growth was constrained by the dominance of London and the marshy nature of its low-lying site, and the lack of security, for the merchants preferred to be within the safety of London's walls. On the other hand, its position was ideal for travellers arriving from the south, or leaving, and inns and hostelries were established to cater for them. The district also contained many alehouses, and was known for its brothels by 1162, when Henry II issued regulations governing 'the stews in Southwark'. In 1504, eighteen brothels were closed down, but they were soon reopened. Because of those

in the Bishop of Winchester's liberty, the prostitutes were known as 'Winchester Geese'. An alternative name was 'Flemish Frows', as many of the women were from the Low Countries.

Along the river to the west of the bridge was St Mary Overy's priory, founded around 1106, and beyond that Winchester Palace and then Bankside. East of the bridge was St Olave's church alongside Tooley Street, leading to Bermondsey and its abbey. Off the east side of the street was St Thomas's hospital, originally part of the priory but moved to a new site after a fire in 1212. A prison built close to Winchester Palace was known as the Clink, a name which came to be applied generally to small gaols. Two royal prisons were also established in Southwark, the Marshalsea and King's Bench. By the nineteenth century the borough contained nine prisons, including the county gaol for Surrey. The priory was dissolved in 1539; its church became the parish church of St Saviour, and in 1905 Southwark Cathedral.

Southwark Fair was held annually from the mid-fifteenth century and was granted a charter in 1462, as a three-day event. It continued to be held, around 8 September, until the corporation suppressed it in 1763, because it caused rowdiness in the streets. Southwark's economy was closely related to London's, and as the city grew in the late sixteenth and early seventeenth centuries the borough's population increased threefold, reaching more than 5,000 by the 1630s, including immigrants from the Low Countries and Germany. This put it comfortably within the top ten English towns by population size. The corporation's sporadic attempts to extend its influence over its near neighbour across the bridge came to fruition in 1550, when Southwark became one of the City's wards, designated Bridge Ward Without.

John Stow described Southwark, in 1598, as consisting of 'divers streets, ways, and winding lanes, all full of buildings, inhabited', with the riverfront built up for about half a mile, on both sides of the bridge, and development southwards from it extending for about a mile. The area around the High Street was swept by a fire in 1676, which destroyed 624 houses, although rebuilding was swift, based on the regulations imposed after the Great Fire ten years earlier.

In 1720 John Strype summarised its economy as consisting of 'a very considerable Trade, and the rather as being so great a Throughfare out of Kent, and Sussex, into London; which makes it to be very well Inhabited by Tradesmen of repute, with Buildings answerable'. Shortly afterwards, Thomas Guy established his new hospital, close to St Thomas's, which opened in 1724. The parish of Christ Church was created in 1671, between the Borough and Lambeth. Although that area was not greatly developed at the time, it became so after the opening of Westminster Bridge in 1750; the completion of Blackfriars Bridge in 1769 and Southwark Bridge in 1818 further stimulated development in Southwark. As the district developed it contained both insalubrious parts, such as Kent Street, described by Tobias Smollett in 1763, as 'a most disgraceful entrance to such an opulent city', and others with an air of gentility,

such as the houses in Trinity Street and Trinity Square and the later development of Merrick Square, built in 1853–56.

St Saviour's church was largely rebuilt between 1818 and the early 1840s; the process included demolition as well as restoration. The chapel of St Mary Magdalene on the south side was pulled down in 1822 and, because the alignment of the new London Bridge brought the approach road much closer to the church's east end, the Bishop's chapel was demolished in 1830. The nave was demolished in 1838 and a new one was erected in 1839–40; it was greatly derided, not least by A. W. Pugin, who condemned it with the comment that it was 'as vile a preaching place as ever disgraced the nineteenth century'. It proved to be so unsatisfactory that in 1890–97 it was rebuilt, to Sir Arthur Blomfield's designs, which were much more acceptable, albeit with the reservation, in the words of the author Edward Foord, that 'it is perhaps open to the charge of lifelessness'.

In the late eighteenth century the long-standing trades of tanning, leatherworking, brewing, printing, gloving and hat making were supplemented by other industries, including glassmaking, flour milling and general engineering, on a far larger scale, in bigger premises and generating more employment and greater pollution. Coal was brought both up the Thames and downriver from the Grand Union canal at Brentford. The supply of coal and other raw materials along the Thames and, from the mid-nineteenth century, on the railways, which cut across the district on viaducts, facilitated the growth of industries, especially along the riverside. London Bridge station was built in 1836 and was later expanded, Blackfriars railway bridge was opened in 1864 and the St Paul's railway bridge alongside it in 1886.

Southwark became entirely built up with housing, warehouses and factories, including gasworks. Its population had risen to around 40,000 by the early eighteenth century and to 66,000 in 1801; it then increased to 206,000 by 1901. Its social problems attracted attention. At the end of the nineteenth century Charles Booth described the area between the High Street and Red Cross Street as being inhabited by 'waterside labourers and market porters and others of the lowest casual and loafing class, including thieves and the bullies who live on the earnings of prostitutes'. In the early 1930s the artist Paul Cohen-Portheim described the district as containing 'nothing but warehouses and wharves, slums, and a few broad thoroughfares of no great character. But … "The Borough" is full of a popular life … and of a roughly humourous vitality.'

Despite its liveliness and history, the district came to be shunned by those who sought the picturesque in London. Some ignored it, while W. W. Hutchings, in the early twentieth century, dismissed south London generally, because there 'for the most part industry tends to be amorphous' and its lack of bright shopping streets gave it a 'sense of monotony'. He commented of Southwark in particular that the visitor 'who expects to find here abundant relics of distant days will be woefully disappointed'. Even the galleried inns, survivors from the rebuilding after the fire in 1676, had not been spared, with the White Hart, which featured in Dickens's *Pickwick Papers*, and the north wing and centre of the George, demolished by the Great Northern Railway Company in 1889. And awareness of the history of St Olave's, founded in the mid-eleventh century, was not enough to save the church, which was pulled down in 1926.

For much of the twentieth century planners regarded Southwark as a predominantly industrial district. Only with the gradual closure of the industrial premises and wharves in the later part of the century did the earlier perceptions begin to alter and the growing sense of dereliction was reversed. The change was stimulated by the construction of a riverside walkway between Lambeth and Tower Bridge, the erection of the new Globe Theatre, based on the original of 1599, the transformation of the Bankside power station of 1957–60 into a gallery for modern art, the conversion of surviving warehouses and the construction of the Millennium Footbridge linking Bankside with the City. Together with a greater appreciation of such survivals as the George Inn, Hopton's almshouses and the remains of Winchester Palace, and the rediscovery of the Globe and Rose theatres, those developments helped to transform the riverside into a visitor attraction and produce the sense of brightness which Hutchings had found lacking a century earlier.

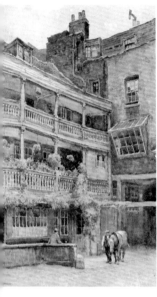

Left: 347. The George Inn was one of several inns in Borough High Street, Southwark. It was partly demolished by the Great Northern Railway Company in 1889, although one galleried range remained, painted by E. W. Haslehust around 1924. (Stephen Porter)

Below: 348. Borough High Street, Southwark, looking north, with St George's church on the right and the tower of St Saviour's church in the distance, shown by William Know in 1826. (Stephen Porter)

Right: 349. The church of Southwark priory became the parish church of St Saviour's after the Dissolution of the Monasteries. The nave was rebuilt twice during the nineteenth century, in 1839–40 and again in 1890–97, and the chapel of St Mary Magdalene on the south side was pulled down in 1822, as was the Bishop's chapel at the east end in 1830; plans to remove the adjoining Lady chapel were only narrowly defeated. The tower dates from the late fourteenth and fifteenth centuries. (Stephen Porter)

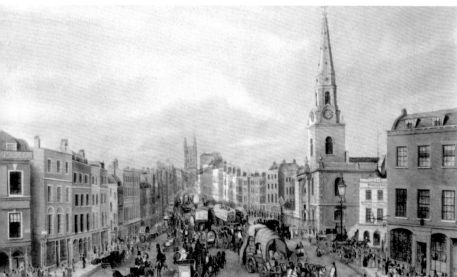

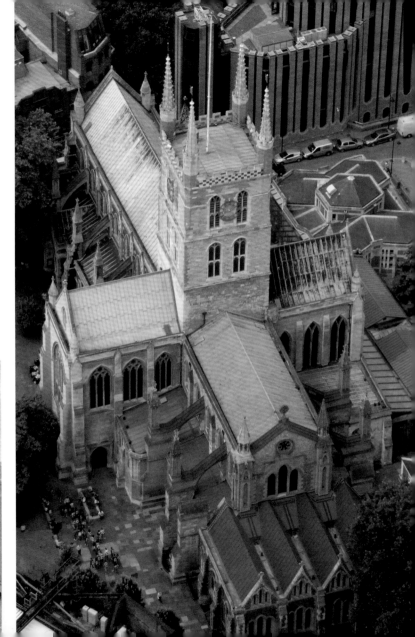

35

BANKSIDE

The area west of Southwark became known as Bankside, protected by an embankment probably raised in the early thirteenth century. Bankside was only sparsely developed before the mid-sixteenth century, but it then attracted increasing numbers of Londoners for recreation, with bull- and bear-baiting from the 1540s, and then theatres prominent. There were two arenas for animal baiting; in 1583 one of them 'fell suddenly down', killing eight people. It was swiftly rebuilt, as an octagonal arena.

With Londoners already drawn to the area, and the ease of bringing audiences to its landing stages by boat, Bankside was a suitable place for theatres, beyond the restrictive controls of the City. The Swan was built in 1595 by Francis Langley, and the Globe was rebuilt here in 1599, having been dismantled and moved from Shoreditch. The impresario Philip Henslow acquired a controlling interest in the Bear Garden in 1594 and in 1613 replaced the building with a theatre called the Hope, used for both plays and animal baiting. The Swan was disused and reported to be decayed by 1632, the Globe was rebuilt in 1613 after a fire and demolished in 1644, and the Hope was demolished in 1656. The Bear Garden was forcibly closed in 1656 but was reopened after the Restoration and continued to be used for recreation, including prize fights, until around 1690.

In 1720 John Strype described the district as 'a Place not over well built, or Inhabited, except by some few Dyers there seated for the Conveniency of the Water'. But the opening of Blackfriars Bridge in 1769 stimulated development and the area gradually was built over, with factories and mills as well as housing. They included the Albion Mill, a large flour mill opened in 1786 close to Blackfriars Bridge by Matthew Boulton and James Watt, with the engineer John Rennie to supervise the steam engines. The mill burnt down in 1791 and stood in ruins for eighteen years before a row of houses, Albion Terrace, was erected on the site. During the intervening years the poet William Blake lived in Lambeth Marsh and would pass the ruins as he walked to the City; perhaps they were the inspiration for the 'dark satanic mills' in his poem 'And did those feet in ancient time', which is better known as the anthem 'Jerusalem'.

In the nineteenth and twentieth centuries the riverfront was occupied by mills and factories, and Bankside power station. As the industrial premises were closed down and the power station was decommissioned, the district came to be pervaded by an air of decay and decline, although that had been reversed before the end of the century, with the power station converted into a gallery of modern art, Tate Modern, opened in 2000.

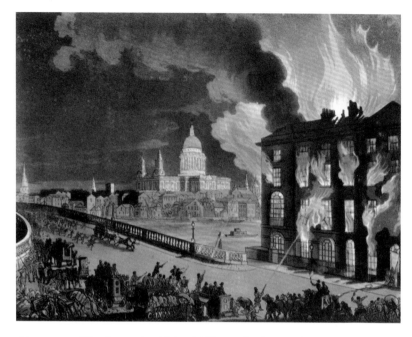

Above: 350. The fire at the Albion Mills, Bankside, Southwark, in 1791, was a spectacular blaze; the ruins stood empty for several years. The scene was illustrated by Augustus Pugin and Thomas Rowlandson. (Stephen Porter)

Right: 351. A section of Wenceslaus Hollar's *Long View* of 1647, looking west from Southwark, across Bankside. (Stephen Porter)

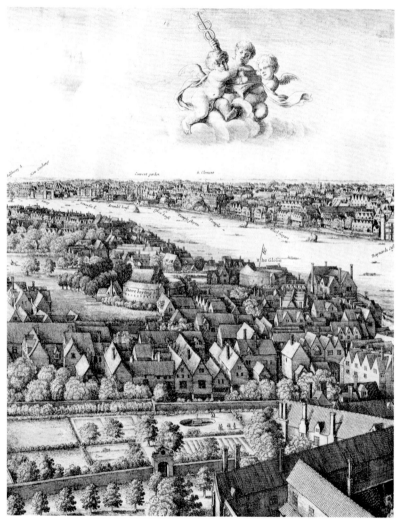

36

LAMBETH

Lambeth was mentioned in the Domesday survey of 1086, when a new church was being erected there by Edward the Confessor's sister, Countess Godgifu. Shortly afterwards William II gave Lambeth to the bishop and monks of Rochester and the bishop's London house, Rochester Place, was built at the end of the twelfth century. That stood to the north-east of the site where Lambeth Palace was to be built, as the London residence of the archbishops of Canterbury. They were largely peripatetic before the eleventh century, but subsequently built a number of houses in south-east England and Lambeth was ideally placed, on the opposite side of the Thames to the royal palace and the abbey at Westminster.

From at least the early twelfth century the archbishop had a hospice at Lambeth, with a chapel, where bishops were consecrated. Work on a college of canons and church during the 1190s was abandoned and in 1197 the manor was acquired by the See of Canterbury, in an exchange of properties with the monks of Rochester. In 1199 an abbey for up to twenty canons of the Premonstratensian order was founded and it may be that its buildings formed the core of the later archbishop's palace, which was largely built during the archiepiscopate of Stephen Langton (1206–28). It included a chapel, great hall, kitchen and other service buildings, and by 1270 buildings described as 'the archbishop's houses' had been erected.

The parish church of St Mary was separate from the palace and was rebuilt in the 1370s. Medieval Lambeth consisted of a small village south of the church. Additions to the palace in the fifteenth century included the lower stages of the Lollards' Tower, during the archiepiscopate of Henry Chichele (1414–43), which also saw the rebuilding of the quay, or landing stage, adjoining the palace. The upper part of the Lollards' Tower may date from the archiepiscopate of John Morton (1486–1500), together with the great gatehouse which bears his name; Laud's Tower is possibly of sixteenth-century date.

William Laud was appointed Bishop of London in 1628 and Archbishop of Canterbury in 1633. He was one of Charles I's leading advisors and was a key figure in the disastrous decision to impose the Book of Common Prayer on the Scots, provoking a resistance which led to the king's attempt to impose his will by force in the two Bishops' Wars of 1639 and 1640. Not only were the English armies ineffective, so that Northumberland and Newcastle were occupied by the Scots, but the already fragile royal finances were unequal to the extra costs of the wars and Charles was obliged to call Parliament. By then Laud was one of the most unpopular men in the country and in May 1640 Lambeth Palace was attacked by a crowd of what he termed 'rascal routers', which he estimated to number 500, but he had been forewarned and so 'had no harm'. But in March 1641 Laud was imprisoned. Civil War followed and he was tried and executed in 1645; the archbishops and bishops were abolished in the following year and their property was confiscated and sold, to help pay for the war. The palace and manor were bought by Thomas Scot and Matthew Hardy for £7,073; the great hall was dismantled around 1650.

Lambeth had attracted attention before the Civil War because of the plant nurseries there of John Parkinson and his friend John Tradescant. Parkinson was the author of the first book on English gardening and Tradescant had travelled widely in Europe and North Africa to collect plants for the gardens of his aristocratic patrons. Assisted by his son, also John, Tradescant opened his premises in Lambeth to display the various items, described as 'Rarities and Curiosities', which he had picked up during his travels, such as clothes, carvings, coins, medals and fish. The elder John died in 1638 and his son in 1662; their collections then came into the possession of Elias Ashmole and formed the core of the Ashmolean Museum in Oxford.

After the restoration of the monarchy in May 1660, the Church was re-established and its properties were recovered. William Juxon was appointed archbishop in September and he oversaw repair of the palace and the construction of a new great hall; his successor, Gilbert Sheldon, completed the work and added a library. Although the palace had become the archbishop's principal residence, rather than that at Canterbury, the buildings were neglected during the eighteenth century. In 1829–33 the architect Edward Blore carried out a programme of restoration and new building which included pulling down roughly a half of the medieval and Tudor buildings and erecting a three-storey block in a Gothic style. Blore's range was badly damaged during the Blitz, as were the chapel, the Lollard's Tower and the great hall, with further damage throughout the buildings, added to by flying bombs in 1944. The post-war restoration was carried out by Seely & Paget and was completed by 1955.

Lambeth contained roughly 4,000 inhabitants by the 1660s and was slowly developed thereafter, with industries established along the riverside and around the High Street. The process accelerated with the improvement in communications. Westminster Bridge, to the north, was opened in 1750; Lambeth Bridge was built in 1862 and replaced in 1929–32, and the construction of the Albert Embankment in 1866–70 provided a roadway along the river. St Thomas's Hospital was built alongside the embankment north of Lambeth Palace gardens in 1868–71. What was to become the Royal Doulton Company was established in Lambeth in 1815, specialising in stoneware and fine ceramics, especially after Henry Doulton nurtured a connection with the Lambeth School of Art, which was opened in 1854. Lambeth was the company's principal site until the demolition of its factory there in 1978, which was part of the process of de-industrialisation of the district. The art school developed into the City and Guilds of London Art School, which has been in Kennington Park Road since 1879.

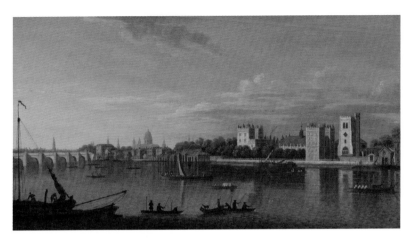

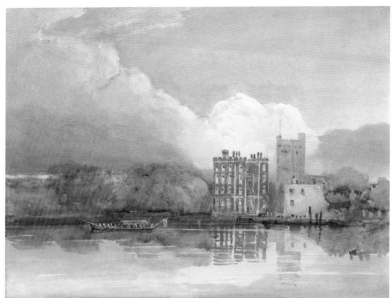

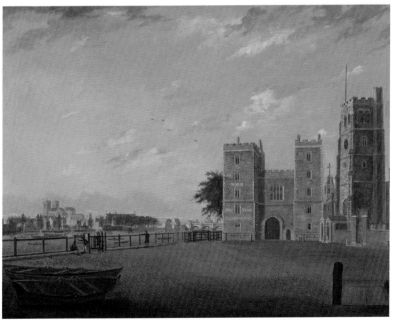

Above right: 352. A view of Lambeth Palace and St Mary's church from the river in the 1820s, by David Cox. (Yale Center for British Art, Paul Mellon Collection)

Above left: 353. The Thames at Westminster, looking across to Lambeth Palace, with Westminster Bridge, opened in 1750, and St Paul's Cathedral in the distance, by an unknown artist. (Yale Center for British Art, Paul Mellon Collection)

Left: 354. The gatehouse of Lambeth Palace built by Archbishop Morton around 1495 and the tower of St Mary's parish church, looking across the Thames to Westminster, by Daniel Turner, 1802. (Yale Center for British Art, Paul Mellon Collection)

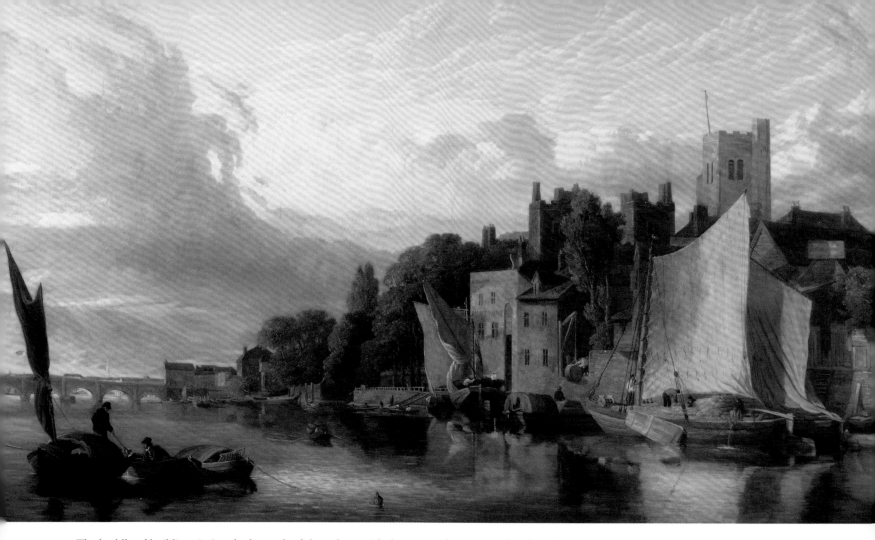

355. The huddle of buildings in Lambeth, south of the palace, with the tower of St Mary's church and Westminster Bridge beyond. The painting, of 1818, is by James Stark. (Yale Center for British Art, Paul Mellon Collection)

37

CHELSEA

The village of Chelsea, two miles upstream from London, was readily accessible along the Thames and by road from the city and Westminster. By the early sixteenth century it had become attractive to members of the court; Henry VIII acquired the manor and the Duke of Norfolk and the Earl of Shrewsbury had houses there. Sir Thomas More built a large house in the 1520s, with a separate library and a chapel in the grounds.

From the late sixteenth century market gardens were established, supplying London's markets, and the Society of Apothecaries laid out a physic garden in 1676. The parish then contained more than 160 houses. Chelsea College was founded by James I as a theological college, but was still unfinished by the Restoration. It housed prisoners of war during the Second Dutch War and was presented by Charles II to the Royal Society in 1667. It was reacquired by the king as a site for a new home for Army veterans, the Royal Hospital, which he established in imitation of Louis XIV's Hôtel des Invalides. Sir Christopher Wren was appointed architect and the foundation stone was laid on 17 February 1682. The first soldiers moved into the buildings ten years later. Daniel Defoe described the hospital as 'the noblest building, and the best foundation of its kind in the world'.

In 1748 the Swedish traveller Peter Kalm thought that Chelsea 'resembles a town, has a church, beautiful streets, well-built and handsome houses, all of brick, three or four storeys high'. The pleasure garden of Ranelagh was opened adjacent to the hospital in 1742 and proved to be immensely popular, drawing large numbers of visitors from a wide social background. When Samuel Johnson was told that there was not half a guinea's worth of pleasure in seeing Ranelagh he replied, 'No, but there is half a guinea's worth of inferiority to other people in not having seen it.' When the gardens closed in 1803 the site was absorbed into the hospital's grounds.

Chelsea remained fashionable and in the nineteenth century was home to members of the literati, including Thomas Carlyle and Dante Gabriel Rossetti, and artists, perhaps most notably Walter Greaves and James McNeill Whistler. The literary and artistic community continued to favour the district into the twentieth century, and, according to the writer Elizabeth Montizambert, 'do not remove to more fashionable Mayfair streets when they have "arrived"'.

The district was steadily absorbed into the metropolis, and although Nathaniel Hawthorne could describe it in the 1850s as 'an old town endowed with a prodigious number of pothouses, and some famous gardens', many of its older buildings were demolished, with More's house replaced by 'great blocks of industrial dwellings'. A suspension bridge across the Thames was built in 1851–58 and was described as forming 'so beautiful an ornament to this part of the river'. Nevertheless, it was replaced in 1934. Chelsea became a borough in 1900, which was superseded by the London Borough of Kensington and Chelsea in 1965.

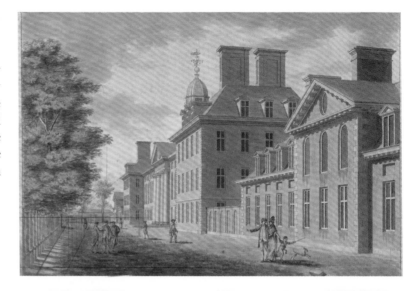

Top: 356. The north front of Chelsea Hospital, for Army veterans, designed by Sir Christopher Wren and built between 1682 and 1692; painted by Thomas Malton (1726–1801). (Yale Center for British Art, Paul Mellon Collection)

Bottom: 357. The great hall in the Royal Hospital, decorated with captured standards, painted by Charles F. Flower around 1910. (Stephen Porter)

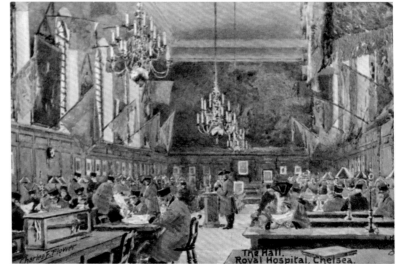

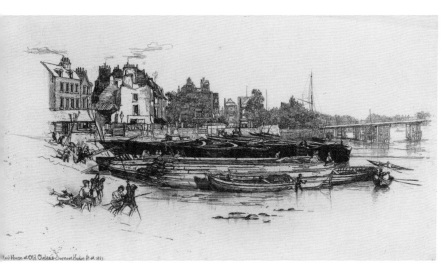

358. James McNeill Whistler was one of the colony of artists who lived in Chelsea; the drawing of his house and nearby buildings on the river was by Francis Seymour Haden, dated 1863. (Yale Center for British Art, Yale Art Gallery Collection, Gift of Leonard C. Hanna, Junior)

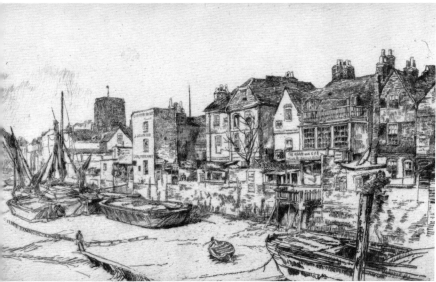

359. James McNeill Whistler's drawing of the jumble of buildings on the riverfront at Chelsea, including the Adam and Eve Tavern and the coal merchant J. Johnson's Old Ferry Wharf. (Yale Center for British Art, Gift of Donald and Willi Holden)

38

GREENWICH

The fishing village of Greenwich, at the foot of the high ground of Blackheath, was occupied by the Danish fleet in 1011–12, and there they murdered St Aelfeah, or Alphage, Archbishop of Canterbury. During the Middle Ages it developed royal connections and in 1426 Henry V's brother Humphrey, Duke of Gloucester, built a grand house, which was to develop into Greenwich Palace. In 1433 he enclosed around 200 acres as a deer park. Henry VIII was born at Greenwich in 1491, as were his daughters, Mary in 1515 and Elizabeth in 1533. He favoured the palace there partly because of his development of the Royal Navy. Henry established the King's Yard in nearby Deptford, where the *Great Harry* was built in 1512, and in that year he created the royal shipbuilding yard downstream at Woolwich.

In 1605 James I granted the palace to the queen, Anne of Denmark, and in 1616 she began the building of the Queen's House, designed by Inigo Jones and completed in the 1630s. It was enlarged after the Restoration, in 1662; another block erected shortly afterwards, to John Webb's designs, was intended to be part of a palace for Charles II, which was not finished.

The manor house of West Greenwich at Deptford became Sayes Court, the home of John Evelyn. Both the fine garden and the house were damaged by rough and careless behaviour by Peter the Great of Russia and his entourage, when they stayed there during a visit in 1698. Peter's interest was in the shipbuilding industry; Deptford then had a double dry dock, a wet dock of two acres, a mast house and more than a dozen storehouses, and, as well as its shipyard, the royal arsenal was developed at Woolwich from the late seventeenth century.

Greenwich's connection with the Royal Navy was greatly enhanced by the establishment of the Royal Naval Hospital, facing the river. The new buildings were designed by Sir Christopher Wren, who retained the Queen's House and Webb's building, but demolished the remainder of the Tudor palace. The hospital was built in 1694–1705; Wren had earlier designed the observatory in Greenwich Park, erected in 1675. The parish church of St Alphage was newly built in 1711–14 by Nicholas Hawksmoor.

Deptford and Woolwich grew as workaday dockyard towns, while Greenwich and the village of Blackheath to the south-east cultivated a more genteel character. Even their almshouses were noteworthy. Henry Howard, Earl of Northampton, established Trinity Hospital in Greenwich for twenty poor people in 1613 and Morden College at Blackheath was founded in 1695 for 'decayed Turkey merchants'.

'Of all London's surprises, Greenwich is perhaps the greatest,' wrote Paul Cohen-Portheim around 1930. 'After an endless ride through mean and poor quarters you see a fine Baroque church, and suddenly, round a corner, lies Greenwich Palace, one of the grandest Baroque palaces of Europe.' Those distinguished buildings have constantly drawn admiration from writers and, like so much of London, have proved to be irresistible subjects for artists and draughtsmen for more than three hundred years.

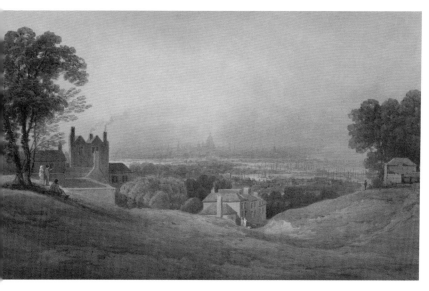

360. London seen from the high ground of Blackheath, looking across Greenwich, by Francis Nicholson (1753–1844). (Yale Center for British Art, Paul Mellon Collection)

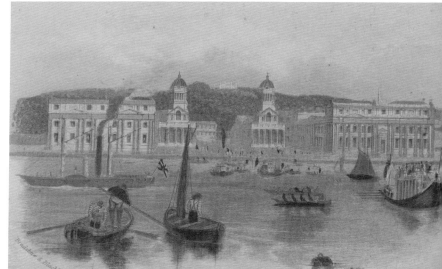

361. A steamboat and a variety of other vessels are shown on the river in front of Greenwich Hospital in the mid-nineteenth century. In Greenwich the Trafalgar Hotel provided whitebait dinners to excursionists, 'served on a verandah overlooking the river ... Numerous small craft glided to and fro, their sails sharply outlined against the flaming sky.' (Yale Center for British Art, Paul Mellon Collection)

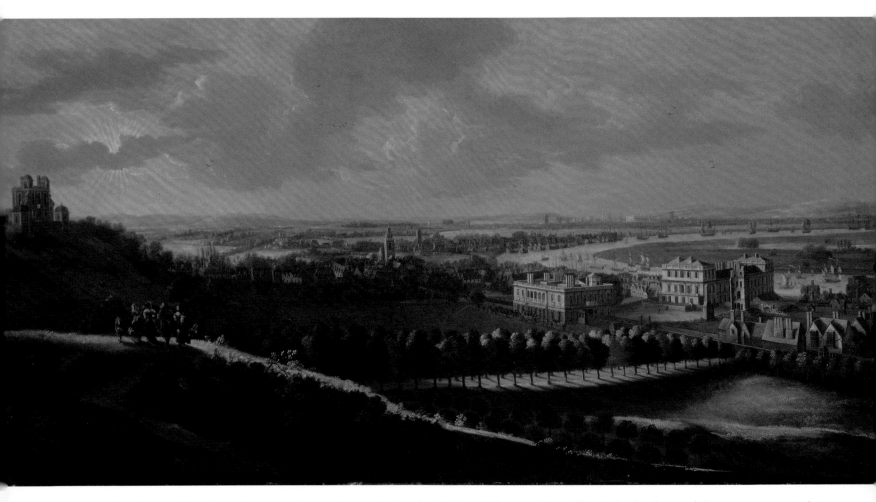

362. Greenwich Palace and the village of Greenwich around 1680, before the building of the Royal Naval Hospital. The cluster of shipping upstream is lying off Deptford. Painted by an unknown artist. (Yale Center for British Art, Paul Mellon Collection)

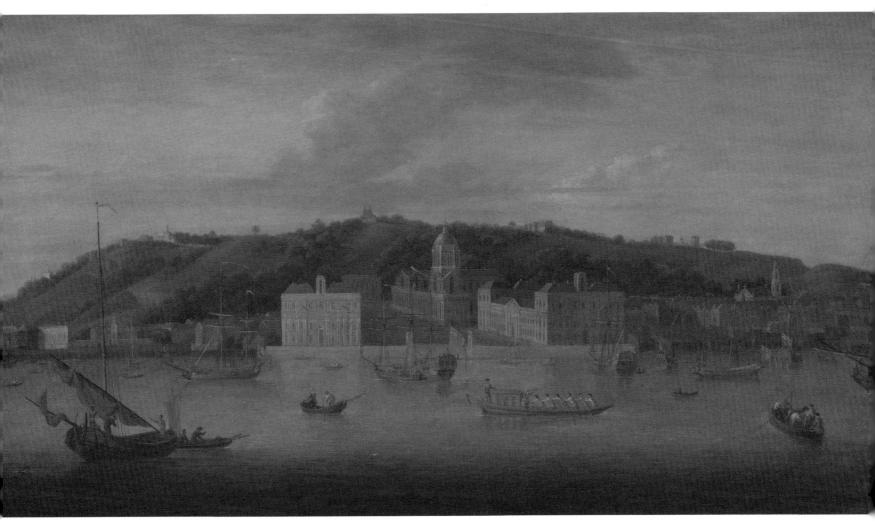

363. The buildings of Greenwich Hospital were erected in 1695–1705 and were painted, probably before 1710, by Jan Griffier the elder, a Dutch painter who was in England from at least 1677. (Yale Center for British Art, Paul Mellon Collection)

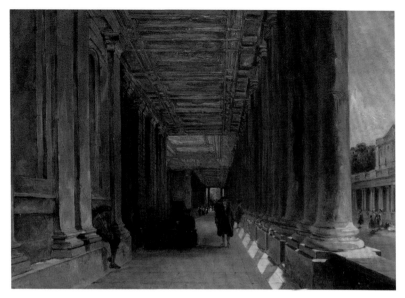

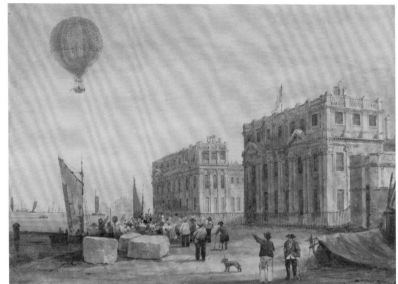

Above left: 364. The colonnade of the Jacobean Queen's House at Greenwich, painted by James Holland in 1833, after it had been incorporated into the Royal Naval Hospital for seamen, designed by Sir Christopher Wren and built in 1694–1705. (Yale Center for British Art, Paul Mellon Collection)

Above right: 365. Ballooning became popular in the eighteenth century, and this ascent is being watched by a considerable crowd on the Thames foreshore near the Royal Naval Hospital at Greenwich, around 1800. (Yale Center for British Art, Paul Mellon Collection)

Right: 366. Thomas Rowlandson depicts a holiday atmosphere by the river at Greenwich, probably in the late 1790s. Greenwich was a popular place for excursions by boat from London. (Yale Center for British Art, Paul Mellon Collection)

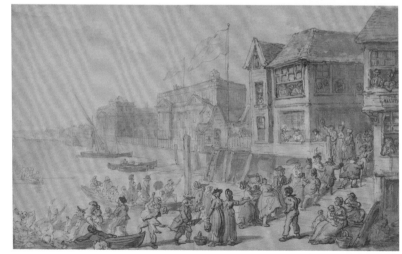

SOURCES QUOTED

The Anglo-Saxon Chronicles, ed. Michael Swanton (London: Dent, 1996)

Bacon, Sir Francis, *The History of the Reign of King Henry the Seventh*, ed. Roger Lockyer (London: Folio Society, 1971)

Besant, Walter and G. E. Mitton, *The Fascination of London: The Strand District* (London: Adams & Charles Black, 1903)

Booth, Charles, *Charles Booth's London. A portrait of the poor at the turn of the century drawn from his 'Life & Labour of the People in London'*, ed. Albert Fried and Richard M. Elman (London: Hutchinson, 1969)

Chronicle of London, from 1089 to 1483 (London: 1827, reprinted Felinfach: Llanerch, 1995)

Clunn, Harold P., *The Face of London: The Record of a Century's Changes and Development* (London: Simpkin Marshall, 1932)

Cohen-Portheim, Paul, *The Spirit of London* (London: Batsford, 1935)

Conan Doyle, Arthur, *The Sign of Four* (London: Penguin, 1982)

Croker, John Wilson in Bernard Darwin, *British Clubs* (London: Collins, 1943)

Defoe, Daniel, *A Tour through the Whole Island of Great Britain* (Harmondsworth: Penguin, 1971)

Dickens, Charles the younger, *Dickens's Dictionary of London 1888: An Unconventional Handbook* (Moretonhampstead: Old House Books, 1993)

D'Israeli, Isaac, *Curiosities of Literature* (London: Richard Bentley, 1838)

Farley, Henry and Pamela Tudor-Craig, *'Old St Paul's': The Society of Antiquaries' Diptych, 1616*, ed. Penelope Hunting and Ann Saunders (London: The London Topographical Society and The Society of Antiquaries of London, 2004)

Fitzstephen, William in John Stow, *The Survey of London*, ed. H. B. Wheatley (London: Dent, 1987)

Foord, Edward and Chancellor E. Beresford, *St Paul's Cathedral … Southwark Cathedral and Notable City Churches* (London: Dent, 1925)

Gronow, Rees, *Captain Gronow: His Reminiscences of Regency and Victorian Life 1810–60*, ed. Christopher Hibbert (London: Kyle Cathie, 1991)

Hawthorne, Nathaniel, *Our Old Home and English Note-Books*, 2 vols (Boston and New York: Houghton, Mifflin, 1897)

Hutchings, W. W., *London Town: Past and Present* (London: Cassell, 1909)

Huygens: *Lodewijck Huygens: The English Journal 1651–1652*, ed. A. G. H. Bachrach and R. G. Collmer (Leiden: Leiden University Press, 1982)

Kalm, Peter, *Kalm's Account of his visit to England on his way to America in 1748*, ed. Joseph Lucas (London and New York: Macmillan, 1893)

Lucas, E. V., *A Wanderer in London* (London: Methuen, 1913)

Mackay, John Henry, *The Anarchists: A Picture of Civilisation at the Close of the Nineteenth Century*, ed. George Schumm (Boston, Mass.: Benjamin R. Tucker, 1891)

Maré, Eric de, *London's River: The Story of a City* (London: Bodley Head, 1964)

Milton, John, *Areopagitica; A Speech of Mr John Milton For the Liberty of Unlicensed Printing, To the Parliament of England* (London, 1644)

Misson, Henri, *Memoirs and Observations in his Travels over England* (London, 1719)

Montizambert, Elizabeth, *Unnoticed London* (London: Dent, 1923)

Moritz, Carl Philip, *Journeys of a German in England*, ed. Reginald Nettel (London: Eland Books, 1983)

Munby, Arthur and Derek Hudson, *Munby Man of Two Worlds: The Life and Diaries of Arthur J. Munby 1828–1910* (London: John Murray, 1972)

Pennant, Thomas in Edward Walford, *Old and New London*, vol. 4 (London: Cassell, 1878)

Pepys, Samuel, *The Diary of Samuel Pepys*, ed. R. C. Latham and W. Matthews, 11 vols (London: Bell & Hyman, 1970–83)

Platter, Thomas and Clare Williams, *Thomas Platter's Travels in England* (London: Cape, 1937)

Pollnitz, Carl Ludwig, *The Memoirs of Charles-Lewis, Baron de Pollnitz*, II (London, 1739)

Rochefoucauld, François de la and Jean Marchand, *A Frenchman in England 1784* (Cambridge: CUP, 1933)

Rouquet, Jean André, *The Present State of the Arts in England* (London: J. Norse, 1755)

Rugg, Thomas, *The Diurnal of Thomas Rugg 1659–1661*, ed. William L. Sachse (Camden Society, 3rd series, XCI, 1961)

Rush, Richard, *A Residence at the Court of London*, ed. Philip Ziegler (London: Century, 1987)

Saussure, César de, *A foreign view of England in the reigns of George I. & George II. The letters of Monsieur César de Saussure to his family*, ed. Madame Van Muyden (London: John Murray, 1902)

Schellinks, William, *The Journal of William Schellinks' Travels in England 1661–1663*, ed. Maurice Exwood and H. L. Lehmann (Camden Society, 5th series, I, 1993)

Shore, William Teignmouth, *Touring London* (London: Batsford, 1930)

Smollett, Tobias, *Roderick Random*, ed. H. W. Hodges (London: Dent, 1927)

Southey, Robert, *Letters from England* (Gloucester: Sutton, 1984)

Steele, Richard, *The Spectator in London: Essays by Addison and Steele* (London: Seeley, 1906)

Stow, John, *The Survey of London*, ed. H. B. Wheatley (London: Dent, 1987)

Strype, John, *A Survey of the Cities of London and Westminster … By John Stow* (London, 1720)

Voltaire, *Letters on England*, ed. Leonard Tancock (London: Penguin, 1980)

Waldstein, *The Diary of Baron Waldstein: A Traveller in Elizabethan England*, ed. G. W. Groos (London: Thames & Hudson, 1981)

Walpole, Horace in Bernard Darwin, *British Clubs* (London: Collins, 1943)

Wey, Francis, *A Frenchman sees the English in the 'Fifties*, ed. Valerie Pirie (London: Sidgwick & Jackson, 1935)

Witts, Francis, *The Complete Diary of a Cotswold Parson: The Diaries of the Revd Francis Edward Witts*, vol. I, ed. Alan Sutton (Stroud: Amberley, 2008)

Woolf, Virginia, *The London Scene* (London: Snow Books, 1975)

INDEX

London History from Amberley

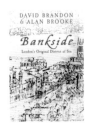

Bankside

978-1-4456-1384-0 £12.99

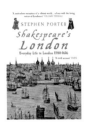

Shakespeare's London

978-1-84868-200-9 £9.99

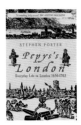

Pepys's London

978-1-4456-0980-5 £10.99

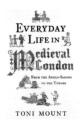

Everyday Life in Medieval London

978-1-4456-1541-7 £20.00

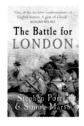

The Battle for London

978-1-4456-0574-6 £12.99

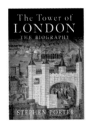

The Tower of London

978-1-4456-0381-0 £20.00

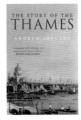

The Story of the Thames

978-1-4456-1194-5 £16.99

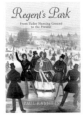

Regent's Park

978-1-4456-1024-5 £20.00

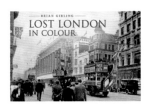

Lost London in Colour

978-1-4456-1502-8 £15.99

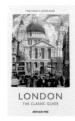

The King's England: London

978-1-4456-4217-8 £9.99

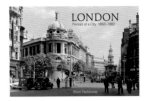

London: Portrait of a City

978-1-4456-3587-3 £20.00

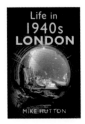

Life in 1940s London

978-1-4456-4378-6 £9.99

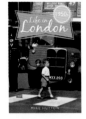

Life in 1950s London

978-1-4456-2124-1 £20.00

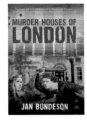

Murder Houses of London

978-1-4456-1485-4 £20.00

Available from all good bookshops or to order direct. Please call **01453-847-800**   **www.amberleybooks.com**